100 DAYS SMART

A kindergarten teacher
shares lessons on life, learning,
and community during the
COVID-19 outbreak in bella Italia

A memoir by

KARIN TRAMM

Elva Resa ✳ Saint Paul

Senior editor Christy Lyon.
Cover design by Brenda Harris, based on a kindergarten morning board.
Back cover kindergarten student art by Silvana Gonzalez-Benjumea.

Poem "exodus pandemia" ©2020 Ian Tramm.
Song "Too Fast/Too Slow" ©2020 Will Tramm.
Reprinted with permission.

Library of Congress Control Number: 2023931576

ISBNs 978-1-934617-77-9 (pb), 979-8-88752-016-2 (ebook)

1D 2 3 4 5

Elva Resa Publishing
8362 Tamarack Vlg, Ste 119-106
St Paul, MN 55125

ElvaResa.com
MilitaryFamilyBooks.com

To Gene,
for bringing me a notebook
when I felt a story coming on.

SCHEDULE

ROLL CALL

Karin	Mrs. Tramm; Kindergarten teacher stationed at Caserma Ederle, US Army post in northern Italy
Gene	Karin's husband, retired US Navy, high school physics teacher
Ian	Karin and Gene's oldest son, Peace Corps volunteer in Thailand
Will	Karin and Gene's youngest son, senior at Florida International University in Miami
Mom & Dad	Karin's parents in Florida, USA
Barbara	Karin's sister, military spouse, creative marketing director
Brian	Barbara's husband, retired US Marine, Department of Defense civilian
Morgan	Barbara's daughter, preschool special education teacher at Fort Bragg, North Carolina, USA
Bill	Karin's brother, US Merchant Marine captain, on board a ship in Diego Garcia
Mrs. Dee	Karin's kindergarten aide, veteran and military spouse, aka Wonder Woman
Vickie	Karin's college and lifelong friend, military spouse, US Marine mom
Misty	Kindergarten colleague stationed at Sigonella, US Navy base in southern Italy, veteran and military spouse
Flavio	Karin and Gene's Italian landlord
Stella	The Christmas Elf on the Shelf
Aunt Babe	Karin's aunt, Dad's sister
Friends	From near and far

PROLOGUE

September 3, 2019 was the first day of kindergarten at Vicenza Elementary School, Caserma Ederle, Vicenza, Italy. We began growing a number line, adding a new number each day, counting up to a magic day, the hundredth day of school. It was day eighty when I explained to my five-year-olds that in twenty more days they would be ONE HUNDRED DAYS SMART! They were excited and a bit anxious. I heard an uneasy voice from the back of the rainbow carpet:

"Mrs. Tramm, is that the last day of school?"

I expected this question. I get it every year. I assured my students that even though we would celebrate the first hundred days of kindergarten, it didn't mean it was the last day of school.

"Goodness no, there are a lot of numbers bigger than one hundred," I explained, "and we will be in school for many more days after the hundredth day."

Their apprehensive faces relaxed and we continued on with our Tuesday morning routine.

Three days later the coronavirus quietly raised its ugly head in Bordeaux, France, the first recorded case in Europe.

Friday, February 21, 2020

Finally! It was the day we'd all been waiting for, the hundredth day of school, and the kids were bubbling over with excitement. We'd been counting up and counting down, preparing for a celebration to mark the big day. We sang and danced. We read stories about one hundred days of school. We wrote one hundred words, counted one hundred pennies, made special hundredth-day hats. We were even lucky enough to have our class picture taken for the yearbook that day, a permanent reminder of February 21, 2020, our hundredth day of school.

That afternoon, twenty-one very excited and exhausted kindergartners lined up and marched out to the bus parking lot, hundredth-day hats on heads, singing the "Goodbye Song."

"Goodbye, goodbye! We're so glad you came to school today.
Goodbye, goodbye, See you on Monday!"

"Don't forget to read!" I reminded them as I watched their little feet climb the steep steps as they clambered on board.

"Bye, Mrs. Tramm!"

I walked back to the classroom smiling, thinking about the day. I wished I'd let the kids wear their hundredth-day hats for the class picture. It would've been a memorable yearbook photo.

"A good day," I said to my aide, Mrs. Dee, as I came through the door. "Thanks for everything; I think it went well."

We went over lesson plans for the upcoming week and set up the tables for Monday.

"I hope you've got something fun planned for the weekend. *Carnevale* is still going on in Venice," I called and waved as she headed out.

I busied myself with the usual Friday afternoon tasks, tidying my desk, watering the plants, and feeding the fish. The final item was to write my weekly class newsletter.

From: Mrs. Tramm
To: VES Kindergarten 2019-2020
Subject: Kindergarten News, Friday, February 21, 2020

Dear Kindergarten Families,

Today we marked a kindergarten milestone—can you believe it's been one hundred days since we started school? The children have shown a tremendous amount of growth. They surprise me and make me proud every day. We had lots of fun celebrating our progress—counting to one hundred by tens and ones. We wrote one hundred words, counted objects to one hundred, and wrote numbers to one hundred! […]

I've attached an updated parent email list to use as a resource for playdates, invitations, and keeping in touch over breaks. Thanks all who sent me permission and updated information. Have a great weekend and see everyone on Monday!

Karin Tramm
VES Kindergarten

I clicked send and scanned the room. Everything was laid out and ready to go for Monday, just the way I liked it. I heard my phone ping and picked it up from the charger beside my computer. I saw the text from my husband, Gene.

Gene: I'm here.

Me: OK. On the way.

Perfect timing, I thought, as I gathered up my lesson plan book and files so I could tighten up next week's schedule over the weekend. I packed my schoolbag, clicked off the lights, and made my way out to the parking lot in the back of the school.

"How was the hundredth day?" he asked knowingly. Being a high school teacher, he enjoyed hearing my stories of bedlam.

"Over," I replied in a weary voice, "It was a good day, but I'm so glad it's Friday."

We drove the fifteen-minute commute in quiet teacher exhaustion to our home in Bolzano Vicentino.

"No surprises," he said as we turned right and started down the long gravel driveway toward the house.

It was the same wishful thinking we voiced every time we approached the house. As a habit, we braced ourselves for what we might find—a power outage, farm machinery blocking the driveway, or an Italian family bringing their children to jump on our boys' trampoline.

"No surprises," I echoed, with no inkling of what the next one hundred days would ultimately bring.

~

Friday night was time to power down, and that meant pizza and a movie at home. This was a long-standing family tradition ever since moving to Bolzano Vicentino in 2006. We loved our little *comune*, one of the dozens of small rural villages that stretch out like grapevines on the outskirts of Vicenza. We had embraced our space there in the shadow of the Dolomite Mountains. We loved the sense of family and community shared by the Italians, we loved the travel, we loved the art, and we loved the culture. We loved the wine and the food, probably a little too much.

Gene called our favorite pizzeria, ordered the usual, and made the three-minute drive for pick up. He used to arrive home with a tall stack of pizza boxes, depending on how many kids we'd adopted for the weekend. Now that it was just the two of us, the stack was much smaller and pizza night less boisterous. I missed the mayhem and mischief.

After cutting the pies, we poured wine, built a fire, and settled into our familiar Friday night routine. Yes, please, to another glass of wine. After the movie, I sank deep into the sofa, ready for bed but not wanting to make the trek up the stairs.

Yawning, Gene asked, "Still awake?"

"Yes, and glad we don't have to do dishes," I replied.

I flipped through the news on my phone and noticed a blurb about the coronavirus. In Italy. We'd been carefully watching as the story was unfolding in Asia, because our older son, Ian, was a Peace Corps volunteer teaching in Thailand. The reports coming out of China were a little too close to him. I was keeping my eye on the developments in a mom sort of way. We had talked to him about the first confirmed case of human transmission in Thailand, a taxi driver in Bangkok, and even though Ian lived two and a half hours away from the capital, I was still nervous about it.

"Please don't go to Bangkok for now," I implored him, "just wait until we get there in April; by then all this will have died down." Ian didn't seem to be concerned.

Gene and I had planned a trip to Thailand to visit Ian over our upcoming spring break. We hoped to continue on to Cambodia with him while we were there. It had been over a year since we'd seen him, and we were getting more excited as the trip drew near. We'd never been to Cambodia, so all three of us were looking forward to it.

We'd heard that there were a few cases of coronavirus in Europe, but it seemed to us they were few and far between and, so far, contained. The news story named two locations in Italy where the virus was a concern and may be spreading. One was Codogno, near Bergamo, about an hour and a half away. The other was a town called Vo'Euganeo. That name leapt out because there was a sleepy little town called Vo' right down the road. Surely it couldn't be the same Vo', the Vo' where we liked to take our out-of-town guests, where we bought our wine and prosecco, where we went for springtime happy hours, sat under the wisteria, and took in the late afternoon sun.

A new notification appeared from the United States Embassy. It became quite apparent, there was no second Vo'.

Health Alert—US Embassy Rome, Italy, 21 February 2020

Location: Region of Lombardy, Codogno and surrounding towns of Castiglione d'Adda, Casalpusterlengo, Fombio, Maleo, Somaglia, Bertonico, Terranova dei Passerini, Castelgerundo, and San Fiorano.

Location Two: Vo'Euganeo in the Veneto region.

Event: On February 21, the Italian Ministry of Health announced fourteen confirmed cases of novel Coronavirus (COVID-19) in the town of Codogno in the Lombardy region and two cases in Vo'Euganeo near Padua.

Public schools and offices have been closed in the affected areas and Italian health officials have advised residents in these areas to avoid public spaces. Travelers in the area should be prepared for travel restrictions to be put into effect with little or no advance notice.

And just like that, little did we know, life changed forever.

Saturday, February 22, 2020

We had heard a few days before that some of the American military schools in Korea had temporarily closed due to the coronavirus outbreak in Daegu. Would we face similar closures here in the Italian schools? We watched the local news with concern as two cases turned to twelve then to more than one hundred cases. Then came the first death … in Vo'.

The rest of the world seemed to have little awareness of what was happening around us. That evening I received a message from my longtime friend Vickie.

Vickie: Arrived on Guam on Wednesday and will be here until March 3rd, staying with friends. Will send pictures. I'll be staying at the Westin next week while John is working at the Naval Station. You must google it! It's built on the cliff line in Tumon above our old favorite hangout—the Blue Lagoon Bar. Let's video chat while I'm here so we can stroll down memory lane!

Sunday, February 23, 2020

As Italy's confirmed cases surged, rumors started to fly that the local Italian schools would be closed for the upcoming week. Speculation grew that the American schools on Caserma Ederle, the army post where Gene and I both taught, would follow the Italian schools.

We were surprised to learn that the last two days of the *Carnevale* celebration in Venice were canceled. When had that ever happened? Maybe during the black plague? Roadblocks were set up and trespassers would face three months in prison for attempting to circumvent the barriers. Trains were being stopped at the border of Italy and Austria. We were in disbelief. This sounded more like a Netflix series than real life.

I called my parents in Florida just in case they had seen the news and might be worried. Fortunately, like most of America at the time, they had not heard a thing. I sent a message to our younger son, Will, a senior at Florida International University in Miami. He called back and said he hadn't heard anything either. We checked the FIU news site and read:

> There are fifteen cases of coronavirus in the US. It is important to note that no coronavirus cases have been reported at FIU and there are no confirmed cases in Florida.

Okay then, I felt better. FIU seemed to be tracking the coronavirus, which was a big relief for us as parents. It was one thing for us to be in the danger zone. It was something else completely when it was our child and he was on another continent.

The hardest thing about life overseas is family separation. When the boys left to go to college in the States, I didn't think I could bear it. Ironically, it was what Gene and I had strived so hard for. We wanted the boys to be confident, competent, and independent, to spread their wings and fly. And that they did.

In the evening I received a message from my sister, Barbara.

Barbara: Brian and I are still talking about visiting in October. Just wanted to double-check dates with you. Maybe London first and then come over. Would that work?

Me: Yes, yes, and yes! Just come when you can; we'll be so happy to see you. We can work it out whenever you're here. On another note, our school may be canceled tomorrow due to the coronavirus.

Barbara: Oh no! Did they find an active case there?

Me: Yes, in Vo'. Remember our favorite prosecco villa in Vo'—Villa Sceriman? Today there are more than a hundred cases here in Italy. *Carnevale* has been canceled.

Barbara: Stay home!!

Me: I think we have to. Thank goodness we're stocked on vino.

Barbara: Yes, that's most important.

From Thailand, our son Ian sent news articles with headlines that screamed out:

"Italians Scramble to Find Patient Zero"
"Italian Authorities Announce Sweeping Closures in the North"
"Europe's Biggest Outbreak of the Novel Coronavirus"

Ian: Be careful out there; looks like you guys have more confirmed cases than we do now.

Me: We do. It's close by, in Vo'. The schools are closed.

Ian: Wait, like the Italian schools or the base schools?

Me: Not sure but I think both.

Right then, as if on cue, the computer dinged, Gene's phone pinged, followed by my own. We were being barraged by emergency messages:

US Army Garrison Italy Update

United States Army Garrison Italy will close all Vicenza Military Community schools and activities, Child Development Center, Child and Youth Services activities from Monday through Wednesday, February 24-26, 2020. These actions are in response to a potential ongoing community transmission within the Veneto region of Northern Italy and are aligned with our host nation's actions to protect our communities.

Press 1 to acknowledge receipt.

I was incredulous. I looked down at my phone, attempted to focus, and returned to my text message conversation with Ian.

Ian: Seriously?

Me: Yes, both.

PART 1

THE BEGINNING OF THE BEGINNING

"You are braver than you believe, stronger than you seem,
and smarter than you think."

The House at Pooh Corner, A. A. Milne

WEEK 1: THE BUS STOPS HERE

Monday, February 24, 2020

The coronavirus had pulled up to our bus stop.

When my body clock said WAKE UP at five thirty in the morning, I stayed in bed. It was a relief, lying there knowing I didn't have to get up in the dark, but the giddiness of a snow day wasn't quite there. I couldn't go back to sleep. I watched daylight tiptoe through the bedroom window. Black to grey today.

I felt uncertainty, uneasiness, a bit of annoyance that I would have to rewrite my lesson plans. This was definitely not in the plans, and I disliked it when my plans got changed. I always said it was the children who needed predictability and routine, but more and more I realized that I was the one who needed it. I was the one set in my ways, and I was definitely the one who didn't deal well with change.

I glanced up at the ceiling where an alarm clock cast the time in glowing red. At seven o'clock on any other day I would be gathering up my purse and school bag, scrambling to leave the house about now. Phone? Check. Lunch? Check. ID card? Check. Keys? Check. Then eight o'clock, arrival time. The kids would be coming in from the buses, crowding through the door, excited, needing to tell me about their big adventures over the weekend. At nine o'clock, story time. They were missing the book *One Hundred Days (Plus One)*. My eyes were fixated on my watch throughout the morning. At ten o'clock they would've been going to recess. At eleven o'clock, bouncing into the cafeteria for lunch. Throughout the day my mind was at school even though my body was home.

The calendar reminded me that I had an appointment at the nail salon in the late afternoon. If schools were closing down, I wondered if my appointment was canceled as well. I scrolled through my phone contacts and called.

Teachers have a challenge trying to keep nice fingernails. My nails were constantly stained with paint and markers, broken and chipped from pulling staples, and dried out due to the continuous handwashing with the very harshest industrial school soap ever. Honestly, presentable nails were probably a lost cause, but I tried. Perhaps it was just an exercise in mental health. After a long day of taking care of young children, it felt nice to carve out an hour once a month for this type of self-care.

"*Pronto!*" I was relieved to hear a click, followed by the sunny voice on the other end of the line.

"*Buongiorno,*" I answered. "*Sieti aperti oggi?*" Are you open today?

Yes, they were still open, but it wasn't really business as usual.

"Can you come in a little early?" the manicurist asked, explaining that the appointment before mine had been canceled; many appointments had been canceled that day, she told me in a disappointed voice.

Arriving at the salon, I was happy to see an old friend there, someone I had met fourteen years ago when I first moved to Vicenza. I loved chatting with her because she had been in the Philippines, as had I, many years back. I always welcome a chance to reminisce, having so many fond memories of living and working there.

Gene was a newly-commissioned officer assigned to a survey vessel, USNS Chauvenet, when I met him in that beautiful island nation. He was gregarious, adventurous, and quick with a joke. We hit it off right away but unfortunately our time together was short-lived. The ship soon departed the base at Subic Bay for Indonesia. He went on to Somalia and finally to Naples, Italy. After a two-year long-distance relationship, I was able to transfer to Strullendorf Elementary, an American military school located in Bamberg, Germany. I was happy and grateful that we were finally living on the same continent, in the same time zone.

The following February we were married. At the end of the school year, I moved down to Naples, stepping into a job teaching kindergarten at the base elementary school. We then wandered the globe as most military families do. I was thrilled when we got orders to Guam, my old stomping grounds, where I taught for the Guam Department of Education again. We moved on to Monterey, California, where both boys were born. From there we transferred to Keflavik, Iceland, then to Virginia Beach, where Gene was stationed on board the aircraft carrier USS Theodore Roosevelt.

Following that tour, the navy moved us to Rota, Spain.

As proclaimed on many a doormat in navy housing across the world, "Home is Where the Navy Sends You." And it was.

When the boys were born, I stopped teaching and became a full-time stay-at-home mom. I was lucky to be able to take advantage of this gift of time, thanks to the military, which always provided Gene with a job, a home, and healthcare for our family. I missed the classroom, but I knew those precious days in my boys' lives were a time to cherish.

When Ian was in second grade and Will was in kindergarten, I dusted off my school bag and went back to work for the elementary school in Rota, Spain. Gene and I dreamed that one day I would get back into the military school system and we could stay overseas. Maybe in Italy, we thought, because we had loved living in Naples. And maybe Gene could manage to get a teaching job, too.

In 2006, Gene retired from the navy. I was able to get a transfer and we moved from Spain to Vicenza, where I continued to teach kindergarten. Gene, a meteorologist while in the navy, took classes to earn a credential to teach math and physics. Our boys were able to stay in the same location throughout their teen years and both graduated from Vicenza High School. We were living the dream, teaching overseas and having big adventures. Life was good.

"It's a little bit crazy out there," my friend commented as the manicurist worked her magic. "People won't even eat in a restaurant because they're afraid of getting the coronavirus from the food."

There was already much misinformation and fear in Italy, even before things got really scary.

Pleased with my new nails, I paid and wandered into the small grocery store across the way to buy pepperoncini. I loved the long greenish-yellow peppers, a little spicy but not too much. I believed they boosted my immune system, so I always kept a couple of jars on hand at home and at school so I could snack on a few every morning, especially during the cold and flu season. A kindergarten classroom is basically a petri dish, and I needed all the help I could get. This store carried my favorite brand, so I ducked inside to get a jar or two while I was there. I would especially need them now, and even more so when we were back in school on Wednesday.

This was the first time I saw fearful faces, stylish scarves wrapped over mouths as makeshift masks, eyes peeking out with uncertainty. Unsettled, I bought four jars of peppers and hurried home.

I backed the car into the Batcave, our makeshift carport, named for the real bat house nailed to a post in the rear. As I unbuckled my seatbelt my phone rang, my sister Barbara calling from Florida.

"Did Ian get through to you? He was trying to call you but called Morgan by accident."

Ian was close to his cousin Morgan, so I was happy he'd talked with her, even if it was by accident.

"Yes, we managed to talk to both boys yesterday. They hadn't heard anything, no surprise there, but now they're aware. I also called Mom and Dad; they hadn't heard anything either. Now everybody knows and no one's going to panic when they see the news stories coming out of the Veneto. We're good, no worries."

"Okay, then." She didn't sound convinced.

"Seriously, we're fine."

"What about school tomorrow?" she asked.

"School was canceled today and we're out tomorrow, too. I'm practicing for retirement."

Tuesday, February 25, 2020

As the hours passed, my feelings wavered between excitement to have another day off and worry about what would come next. Gene and I puttered around waiting for word, not really focused on any worthwhile tasks. We finally received an update in the evening:

Vicenza Staff Update for tomorrow, Wednesday, 26 February 2020

All Vicenza teachers and staff will report to the Vicenza Middle School Multipurpose Room tomorrow morning, Wednesday, 26 February, at 8:00 a.m. At that time more information will be provided regarding continuity of education services and work schedules. This is an important meeting for all staff; the only attendance exceptions should be those on a previously excused absence or those not feeling well. Please inform your school's leadership if you will not be in attendance. We look forward to seeing you all in the morning.

I didn't look forward to getting up early again, but at least now we would have some guidance. I sent a message off to Barbara, to keep her in the loop.

Me: Teachers have to report to school tomorrow but no students right now. I think we have to come up with some sort of virtual lesson plans that the kids can do at home. Panic isn't as bad here as in some other places. People are hoarding hand sanitizer, wipes, and toilet paper. And of course, pasta. You should keep that in mind next time you go to the store because coronavirus isn't there yet but it's coming. Stand by, things are happening very quickly here and when it gets to you it'll be quick as well. I really worry about Mom and Dad because they're the demographic most affected. They need to be prepared to stay inside for a while. They have enough food for a zombie apocalypse, but they will need toilet paper. LOL.

Barbara: Thanks for the update. I'm so glad you're ready. We'll start hoarding toilet paper and vino so we're well prepared.

Later, an email appeared from FIU reporting they had restricted travel to Italy, Japan, and South Korea over coronavirus concerns. All travel, individual trips or study abroad programs, to Singapore, Japan, South Korea, and now Italy, were canceled effective immediately.

Not that Will was planning on coming home anytime soon, but seeing this in writing left me with an ominous feeling. We already had his return ticket booked for August, after his graduation. Surely, coronavirus would not be a problem by then. Will would be coming home.

Wednesday, February 26, 2020

With the five-thirty alarm, our new life began. We chugged coffee, stashed a small bottle of hand sanitizer in the console of the car, and left for work. Traffic seemed normal on the drive to school, or, I should say, as normal as driving gets in Italy. All sense of normalcy ended upon arrival, however. We entered the school building where the faculty of all three schools—elementary, middle, and high school—were guided into the multipurpose room. We were greeted at the door by school administrators and, with a squirt of hand sanitizer, ushered in and told to distance ourselves. Packets of papers were spaced out on the tables three feet apart. More than a hundred of us packed in, conferring in hushed voices as we shared rumors and tried to figure out what might come next.

We were briefed by army officials, the community school superintendent, and a healthcare professional from the clinic. We were reminded to maintain a social distance of three feet at all times, to wash hands or sanitize regularly, and that it was not necessary to wear masks. We were dismissed to our classrooms with two assignments: to come up with two days of online lessons that we could post by the next morning and to make a tentative plan for the next week if school continued to be closed. We were given a template, and the educational technologist roamed the building offering support. Our team worked hard but I soon realized I was in way over my head. Over thirty years in the classroom had not prepared me for the educational upheaval that was about to happen. Oh, and did I mention that I don't do well with change?

During the day, a notification was sent to parents informing them that school would be out for the remainder of the week.

Vicenza Schools closed to students through 28 February 2020

As a precautionary measure, we will continue to follow garrison guidance regarding coronavirus concerns. All schools in Vicenza will, therefore, remain closed to students through Friday, 28 February 2020. This includes any scheduled events for the rest of week. We will continue to update you as more information becomes available. Please continue to check for these updates prior to making any decisions regarding future schedules. We are working closely with our garrison and host nation partners to monitor the situation. All decisions will be made with the health of our staff, students, and community in mind. Thank you for your support.

Gene and I had been kicking around the idea of retiring in a year or two. I had been in and out of the military school system since I started teaching in the Philippines in 1986, ages ago it seemed. By now I had enough years in to make the move, so we'd been discussing it and doing some preliminary planning. It had been almost fourteen years since Gene retired from the navy and for the past few years his teaching salary had flowed directly into the Florida State University system. Will was ready to graduate, so we needed a little bit of time to refill the family coffers and then our days of sleeping in would be on the horizon. We didn't own a house, so we planned to go back to Florida in the summer and buy something in preparation for our final move back. We needed an address and a place to send our belongings. That would put us one step closer.

Barbara and her husband, Brian, had recently purchased a home and knew a real estate agent who was keeping her eyes open for us. Each week Brian forwarded information from her as well as several Zillow links so we could see what was out there in preparation for our summer house hunting visit. Now I was seeing everything with new eyes. Maybe this was a sign. Maybe now was the time to go.

There was a message from my friend Vickie, still on Guam, where news was just starting to trickle in.

> **Vickie**: Have you been going to work? News here on Guam says some towns in Northern Italy are closed from the virus. Is that you?
>
> **Me**: Yes, it's us. We've been out of school for the past two days. Teachers had to go in this morning for an all-call meeting, but the kids are out for the rest of this week.

Thursday, February 27, 2020

I was awake most of the night, my thoughts spiraling, trying to absorb everything. In the morning the kindergarten team reviewed the lesson plans, posted them on the newly created school splash page, and sent a letter to parents about our next steps, or at least what we thought our next steps might be.

From: Mrs. Tramm
To: VES Kindergarten 2019-2020
Subject: What Comes Next

Dear Kindergarten Families,

Earlier today you received an email regarding our missed days of school and a link to assignments for your child. Some of the links require a log-in, so please find that information below. We are learning this as we go along so thanks in advance for your patience while we work through it together. Please contact me with any issues and I'll try to help you as best I can.

In addition to the lessons outlined on the digital learning page, I would also like to add:

1. Please remember that it is very important that you continue reading with your child each day. I have attached a copy of the reading log for your use.
2. I encourage everyone to get some outside play in each day. Exercise is especially important if the children are feeling stressed being out of their normal school routine.
3. Play with blocks, Legos, and other building toys.
4. Visit the post library—they are still open!
5. Send us pictures of fun things you are doing, your Lego creations, cooking projects, favorite books, etc. We need to stay connected! Please cc Mrs. Dee on them as well.

Finally, and most important, please tell our kids we love them and we miss them and we can't wait to see them back at school soon. Thank you for being a VERY important part of our team!!

Mrs. Tramm & Mrs. Dee
VES Kindergarten

Reinvention is what military spouses do best. In my past lives I've been a teacher, stay-at-home mom, travel writer, bartender, grad student, photographer, and teacher again. Every move to a new duty station required a restart. New home, new friends, new job, new life, and so it goes for a navy wife. Now this job would require a restart as well. As much as I didn't embrace change, I had plenty of experience with it.

Day one of digital learning brought parents and teachers together in a new kind of partnership. Parents had been supporting us in the classroom, assisting with art projects and math games, in the science lab and the library. This would be a different way for parents to step up, since I didn't know what things looked like from the students' perspective.

From: Mrs. Grant
To: Mrs. Tramm
Subject: RE: What Comes Next
FYI...The handwashing video won't open on an iPad nor an iPhone. Asks for credentials & when added it says "Uh-oh, this app can't be used in your classroom." Am I doing something wrong?

From: Mrs. Benson
To Mrs. Tramm
Subject: RE: What Comes Next
So... with the math stuff, I can't find the right practice. It's having her add really big numbers like 286+57.

From: Mrs. Taylor
To: Mrs. Tramm
Subject: RE: What Comes Next
I have not received ANY email or message from the school. Would you mind letting whoever is responsible for it know that I don't get any info? Or let me know who I have to talk to?

From: Mrs. Taylor
To: Mrs. Tramm
Subject: RE: What Comes Next
Sorry, I checked my spam, and the school email alert system went directly there. :) So, I figured it out.

From: Mrs. Lewis
To: Mrs. Tramm
Subject: RE: What Comes Next
Are these assignments just for this week? Is school back in session 3/1? Sorry, I'm just a bit confused.

From: Mrs. Khorman
To: Mrs. Tramm
Subject: RE: What Comes Next
   Something on my laptop doesn't like the math program. Working with both kids back and forth I do trial and error to figure out which laptop works for who in which assignment. Sorry for all my questions. You guys rock!

These parents rocked, too. They had been stalwarts throughout the school year, and nothing had changed about that. We spent most of the day working out the bumps. A lot of bumps. As our team plowed through the digital lesson plans, I felt more and more overwhelmed with the Herculean task at hand and the overload of new technology we were required to make friends with.

The front office rallied our aides to help make posters outlining the new social distancing guidelines and handwashing schedules. I couldn't fathom how I could make twenty-one kindergartners keep their hands off each other and maintain a meter of space between them. I was having dismal luck with that so far this year. This had all the makings of a chicken pox party sponsored by the school. Handwashing seven times a day would be a challenge as well. We put up our posters by the sink and sighed heavily, thinking about the challenges we would face when the kids were back on Monday.

~

At the high school Gene toiled away on his online lessons. In the afternoon someone came by his classroom with a canister of disinfecting wipes.

"Wipe down all the desks and tabletops in your physics lab," he was told, "and anything else the students may have touched. And pass the wipes to the next teacher when you're done."

We went home frustrated and exhausted. Serenity now.

~

I was glad to be home but schoolwork, like laundry, is never entirely finished, and going home didn't mean our day was done.

Many families had more than one student and were sharing devices. Some parents were trying to juggle their own work from home with schoolwork for their kids. Some kids were going to work with their parents. For many, schoolwork continued well into the night. If families were scrambling this hard to make remote learning work, I needed to as well. When I came home, I turned on my computer straightaway and continued answering emails from the kitchen while I prepared dinner.

From: Mrs. Hill
To: Mrs. Tramm
Subject: Math
Sorry to be a bother. What is the math account?

From: Mrs. Tramm
To: Mrs. Hill
Subject: RE: Math
You are never a bother. It's the username and password you see below. When you click on the link it will take you to a log-in site. I know it's confusing and I'm sorry. I'm learning it as we go as well.

From: Mrs. Hill
To: Mrs. Tramm
Subject: RE: Math
I tried that and it said that it wasn't valid. :(

From: Mrs. Tramm
To: Mrs. Hill
Subject: RE: Math
I'm not at school right now so I'm not sure if I can sort it out from home. I'll try and get back to you. Thanks for your patience!

I continued making dinner and thought hard. Searching my memory, I tried to recall what I had done to reset all those passwords, a hundred days ago back in September. I tried a couple of things and emailed her when I thought I was on the right track.

Aah, little victories.

From: Mrs. Tramm
To: Mrs. Hill
Subject: I think I got it!
  I think I fixed it! That was totally my fault, I reset the wrong password but now it should be good to go. Let me know if it works.

Back in Miami, Florida International University was doing a fine job communicating with parents. As soon as I heard the email notification, I stopped what I was doing to read. We were reassured that no coronavirus cases had been reported on campus, and there were no confirmed cases in Florida. That was welcome news.

Later that evening Gene and I received a message from Will. He told us he would be spending his spring break in Tennessee. I was happy he was choosing to leave Miami for the next week instead of staying there in the beach madness I knew would ensue. He was planning to stay in Nashville with a friend and former band member, now living and working there. Will played guitar and was part of a local Miami band called The Hattts, which had recently been chosen to play in a music festival in March. Will was beyond excited, and we were excited for him, although in the back of my mind I wondered how that was all going to play out with coronavirus on the way to the US.

~

Ian messaged to tell us that the Peace Corps had banned travel to Italy. It had been fourteen months since he started his work in Thailand and we were eager to see him over spring break. We looked forward to visiting his work site and meeting the host family that had so graciously accepted him into their own home. We hoped this wouldn't have any impact on our trip, but a bad feeling settled in the pit of my stomach.

Ian: Not that I had any plans to come home right now, but officially now I can't anyway. Additionally, you'll notice there's a restriction on Cambodia so at least for now we should go ahead and put a pin on that part of our trip.

Me: It's bad news but not unexpected. I hope you're having a fun trip with your colleagues.

Ian: Indeed, indeed. Hopefully, it will end up that you guys can still make it out to just Thailand over your spring break. And yes, it's been a good week! It's been good bonding with some of my coworkers I don't get to spend too much time with otherwise.

Gene: OK, I'll cancel the Cambodia hotel. Good thing we didn't have that leg of the plane tickets yet.

Ian: Yeah, it's lucky. Lots of Peace Corps volunteers have travel plans for April, as do their parents. They have been blasted in the last couple of days; lots of frustration over here right now about non-refundable flights and plan changes.

As Ian said, not that he had any plans to come to Italy at the moment, but now, officially, neither of the boys could travel here. Even though I knew they were both safe, I felt anxious about not having the family together during this crisis. It had been a long time since we were all in the same time zone.

Friday, February 28, 2020

From: Mrs. Brown
To: Mrs. Tramm
Subject: PE
   Good morning Mrs. Tramm! We are trying to do the PE lesson but when we click the link it says the requested URL was not found on the server. I'm not sure what the PE teacher's name is, so I was wondering if you could please let her know?

From: Mrs. Smith
To: Mrs. Tramm
Subject: Help
   Hi Mrs. Tramm, our account login is not working. Says invalid username or password. I tried multiple times.

Teaching a kindergartner how to log on to a school computer is not fun. Their username consists of part of their first name and part of their last name combined with part of their student number. The password is made of letters, numbers, and symbols. At the beginning of the school year when we're focused on learning to be little human beings working together in a shared space, I question the value of this complicated task.

Many five-year-olds come to school not knowing all their letters and numbers. Some don't know the difference between a letter and a number. Some kindergartners can't write their names yet. That's all okay; it's my job to teach them those things. However, trying to teach a group of non-readers about a keyboard and a mouse and a login system made for kids who can actually read is another thing entirely.

Many five-year-olds have their own devices and plenty of screen time at home. When they're at school, I believe face-to-face interaction and hands-on instruction is more meaningful and a better use of their time. However, using computers is an expectation for all students, kindergartners included, and something teachers are evaluated on.

So to make things easier, I simplified and reset all the usernames and passwords at the beginning of the school year. We rarely used them; I just logged onto our two classroom laptops myself before school so they were ready to go, one less thing to struggle with each day.

Now that we were working from home, everyone was required to use their own specific log-in. I constantly apologized to the parents because I knew that even when simplified, it was still frustrating for everyone.

From: Mrs. Tramm
To: VES Kindergarten 2019-2020
Subject: Digital Learning Update 1

Dear Kindergarten Families,
   Thanks for all your input to help us work out the bugs in the program. Our internet was down earlier, so if you had a problem accessing the links, please try again. Don't forget to send us some pictures of your kids so we can include them in our Kindergarten News and on our Welcome Back bulletin board. Keep the feedback coming so we can work through this together. Thanks all!

Karin Tramm
VES Kindergarten

The kindergarten team worked late into the afternoon to finish up digital lesson plans for the next five days. If this situation were to drag out another week, and I really couldn't imagine it would, we'd be ready. We also needed to organize the classroom so we would be set for students to return on Monday. Not being sure what would happen over the weekend, we needed to be prepared to pivot with a moment's notice and be ready for both scenarios. I took down the February calendar and put up March. Looking at the shamrocks, I thought March would certainly be our lucky month, when kids would be back and things would return to normal.

I left out all the activities I had planned for the one hundred first day of school, expecting that we could just write off the last week and move forward on Monday. Later in the day, a box of new reading assessment materials was delivered to my classroom. I couldn't bear the thought of testing right now. That was my cue to send my Friday newsletter, lock the door, and go home.

Friday, February 28, 2020

From: Mrs. Tramm
To: VES Kindergarten 2019-2020
Subject: Kindergarten News

Dear Kindergarten Families,

Thank you for sharing photos of your child's learning activities this week. I'm glad the learning didn't stop for them—and it certainly didn't for us! I appreciate the feedback on our online lessons. We continue to make adjustments as needed based on your input. Thanks for helping!

I wish I had more news about what's in store for us next week. We won't know until the garrison makes the call, probably Sunday. Either way, we're ready to go. If the children are back in school next week (I hope!) we will continue with our planned unit of study about dental and personal health and hygiene. Very timely indeed. If not, we will continue with online lessons, new and improved as each day passes.

Please tell our kids we miss them and we will see them soon!

Karin Tramm
VES Kindergarten

Friday! Arriving home, I plopped down on the sofa and thought about the past week with amazement and a bit of awe. We had navigated the challenges and made it through the week. I perused the pizza menu because unlike Gene, who had ordered the same pizza for the last fourteen years, I liked a little variety. Besides the normal options, there was pizza with seafood, pizza with bacon and eggs, even pizza with french fries on top. So many pizzas, so little time.

Our Friday night go-to pizza spot was Gioia Pizza. *Gioia* translated means joy, and we were joyful every Friday when we placed our order. Gioia's was take-out only, perfect for us because we liked to eat and then melt away on the sofa.

"What're you having?" Gene called to me from the kitchen.

"I'll have a *capricciosa*," I decided, "with extra peppers."

It was a favorite covered with pepperoni, artichokes, mushrooms, and sausage. Gene's job was to call in the order and pick up the pies, Friday being my night off in the kitchen.

My phone pinged and I saw a message from my friend and former colleague, Dana, recently retired and living in Georgia. She'd taught kindergarten across the hall from me and we'd shared over a decade of work, travel, and friendship. She went back to the States the year before and I missed her spirit and her often cheeky attitude. I especially missed her for our early morning hallway dance parties.

Dana: Seriously, y'all have to do virtual learning? I just saw the superintendent on Facebook telling the community all about the potential for virtual learning. What has this week been like? What kind of living hell are you going through?

Me: The K team is working together to get the job done. Yesterday was work like a dog day, today the same. I hope school gets back to normal next week. I need to be done with this.

I could only imagine how grateful and relieved she was that she retired when she did. As much as she said she missed Italy, I knew she wouldn't be missing this.

Gene picked up the pizza and started a fire. We tried to watch a movie, but it was hard to focus. My thoughts were bouncing around like kindergartners on the morning after Halloween.

Then we saw the stock market vomit. Had it really only been just one week?

Saturday, February 29, 2020

Buongiorno Italia! Happy Leap Day! But not really.

In many countries, Italy included, leap year is believed to be a year of bad luck. It's a year to be careful about making important decisions, getting married, or making financial investments. This year, 2020, was certainly living up to its reputation. The Italians have a saying, *anno bisesto, anno funesto*. It means, literally, leap year, doom year. As if to highlight that point, on leap day the coronavirus cases in Italy topped one thousand. In retrospect, it was a small number compared to later stats, but at the time it was significant.

Spanish has its own version of the saying, *año bisiesto, año siniestro*, meaning leap year, sinister year. Spaniards weren't aware of it yet, but their turn was next.

In the evening another notification from the American embassy lit up my phone screen.

Updated Travel Advisory, US Embassy Rome, 29 February 2020

Level 3: Reconsider travel to Italy due to a recent outbreak of COVID-19.

Level 4: Do Not Travel to Lombardy and Veneto due to the level of community transmission of the virus and imposition of local quarantine procedures.

We were grounded.

One of the things we appreciated most about our overseas military schools was the opportunity students had to travel. Our boys had both benefited from school events that required passports and plane tickets. For the past few years Gene had accompanied a select group of students to attend the International Student Leadership Institute in Germany. The 2020 assembly was slated for the first week of March.

Youth from schools all over Europe attended, as well as students from the American overseas schools. It was a powerful program that allowed our students to work closely with their international peers. They sharpened their critical thinking and problem-solving skills, learned to view themselves as part of a larger community, and strove to become world citizens. Earlier in the week Gene received a disappointing call from the director. Due to the rising number of coronavirus cases in Vicenza, the high school wouldn't be participating in the program in 2020. Gene began the difficult task of contacting parents and students to share the bitter news. Shortly after, it was communicated that no schools from Italy would attend, and later followed the unfortunate announcement that the entire ISLI event had been canceled. 2020 was indeed an unlucky year.

With Northern Italy all over the news, friends from the States continued to reach out to us.

Mari: Hey guys! I have been thinking about you two since the whole coronavirus thing started. I hope you have enough vino running through your veins to kill it. LOL.

Me: We're hunkered down and hoping we don't have to break into the good stuff. There was no school this past week for the kids. We had to go in and provide online activities for them. Not sure if the kids will come back Monday or not. The garrison will follow the Italians. Stay safe and healthy!

Mari: It's just crazy! Put Gene in one of those hazmat suits. I hope it's just a lot of hysteria and in a month, this won't be a problem at all. Positive vibes to get this under control. Love you guys—peace and love and wine.

Throughout the weekend, emails from students' parents continued to flood my inbox. I honestly didn't mind; I was happy they were reaching out and trying to make this work.

From: Mrs. Khorman
To: Mrs. Tramm
Subject: Thanks
Hi Mrs. Tramm! I hope everything is well with you and Mrs. Dee. We

miss you both and although the kids are excited to be home, they miss being in school too. I love the PE assignment, just 60 minutes physical activity, correct? This has truly helped me with keeping them OFF electronics! Thank you all for continuously working very long and hard to help our babies continue their education! YOU ALL ROCK!

From: Mrs. Wright
To: Mrs. Tramm
Subject: Missing you!

We will get to the work this weekend. This week we found some other sites to make sure we were exercising our brains :). Wren said that she misses you two and her classmates. She's been spelling their names on our fridge with magnet letters. Hopefully they go back to school Monday! We picked up more books from the library yesterday.

From: Mrs. Nunez
To: Mrs. Tramm
Subject: RE: Kindergarten News

Thanks for the update. I just went online and found stuff to do on other websites because we weren't able to log on to everything, just the math. Is there any math missing? The first day was a little chaotic. We finished the assignment and the program just kept going. I told Sara to wrap it up because her sister needed to use the computer, but it just kept on like there was no end to the game. She was not so happy with me when we clicked DONE. She is excited to get the new math lesson for tomorrow.

From: Mr. Lewis
To: Mrs. Tramm
Subject: password

Mrs. Tramm, Layla's password didn't work.

From: Mrs. Tramm
To: Mr. Lewis
Subject: RE: password

Please try again and check the caps lock. Let me know if that was the problem.

From: Mr. Lewis
To: Mrs. Tramm
Subject: RE: password
   Yep, and thank you. We are now able to log into her account.

Sunday, March 1, 2020

I felt overwhelmed by what I needed to do to keep up with everything new. I went into school to try to work while no one else was there. I needed quiet time to contemplate, process, and plan.

Upon arrival, I noticed the parking lot was full, many others having had the same idea. Classroom teachers were hunkered down, not panicked, but anxious. There was no socializing in the hall, just a group of dedicated professionals pounding out a plan for what came next. Whatever that was.

My self-talk sustained me: Change is good, I can do this, I am learning new things, it'll all be over soon.

Vickie messaged that she and her husband might be stuck on Guam because flights to Korea were being canceled. They had connected through Seoul and weren't sure if they would make it out as planned. I messaged back:

Me: Maybe you will get a few extra days of fun in the sun. I hope you had a great time. Sorry we couldn't chat; this week has been complete chaos. Did you take any pictures? We are back at work but still no kids; now conducting virtual school. Not sure what that is going to look like or how long it will last. Do you have to wear a mask on the plane? Safe travels!

In the evening, we received another update from the school. At least now we knew what to expect in the morning.

1 March 2020 Update

Schools in Vicenza are now closed to students through Saturday, March 7. Teachers will report to work as scheduled to plan, deliver, and assess digital learning for students. District expectation of at least two synchronous learning experiences for the students each week remain in effect. Teachers with childcare issues should contact their administrator. Teachers who are not feeling well should stay at home and contact their healthcare professional.

Uncharted waters. Sink or swim. I might need my scuba gear.

WEEK 2: ROBO-TEACHER

Monday, March 2, 2020

I loved my kindergarten team. They were professional, passionate about early childhood education, and most importantly, fun-loving. We prided ourselves on our morning dance party in the hallway before the students arrived. We knew we could gather outside our doors and complain, or we could dance and start the day with a little bit of spunk. Manning our stations before the bell rang, Dana would choose an appropriate song of the day, start the music, and we would sing and make up lyrics to suit us. The kids would laugh when they caught their teachers dancing in the hall and we would all start the day with a fist bump and a giggle.

Entering the building now, the contrast was stark. The halls were cheerless and still, a freeze frame of life interrupted. I unlocked my classroom door, scanned the emptiness, and tried to plan for what came next. The tardy bell rang, startling me as it cut through the silence. As if to mock me, the internet cut in and out. The box of reading tests laughed at me from my desk, and piles of books and papers were strewn willy-nilly across my workspace where I had abandoned them the day before.

Our team was organized and had a week's worth of lessons ready to post. Our task for the day was to unscramble how to hold virtual meetings with our students this week as well as to set up a tentative schedule. But first to figure out what was working and what was not working with the online lessons. I took a breath and opened my email.

From: Mrs. Lewis
To: Mrs. Tramm
Subject: Good morning!

Good morning, are the kids supposed to be online at the same time as school? Will you be teaching virtually? I'm pretty confused. I know the middle schoolers are, but I was not sure about elementary.

From: Mrs. Tramm
To: Mrs. Lewis
Subject: RE: Good morning!

Not for the elementary. We will post new assignments today. Did you ever get into the math program? I'm going to check the account right now and I'll get back to you. Please make sure you go in through the link provided in the kindergarten daily lesson plan.

From: Mrs. Hill
To: Mrs. Tramm
Subject: computer

I am wondering what the procedure is for getting a computer from the school for the week. I was having the kiddos share my computer but then the schoolwork takes FOREVER! I am actually at the school now. Trying to figure it out.

From: Mrs. Tramm
To: Mrs. Hill
Subject: RE: computer

Someone is on the way down to help you.

From: Mrs. Simpson
To: Mrs. Tramm
Subject: where is the math?

Good morning. I can't find the math portion of the lesson plan.

From: Mrs. Tramm
To: Mrs. Simpson
Subject: RE: where is the math?

You're right, it disappeared!! I don't know what happened!! Check back in a few minutes. Thanks for letting me know—*ARGHHHH!!!*

The entire math section of the lesson plan had evaporated. Thank goodness we had kept a backup. As the day wore on, more and more sections continued to get moved around or disappear, like a little mouse nibbling away at our hard work. I couldn't understand how that was happening. Was it my fault? Did I do something while trying to fix it and accidentally delete parts of the document? We really were flying by the seat of our pants. One false move, one innocent click, and things were upended. All. Day. Long.

My aide, Mrs. Dee, had been by my side for two years. She was kind and patient with the kids and with me. She was working on a master's degree online, so she was already familiar with virtual learning and incredibly tech savvy. She saved me on a number of occasions when I had given up on computers and the world. Today she might as well have been wearing a cape as she used her superpowers to make things right.

From: Mrs. Grant
To: Mrs. Tramm
Subject: help
Good morning! I can't get into the meeting.

From: Mrs. Tramm
To: Mrs. Grant
Subject: RE: help
Don't try to log in right now. We are still setting it up. You won't need to log in with an email or password. Hang on and I'll get back to you.

From: Mrs. Grant
To: Mrs. Tramm
Subject: RE: help
Okay great! Also, I know this is not ideal for you and I just want to say thanks for even making this possible. You guys are greatly appreciated!

From: Mrs. Taylor
To: Mrs. Tramm
Subject: three pigs
Good morning! I wanted to let you know that the *Three Little Pigs*

assignment isn't in the work folder. Those pigs must be hiding from us. Hahaha!

From: Mrs. Tramm
To: Mrs. Taylor
Subject: RE: three pigs
   I just reassigned it, so log out and log back in and see if that works. Please let me know. Also, I know that the online journal for the science lesson did not connect. We are troubleshooting that right now as well.

From: Mrs. Taylor
To: Mrs. Tramm
Subject: RE: three pigs
   And I will try another laptop. According to my husband, this program doesn't work with my computer. I will keep trying and get back to you.

From: Mrs. Grant
To: Mrs. Tramm
Subject: help again
   Hi! The art program doesn't seem to be working for us. The page loads, but when we try to create a new project to play around with the features, it doesn't work.

From: Mrs. Tramm
To: Mrs. Grant
Subject: RE: help again
   Maybe it's the browser. Chrome works best; are you using Chrome or Explorer? When you click NEW what happens?

From: Mrs. Grant
To: Mrs. Tramm
Subject: RE: help again
   It was my browser. I am using Chrome now and it works fine. Thanks for the tip!

From: Mrs. Hill
To: Mrs. Tramm
Subject: UGH

Ugh … school is hard, haha. Where do I find the online journal template? Am I in the right area?? Please don't get annoyed with me.

From: Mrs. Tramm
To: Mrs. Hill
Subject: RE: UGH

I know, school is really hard for me right now, too, haha. We are working on this problem as I write—the journal did not transfer for some reason. We are aware and trying to fix it. Please don't get annoyed with us either.

From: Mrs. Adams
To: Mrs. Tramm
Subject: sorry

Hello, Mrs. Tramm. We did last week's homework and then I tried to sort out today's work, but it was a challenge. I'm helping out a friend and watching her kids while she is at work. Right now, I have seven kids in the house and unfortunately not enough hands and eyes. I hope it's okay that we finish it tonight when it's a quieter. Please know we are working on it. Our days have been filled with painting, hide and seek, story time, bike rides, and walks. Honestly, it's been fun. I will work on setting up a study area and we will get going on these assignments tonight after dinner. Thank you to the kindergarten team for all your hard work. We are looking forward to this week's digital learning.

From: Mrs. Tramm
To: Mrs. Adams
Subject: RE: sorry

Thanks for touching base. I know you have a full house. Finish the assignments when you have time. You are doing all the right things :)

The parents were champs. But what else did I expect from military families that spend a lifetime navigating the curveballs of chance and circumstance? They were working as hard or harder than I was.

When I was semi-confident I had my act together, I sent out an email letting them know the plan for the group meeting the next morning.

From: Mrs. Tramm
To: VES Kindergarten 2019-2020
Subject: Digital Learning Update 2

Dear Kindergarten Families,

Tomorrow morning I will send you a link for a group meeting check in. We will be touching base with all kindergarten parents from 9-9:30. If you are unable to connect, because of technical issues or because of the time, please email me so we can figure out what to do.

We appreciate all your hard work and patience. We continue to work and learn together on this, so thank you for your input and teamwork. Thanks also for all the pictures you sent in today, keep them coming!

Karin Tramm
VES Kindergarten

From: Mrs. Yates
To: Mrs. Tramm
Subject: RE: Digital Learning Update 2

Good afternoon, Mrs. Tramm. I read the last email and we might have a problem with checking in. My husband and I are dual military and unfortunately our two children are going to work with us. I hope there is an exception. We will do all the assignments, but the meetings might be a problem.

From: Mrs. Tramm
To: Mrs. Yates
Subject: RE: Digital Learning Update 2

Thanks for letting me know, I was thinking about your family. Don't worry, I will figure out a way to connect.

From: Mrs. Khorman
To: Mrs. Tramm
Subject: thank you

Thank you for all your hard work. We are looking forward to the group chat.

From: Mrs. Tramm
To: Mrs. Khorman
Subject: RE: thank you
   Once we know this is working for everyone, each teacher will send
out the link for their own class. It's a step-by-step process and we hope
to be proficient at it soon. In my perfect world, I will try to do a read
aloud and if we get really good at it, maybe a morning message.

Things were still a mess, but at least now my mess was organized into
piles. There was the online lesson plan pile, virtual meeting pile, and
family pile. My family mess was not as critical as that of some of my
colleagues. At least not yet.

Many teachers were trying to juggle virtual lesson plans at work and
online learning at home with their own children. Some of the lucky ones
found childcare with a friend, but many had no other choice than to
bring their younger children to work with them. They were burning the
candle at both ends, holding virtual meetings on one screen and checking
second grade math assignments on another, attending to squabbles, and
making lunch. They were surviving, making it work, because what else
could they do? I felt their anxiety but at the same time thought how lucky
they were to have their kids close by. I was struggling to keep in touch
with my boys, one being six hours ahead and the other six hours behind.
Doing the time zone shuffle was a challenge in normal times and now, a
woeful exercise in frustration in the midst of this reality whiplash.

On the way home I stopped at my favorite Italian grocery store, the
Alì, to pick up a few necessities. Although we were still being advised
otherwise, some people were wearing masks and I could feel the layers of
fear and apprehension in the air. I quickly filled my basket and rolled up
to the *cassa*, careful to keep a proper distance between myself and other
customers.

"*Buona sera*," I greeted the cashier as I unloaded the last of my items
and handed him my Alì customer card.

"*Salve*," he responded warmly but wearily, scanning the card, and
handing it back to me. He must've had a long day, too.

To my annoyance, I felt a tickly sensation starting in the back of my throat. It was that prickly dry allergy-season feeling that can only be alleviated by a swig of cold water or a good hearty cough. I tried a mini cough, then cleared my throat. He looked at me and I smiled weakly, my eyes starting to water as I tried with all my might not to cough.

This was the last place I needed to have a hacking spell, but the harder I tried to hold it in, the more tears gushed from my eyes. My nose began to run. I had to let it out, but gently. I covered my mouth with my elbow, coughed a few times, and tried not to make eye contact with anyone. The couple behind me in line, a man and his elderly mother, stared in abject horror. They had already unloaded their groceries onto the conveyor belt but in response to my coughing they turned and walked away, leaving everything behind. Now it was my turn to be horrified. I handed over my euro, packed my groceries, and fled to the car, throwing my shopping bags into the back seat. I slammed the door and coughed so hard, I was certain my projectile tears hit the windshield.

That was surely my most embarrassing grocery shopping moment since my bickering boys, four and five years old, flipped the grocery cart in the produce section of the Oceana Commissary in Virginia Beach. I hadn't thought of that day in forever, but driving away from the Alì I recalled how I watched my purse cartwheel through the air in slow motion, the contents emptying onto the Pink Lady apples, the bag finally coming to rest in the Granny Smiths. After gathering my belongings, children included, I pulled over into the bakery section and the three of us all had a good cry. Then we each had a doughnut, because when Dad was deployed, sometimes you could have doughnuts for dinner.

If only there were Krispy Kremes at the Alì.

~

Barbara and I tried to communicate each day, keeping each other apprised of our swirling worlds. My phone pinged with a message soon after arriving home from the store.

Barbara: Brian and I are getting ready, stocking up on essentials. How are things in your part of the world?

Me: We're okay here but things are kinda weird. No public gatherings are allowed, and schools are still closed to students. We're required to go to work and provide lessons via the computer.

It's business as usual in many ways. Stores are still open, but people are skittish, especially if you cough or sneeze in public. This afternoon I was in the checkout line at the Italian grocery store and got that itchy throat that makes you want to cough. I tried really hard to hold it back, but my eyes started to water and, I swear, tears started to squirt out of my eyes. I had a little controlled cough and the couple behind me in line left the store. I felt really bad but what could I do?

Glad to see you and Brian are stocking up and preparing. You're going to be fine, but Mom and Dad need to start staying home.

Barbara: Our wine stock keeps disappearing. LOL. The virus is here, only low counts up until now, but I'm sure it will steadily climb. Are you still planning to visit Ian on your spring break?

Me: We haven't canceled our trip yet but just heard there is a fourteen-day quarantine for us to enter Thailand. I don't think we can go. I don't think we'll be able to go anywhere to be quite honest.

Barbara: I'm supposed to fly to North Carolina to see Morgan next month. Even that is beginning to be a little bit concerning.

Me: I don't think anyone's going anywhere for a while.

Message to Mom: Are you home?

Mom: Yes

Me: Good, because you and Dad don't need to be going anywhere right now. I'll call you in a few minutes.

We tried to do a video call, but the connection kept failing. I couldn't figure out if technology was my friend or my foe.

Tuesday, March 3, 2020

Gene and I packed our lunches and our school bags and headed to the car. On the way down the driveway, he slowly rolled to a stop and pointed to something in the sea of grass.

"Look over there," he almost whispered.

Peering out the car window, I glanced at the hayfield, misty and rippling. Halfway across I could see the head of our old friend Mr. Fagiano, a ring-necked pheasant, in the pearly early morning light.

"They're back," I said, "I guess it's that time."

Every year the pheasants returned for mating season, the males resplendent in their plumage and the females in their quiet camouflage. Later, the mother and chicks would appear now and then crossing the driveway in search of berries, seeds, and insects. Our landlord encouraged them to stay by leaving them pieces of cake in the backyard. It must've worked because every year they turned up to raise their brood. We learned the call of the pheasant our first year in the house and smiled when we heard it, knowing spring was right around the corner and the *fagiani* were back. Amid all the madness, the pheasants were still having their dance party.

We continued our drive to post, approaching the first security check. Gene flashed our ID cards and we were waved through. It was always a good morning when we didn't get flagged for a random search, draining our precious minutes of prep time before school. We stopped at the second checkpoint and Gene handed over the ID cards to be scanned.

"*Buongiorno!*" we exchanged morning pleasantries as the gate guard returned the cards.

We drove on, careful to avoid a group of soldiers running in full gear, out for morning PT. Gene pulled up in front of the high school.

"Don't get fired," I called cheerfully as he got out of the car.

It had become our droll goodbye to each other every morning as we'd gotten more and more cynical about the changes taking place in education. I climbed into the driver's seat, backed the car out, and waved to Gene as he strolled over to Pino's, the coffee shop across the street. As I watched him get in line, I thought how lucky he was to have Pino's right there within walking distance of his classroom.

I continued on to the elementary school, five minutes away in the family housing area. Mrs. Dee was already hard at work on our Welcome Back bulletin board. She had printed out pictures parents sent in and stapled them on the bulletin board outside the classroom door.

"So cute!" I said, reading the captions and quotes she'd added. "The kids are going to love looking at these."

They'd been working so hard. We knew they'd be beside themselves to see their pictures, and their friends' pictures, when they came back to school. I could imagine the excitement, the buzz of their voices already. Maybe we could have a quick show-and-tell session out in the hall.

"Let's print out their writing assignments and put them out here, too," I added, "right above their coat hooks."

The children would be delighted to see their work displayed, just as we would be delighted to see their jackets and backpacks hanging on those hooks again.

With high hopes, we attempted to hold our first virtual class meeting. We invited all kindergarten parents to join so we could explain the program and answer questions from families. The parents were patient and trusted we could figure it out together. Still, technology trouble and computer chaos kept us on our toes. During the meeting, emails continued to roll in like waves on the beach.

From: Mrs. Nunez
To: Mrs. Tramm
Subject: meeting

We are unable to access the meeting. Message code is saying, "Video calling is not available in your organization. Try using a different account or contact administrator." I am using Chrome.

From: Mrs. Grant
To: Mrs. Tramm
Subject: unable to connect

Hi! We can't connect. It's asking for email address and password. The technology issues are wearing my patience thin; we've all been in tears at some point every day. Some of the programs will work on an iPad, some won't, and we only have one computer to complete assignments. Neither of my kids is completely able to be self-sufficient and I can't be at two places at once. I can't seem to get this app to work on my phone either. Sorry to vent and I appreciate you!

I could sense their raw frustration, but I could also feel their dedication to making this work for the kids. Their challenges ranged from lack of technology, to dual working parents with no childcare, to sharing devices. My learning curve was surely a stressor to them as well, as I stumbled my way through the assignments. They had been unbelievably adaptable and had shown enormous patience with the process.

Mrs. Dee continued to be a real rock star, too. She had problems fixed in an instant, sometimes before I was even aware of an issue. I thanked my lucky stars she was a part of the team.

From: Mrs. Tramm
To: VES Kindergarten 2019-2020
Subject: Digital Learning Update 3

Dear Kindergarten Families,

We are learning a lot today! Thanks to all who were able to connect to the meeting and to those who let me know about any issues. The next step for our class is to figure out the times that work best for virtual meetings. Understanding that many of you have other students, I will offer a couple of different times during the week so you have options. Please send me a quick reply and let me know the best time for you, next best, and worst time for you (within the school day 8:00-2:40). I will put together a flexible schedule that meets your needs.

Thanks again for all the input, pictures, and videos, and a shoutout to Mrs. Dee who is holding this all together!

Karin Tramm
VES Kindergarten

After sending the newsletter, my thoughts drifted to Florida. It was time to check up on my mom and dad.

Message to Mom: Just checking in to make sure you are staying home. Dad, too.

Mom: Your dad just went to the bank to get some cash.

Me: I heard touching money is bad. Please tell me he washed his hands as soon as he got home.

Mom: He did, and I washed all the doorknobs. We are good.

Me: Okay, just checking. I wish I had some spyware on you guys.

Mom: Good thing you don't.

Me: I know. I'd have a heart attack because you two weren't behaving.

Mom: I am behaving now.

Me: Thank you.

I wanted to think they were being careful, but I still wasn't sure.

~

Gene and I made the drive home in the golden afternoon light. The pheasant was nowhere in sight, but we were confident we would be seeing more of him and hoped that in time we would meet the family.

I went inside, unpacked my school bag, and checked the news before starting dinner. Each time I looked, there was a new blurb that caused concern, and now that concern was in Florida, way too close to home. There was a COVID-19 case in Manatee County, where my family lives. I messaged Barbara to see if she had heard anything on the local news.

Barbara: The person who tested positive is quarantined, but they don't know the source. That means it's still out there somewhere.

Me: Yes, it is. I talked to Mom and Dad about the importance of staying home and washing hands and using hand sanitizer. Mom was at the grocery store this morning and then to the outlet mall. Dad was on his way out the door when I hung up. I told them not to go to church for a while. I don't mean to be an alarmist, but this has the potential to blow up, especially considering the older population of this community. Think about how it has exploded here in Italy in just one week! Anyway, please encourage them to stay home. They're both about to turn 80!

Barbara: I agree. They have enough to eat and drink for months. Are you still teaching remotely?

Me: Yes. Teachers report to work; kids are still at home. I'm providing online lessons and trying to do face-to-face instruction with virtual meetings. The rumor mill says we may be doing this until spring break. Please no, I'm hoping not! I'm praying the kids are back next week. I can't take much more of this robo-teaching.

Barbara: I can't wrap my head around how you'd do that with kindergarten when it's so hands-on. Do you have a Barney suit?

Message from Vickie: We made it! We are back in the US sitting in the Detroit airport for another four hours, waiting to catch our flight to Virginia Beach. Lots of fun on Guam; saw lots of people. Let me know if you're home during the day or at work this week. When is a good time to call?

Wednesday, March 4, 2020

The current update from the Italian prime minister indicated that any Italians over the age of seventy were advised to stay home and avoid even walking outside. Sporting events were canceled for the public; games would continue, but in empty stadiums. The absence of the roaring crowds would be sorely disappointing for diehard soccer fans, but at least they could still watch the games at home on TV or with their *amici* in their favorite sports bar. Other guidance advised citizens not to share drinking glasses and not to shake hands. Then the harshest of harsh—no kissing! This last directive would be most difficult, if not impossible, for the Italians to follow.

From: Mrs. Tramm
To: VES Kindergarten 2019-2020
Subject: Digital Learning Update 4

Dear Kindergarten Families,

We had great input from our class meeting yesterday. We seem to have most of the bugs worked out, so we will start today with our virtual sessions. I have heard back from most of the class on your best available times. Almost all of you prefer the morning, but not too early. I know there are a couple of families where afternoon works best. My plan for today is to meet both in the morning and in the afternoon. The primary goal is to reconnect with each other and learn to use the mute button so we can take turns talking, just like we do at school (just like we try to do at school—haha!). We will practice that first. I will read a story and then we'll sign off until the afternoon, allowing the children to work independently on their digital assignments, which will be posted at ten o'clock.

Someone asked yesterday how long the children should spend on the assignments and I want to reiterate that the answer is different for each child—just like at school some children need more time than others. The most important thing to remember is to take frequent breaks; we don't want them in front of the screen all day. You also know their frustration point, so please be aware and let that guide you.

We will meet again after lunch at two o'clock for another read-aloud and to talk about our day. If your child was not able to attend the morning meeting, please join a few minutes early so we can go over the mute procedures. Your child is welcome to attend one or both of the meetings. If you run into problems during the meeting, as always, please email me so we can troubleshoot them when the meeting is closed. See you soon!

Karin Tramm
VES Kindergarten

The morning meeting with my students did my heart a lot of good. I missed hearing their funny stories, igniting their sense of wonder, and chuckling at their honesty. They seemed to be doing okay, but I could read the anxiety and misunderstanding in their little faces. When the meeting was over, we sang the "Goodbye Song," but I could tell no one really wanted to say goodbye. They needed to tell me something, anything, just to stay in the meeting, just to feel connected. I knew there would be a lot of emotional repair for us to do once we were back in the classroom. It would take a bit of time to restore our sense of community and move forward, but these kids were resilient, and I was confident we would work through this.

The bell rang in my empty classroom as the school day drew to a close. Clouds shadowed the building and cold rain splattered on the playground outside my windows. When Gene texted from the parking lot, I dug out my umbrella, jumped over puddles, and splashed my way out to the car.

The rain eased as we headed north toward Bolzano Vicentino. When I saw sunbeams streaming through the black rain clouds, I knew a rainbow must be somewhere. Sure enough, as we rounded a traffic circle, a magnificent double rainbow spanned the sky. *Andrà tutto bene.* Everything would be fine, I repeated to myself as we made our way home.

Message to Mom: We have at least two more days of no school. Things are tightening down here. Everyone over 70 is supposed to stay home. I hope you both are staying home.

Mom: Well, I have a doctor's appointment at 10:30 and then I will come home. We are taking precautions, don't worry. Thanks for the update.

Message from Vickie: I am home and in a travel fog. Busy weekend, a friend is here visiting, and my youngest is here on his way to spring break. I have great funny stories to tell you from Guam, what a blast from the past. Will call you when we both have a free moment.

Thursday, March 5, 2020

Read Across America Week, marking the birthday of Dr. Seuss, was always a kindergarten highlight. This year I was sorely disappointed that the week had passed and we hadn't been able to come back to school for the fun. The kids delighted in reading Dr. Seuss stories, making hats, and playing rhyming games. Wearing our pint-sized aprons, we cooked green eggs and ham in our classroom kitchen using our homemade recipe books.

The kindergarten team decided to wish Dr. Seuss a happy belated birthday the following week. We hoped the kids would be back and we could get down to business as usual. I got out the mixing bowl, frying pan, and aprons, and laid them on the kitchen table in preparation. The aides got to work with butcher paper and old carpet rolls, turning the kindergarten hallway into a brightly colored Truffula forest. I could already envision our first hallway dance party.

From: Mrs. Taylor
To: Mrs. Tramm
Subject: math again
Something on my laptop doesn't like the math program. Working with both kids back and forth I am just doing trial and error to see

which laptop works for who in which assignment. We are still trying
to have fun with it. Thanks for everything—kinder rocks! But trying to
manage this with kids in multiple grades is getting on my last nerve.

Gene and I arrived home tired but hopeful. Perhaps this would be the
last week of this mess. I started dinner and thought about calling Mom
and Dad, but decided against it, telling myself I shouldn't badger them
so much. I felt sure my nagging was getting tiresome for them, but I
couldn't help checking up. As if reading my mind, the phone pinged.

Message from Mom: FYI just to let you know that I didn't go out with
your dad today. Since he took the car, it's a good thing you don't have a
way to track it. You would think I was out!

Me: I'm glad you're home. I hope he comes straight back and doesn't
go anywhere else. Tell him to wash his hands as soon as he gets home.
Sorry, I know I sound annoying.

Mom: I sent the bottle of hand sanitizer with him.

Me: Thanks. I just want you both to be safe. I realize you're aware, but
this is NOT just the flu.

Mom: I know. Your sister feels the same.

Friday, March 6, 2020

School and breath. School and breath.

"Take a big yoga breath," I liked to remind my students in an effort to
help them calm down. "In through your nose, lick your lips, out through
your mouth."

Today I took my own advice, and just tried to get through the day, to
keep breathing as another week of virtual learning was announced. The
K team scurried to gather *The Cat in the Hat* materials we prepared for
next week's lessons and transform them into packets for the kids to do
at home. If one of us could make it to the post office in a timely manner,
students would have what they needed on Monday. We quickly adapted
the online lessons to use the materials we were mailing out. I sighed as
I busied myself putting away the aprons and cooking supplies. I crossed
eggs off the grocery list.

There were fresh rumors that shipments would stop coming from Germany, causing another run on the commissary. People posted pictures of the jammed parking lot and empty shelves in the cleaning supply aisle. Wasn't everything in that section gone already last week? The checkout line snaked around to the meat section at the back of the store. Toilet paper was wiped out. I said a quick little thank you for the bidet.

From: Mrs. Tramm
To: VES Kindergarten 2019-2020
Subject: Kindergarten News, Friday, March 6, 2020

Dear Kindergarten Families,

It's been quite a week. Thank you all for stepping up and helping out—it was a lot of learning for all of us. If you are noticing things on your end that might help me improve the group meetings, please let me know. I'm trying to adjust the camera so it's good for a story and for the easel. It's also hard for me to know if the sound is okay. Did using an "X" to raise your hand work? I know the kids had to wait awhile for their turns, but I can see that they were interacting with you during their mute time. And great job teaching them to mute! Now I'm wondering how to make a mute button for my classroom for when we return. LOL.

Remember that your child doesn't have to attend every session. I need to see them at least twice a week but would LOVE to see them as much as possible. We miss them!

This week was Read Across America Week, celebrating the birthday of Dr. Seuss and the joy of reading. The kindergarten team does not want to miss out on the fun so we will wish Dr. Seuss a belated birthday next week. We sent your child some snail mail this afternoon, so please check your mailbox on Monday for rhyming games and more fun with Dr. Seuss. Get ready for some outside fun, a delicious cooking project, and more Seuss-on-the-loose adventures. Have a great weekend!

Karin Tramm
VES Kindergarten

Ian called from Bangkok, in a fluster. He was there for the weekend and planned to return to his host family in Prachin Buri by bus on Monday. Upon his return, he'd have to move out of his house for twenty-one days.

There had been some miscommunication, lost in translation, when Ian was planning his trip. He found out about the return quarantine less than an hour before his bus left for the city. A flurry of phone calls concluded with him having to sprint back to his room to make preparations to move. He packed a quarantine bag, fetched his bike, and stashed it at his new place fifty feet down the street.

Ian loved his host family. They had been incredibly accommodating, feeding him, helping him with the Thai language, and even taking him on sightseeing adventures around the area. We had met them via a video call, with Ian translating. We met the host grandma, washing vegetables in the kitchen sink. We met host brother and host sister bopping around the house, giggling, and hanging on Ian like the big brother he was. We met the host parents, both medical professionals, and we hoped they understood our appreciation and relief that they had made him feel a part of their own family. We were a little jealous, too, hearing him refer to them as his host mom and host dad.

However, the host family was rightfully concerned about exposure to COVID-19. There was an elderly great-grandmother, more than ninety years old—they weren't really sure of her age—living in the house. They needed to be sure her health was not compromised. Hence, it was imperative that Ian be COVID-free upon his return. There was a designated place nearby where Ian would live until his time-out was finished. It was spartan at best, but thankfully he had a place to bathe, poop, and sleep—and he would be able to return to work.

Saturday, March 7, 2020

The weekend was upon us and I finally felt like I could catch my breath. I spent two hours on the phone catching up with Vickie, getting the latest gossip, hearing about old friends and new restaurants. Almost thirty years since I had lived on Guam, yet so many things sounded the same.

"There's still construction on Marine Drive," she laughed, and I imagined her rolling her eyes.

Some things never change, I thought, the main thoroughfare always a mess at one end of the island or another. I imagined for a moment I was back at the Blue Lagoon, soaking up sun, grading papers, and snacking on octopus *kelaguen*. Life seemed so uncomplicated back then.

We chatted and filled each other in on the boys' latest adventures. Coincidently, in the crisscross of our lives, two of her sons also lived in Miami. One of them attended FIU, the same university as Will, although a different campus. He would graduate after the spring semester, and so would her youngest son, from the University of Virginia. Both ceremonies were on the same weekend, one on Friday and the other on Saturday. It would require some crazy flights and no sleep, but she and her husband had a plan to make it work.

The conversation reminded me of Ian's graduation from Florida State University nearly two years ago. Gene and I had arrived at Marco Polo Airport in Venice early on a Thursday morning only to discover our flight had been canceled and the check-in desk closed with no one in sight.

After a frustrating exchange of phone calls, a guardian angel from another carrier intervened. We were able to change our itinerary and made it out a few hours later on a partner airline. We arrived several hours late in Tampa, sometime after midnight (six in the morning according to our body clocks), then drove an hour south to my parents' home. We had what amounted to a few minutes of restless sleep, then loaded into a van at five in the morning with my parents, sister, and brother-in-law for the drive up to Tallahassee.

It felt like sliding into home plate when we sped into the civic center parking lot, just in the nick of time, and converged with the rest of the family. Will rolled in from Miami, Cousin Morgan arrived from North Carolina. We found our seats in the massive auditorium and watched Ian walk across the stage. I didn't even care that he was wearing shoes with no socks under his gown. He graduated!

I love how our tribe shows up. We spent a jet-lagged Saturday with the family and left early Sunday morning to fly back to our jobs in Italy. Crazy, the things we do for our kids, but we make it work.

~

I called my parents to touch base and pester them again about staying home.

"I know you're sick of hearing this, I'm sorry. You know when this whole thing started, it was a church service where it first spread."

I imagined the hand shaking, the kissing, the passing of the collection plate, touched by everyone in the church as it went from pew to pew. I thought of the Italians all putting their hands in the holy water and then touching their faces.

"You really shouldn't go to church tomorrow," I continued. "I know your friends are going to be there, but please, please, just do this for me."

A lengthy silence followed. I continued in frustration, "I wish I could just tell you what to do!"

Finally, my dad spoke up, "Well, it sounds like you just did."

~

Over the summer my close friend Misty, a fellow kindergarten teacher, had been transferred to a school down in Sigonella, a navy base in Sicily. I first met her in Vicenza when she joined the kindergarten team. Misty was a former army officer, and her husband was active duty. Her youngest daughter was in my class that year, and Misty worked in the classroom across the hall. We started team-teaching and, more importantly, began a lasting friendship. I loved her sense of humor and her ability to put things into perspective. She was good at saying hard things in a nice way and was a staunch advocate for early childhood education. She whooped it up during our kindergarten hallway dance parties. I missed her. A lot.

Message from Misty: OMG you are still closed? What are you doing?

Me: We post daily lesson plans from the online curriculum resources the school has provided. And anything else we can find online. I'm having live sessions with the kids twice a day.

Misty: Last night we went to a restaurant, and they were moving the tables far apart as per the new social distancing regulations. Meanwhile, we are still scheduled to have a college and career fair, literacy night, and a high school dance! I'm not sure if we are heading toward closure or not but I would love to see your lesson plans, just in case.

Me: Yes, of course, no need to reinvent the wheel. I sent you an email with the link. Miss you!

It was comforting to hear from friends and family and to know they were keeping an eye on our situation in northern Italy. We felt loved and supported but also nervous, knowing we were just a week or two ahead of them in the chaos.

Message to Barbara: Sadly, we are looking at a third week of online teaching. I sure have learned a lot about technology these past two weeks! I do miss my kids but I'm very thankful that I won't be at school this week on Friday the thirteenth with a full moon. I think some parents may be a lot more responsive to behavior issues once all this passes.

I'm glad you already stocked up on supplies. I saw on the news there was a run on toilet paper in the States. And thanks for reminding Mom and Dad to stay home. Not that they will; I suspect they think I am overreacting. Yesterday when I called, I advised them NOT to go to church tomorrow. I don't think they liked that very much.

Barbara: Yep, the last thing I want is for them to get this mess. We'll keep a watch as best we can. Is everything good with the boys?

Me: Will is good. He was in Nashville last weekend but is back in Miami now. His band was playing in the Miami Music Fair that just got canceled. I know he is bummed about it, but I haven't talked to him since I heard.

Ian is Ian. He went on a trip to southern Thailand with some of his coworkers, local teachers. I think he had fun—the part he can tell me anyway. Haha. He went to Bangkok last weekend and is now in quarantine. He's not sick; he's just making sure no one else gets sick. I'm so sad that we have to cancel our spring break trip to Thailand. It's been over a year since we've seen Ian.

There's also a quarantine for us if we travel to the States, so basically, we can't go anywhere except here in the Veneto and that's not really safe right now.

Barbara: I know how hard it must be not to see your kids, especially now. I was checking on flights to North Carolina to see Morgan, but then I thought it might not be a good idea to be in the airport, or an airplane, right now.

Me: I know. And on Tuesday, Mom and Dad are going to Tampa International Airport to pick up their friend who is coming to visit from England! I hate to say this, but I hope she changes her mind and decides NOT to come.

Barbara: I didn't realize that was Tuesday, but I guess it's time. Their plan is to take her around in the motor home to see some of her friends. At least they'll be riding and sleeping in their own environment and not around large groups or a lot of public places.

Me: I know, but she may be infected from the airport or the airplane and pass it around. I'm worried, but they will do what they will do. Maybe she'll decide it's not the best time to come. Or maybe her children will try to talk her out of it. The airports have so-called screening processes in place, but flights continue out of Milan, Venice, and Verona every day. People make connections and then go on to their final destinations. They can be asymptomatic, and there they go, virus and all. Travel is a huge risk at this point. And old people shouldn't be traveling at all right now. Period.

As hard as I tried, I failed in my attempts to stop compulsively checking the news. I poured a glass of wine and curled up on the sofa, pulling out my phone and scrolling through the news stories. It had been a while since I'd seen something to make me laugh, but there it was, and I almost snorted my wine when I read it.

The article detailed a malfunction at a local winery in the northern Italian town of Castelvetro. The glitch caused Lambrusco to accidentally leak into the municipal water supply, causing red wine to flow from the faucets of several nearby homes. Many residents bottled it for later use and some, the article reported, complained that the water company fixed it too quickly. Locals may have considered it divine intervention. I wondered if the residents of Castelvetro also wished for no surprises as they parked their cars each evening. Perhaps this surprise wouldn't have been so traumatic, unless someone was washing a load of whites. I laughed out loud at the write-up and forwarded it to my sister and the boys, hoping it might brighten their day as well. If alcohol killed the virus, perhaps we could bathe in it.

Sunday, March 8, 2020

Waking up to the sun was glorious. I lounged and stretched and reached for my phone to check news updates before getting out of bed. Shocked, I saw the early morning headlines broadcasting to the rest of the world:

"NORTHERN ITALY QUARANTINES SIXTEEN MILLION PEOPLE"

Ironically, northern Italians are all too familiar with the word "quarantine," after all, they were the ones who invented it. Originating in the Veneto, *quarantine* was derived from the word for forty in the Venetian dialect—*quaranta*. Centuries ago, to prevent the spread of the black plague, ships and travelers were required to wait in isolation for forty days before entering the watery cities of the Venetian republic. As the bubonic plague had a thirty-seven-day time lapse from infection to death, it proved to be a successful deterrent against the spread of the disease. We hoped it would be so again.

Messages flew as friends and colleagues woke up and reacted to this new development. What exactly would quarantine mean for us now?

Message to Barbara: Venice, Padua, and Treviso provinces are all locked down now. Vicenza is not in the red zone as of yet, but I bet we will be by tomorrow. We border Treviso and Padua. We have families that live in Padua Province. I wonder how this will play out. Schools in those provinces are closed until April 3.

Barbara: Wow, hopefully this will be a chance to get a handle on this.

Later, a concerned email came from my brother, Bill, a Merchant Marine captain currently on board a ship in Diego Garcia.

From: Bill
To: Karin
Subject: Italy

Karin,

I have been following the COVID-19 saga as it is impacting our crew changes all the way here in Diego. You can't get much more isolated than here, but we are still taking protective measures and screening all new arrivals. I download the World Health Organization's SITREP each day and monitor the cases. I see there was a sharp jump in cases in Italy and it looks like the northern region where you are is hardest hit. Mom told me you were stuck at home, so I just wanted to check in on you and make sure you and Gene are OK. Nothing exciting to report from here, which is good.

Be safe,
Bill

From: Karin
To: Bill
Subject: RE: Italy

Hey Bill, thanks for the email. School has been out for two weeks so far, and we don't know how much longer, but things are not getting any better yet. Even though the kids are at home, we still have to report to work and robo-teach from our classroom via virtual meetings and online resources.

Our trip to see Ian in Thailand is canceled. We would have to quarantine fourteen days to enter. Plus, the airports are closing down here. I'm not even sure if we will be able to travel by summer. We also would have to quarantine if we flew to the States right now.

I'm most concerned about Mom and Dad. Mom is already immune-compromised because of her lymphoma. There is a coronavirus case in Manatee County of unknown origin and that is extremely concerning. I've talked with them about it, but I'm not sure they understand the urgency of this. I have begged them to just stay home right now. Their friend is flying in from the UK on Tuesday and staying with them and I think they are planning on taking her around to visit friends! I really hope she doesn't end up coming right now. They don't need to be out and about, and even if she is virus-free now, who knows what she might be exposed to in the airports. They are all so very vulnerable.

Anyway, you are in a safe and isolated place, I hope. We will see what unfolds in Florida. I think we are just a week or two ahead of them. Stay tuned and I'll keep you posted with the Tramm fam SITREP. Keep washing your hands!

Love,
Karin

Message to Mom: Happy Sunday. Please DO NOT go to church today.

Mom: We are not going. Are you still going into school?

Me: Yes, I still have to go in every day. I do online lessons and meetings, but the kids are still at home.

Mom: How can you tell if they are paying attention? And what kind of lessons can you do for kinders online?

Me: It's a video meeting so I can see them—nose pickers and all. They are pretty hilarious. Sometimes they are in bed or eating their breakfast. But I really don't mind—I just need to connect with them and am grateful we can see each other, even it's only on a computer screen. It's a strange new world.

Mom: It sure is a change. So, are we still a go for Will's graduation? Late July or early August? Surely, they will have a handle on this virus by then. So glad it's in the summer so you will be able to stay a little longer, not like Ian's graduation. Barb told us you aren't going to Thailand to see Ian, but I expected that. The airlines here are refunding money. Can you get anything back?

Me: We don't know about that situation yet. I don't think we can get a refund, but we are trying to get a ticket change and use it to get us to Florida this summer.

And yes, graduation is still a go as far as we know. Thank goodness it's in the summer so this time we will arrive in plenty of time.

In the evening we ventured outside on the terrace to enjoy the crisp night air and the clear sky. Bolzano Vicentino is far enough away from Vicenza to escape the city lights, making stargazing a dazzling diversion. We watched planes overhead and tried to guess where they were headed. To Venice, perhaps? Treviso? Verona? Down to Rome or over the Alps and up to Germany and beyond?

"Check out that one" Gene said, pointing skyward. "Can you see it over there by those trees? And there's another right behind it! Wow!"

I peered up and squinted, catching sight of the faint light gliding across the star-strewn sky. "I see it. Oh yeah, I see both of them."

"There's a third! And a fourth! Okay, this is weird." Gene tried to process the scenario, but it made no sense. It looked to be a long line of high-flying aircraft all traveling northeast in formation, nothing like we'd ever seen.

"Sixteen, seventeen, eighteen …" We continued to count at least twenty and wondered where they were headed, perhaps Aviano Air Force Base? Could this be some kind of evacuation?

When Gene was active duty and our family was stationed overseas, we had to keep a Noncombatant Evacuation Operations (NEO) packet, documents that would facilitate emergency evacuation and repatriation on short notice. On more than one occasion we had participated in NEO drills, going as far as boarding the planes. Was this possible? We knew that American civilians had been evacuated from Wuhan, but would that really happen here? It was hard to imagine, but we were living in interesting times.

"What would you take with a moment's notice?" I asked Gene. "Passports, wallet, phone, military orders, a few days' worth of clothes?"

"Gioia pizza," he answered, always the jokester.

Probably not a bad idea, I thought, recalling some of the Space-A military flights I had endured in days gone by. We laughed and brainstormed a list of things we would need in case of an emergency evacuation.

Before heading off to bed I checked in with my sister.

Message to Barbara: Gene and I just watched a line of at least twenty planes pass over our house tonight. Gene thinks they were military planes. I wonder if we are going to be evacuated? Trying not to be paranoid.

Barbara: If they are going to quarantine your area it might be good to have a free ride out. How does that work anyway?

Me: I don't know. But if we have to leave, Gene and I already decided to just bring our underwear and our good wine. We can get everything else we need there.

Barbara: Great idea! Hope you come home soon!

Me: I'd like that.

Barbara: Me too.

WEEK 3: TIME-OUT

Monday, March 9, 2020

We checked our phones first thing in the morning to see if anything was happening with the planes. There were no emails, no notifications. I googled "military evacuation Italy" but came up with nothing. We looked on Facebook, a source of rumors about COVID-19. *Niente.*

Ian texted from Thailand that he'd arrived in Prachin Buri safely and was now in his time-out location down the street. He was still able to go to work, but couldn't go to his host family's home for twenty-one days. I was relieved he was back from Bangkok and hoped this would serve as a reminder for him to stay put for a while.

We got ready for school, chugged our coffee, and set off on our familiar route to work, weaving with the ebb and flow of Italian traffic. As we approached the gate to Villaggio, the military housing area, we saw the usual security lineup of American military police, Italian gate guards, and *carabinieri*, the machine-gun-toting Italian military police. Gene rolled down the window and held out our ID cards to be scanned. Like us, many of these men and women had been working on Caserma Ederle for years and were familiar faces greeting us as we arrived at work each morning.

"*Buongiorno!*" Gene announced in his booming voice.

"*Buongiorno* teachers!" the guard replied with enthusiasm. He was one of our favorites. This time he did not reach for our ID cards.

"No touch," he smiled and motioned for Gene to flip the card and show the back so he could scan it.

Then he did the same with mine. That was a first, but what was to become standard practice in our new COVID-19 reality. Gene dropped me off at the back door of the elementary school.

"Don't get fired!" I called.

He smirked, waved, and drove away, continuing on to his own empty classroom. It looked like the schools would remain shuttered another week, so we'd make the best of it. I posted the online lesson plans and held virtual class meetings. I tried to fancy up my classroom studio with some props. I arranged the Dr. Seuss books around the easel and placed the Cat in the Hat, Thing One, and Thing Two in the background as if they were planning some new mischief to surprise us.

I thought again about the aircraft we had seen the previous evening. What if I had to leave my classroom in a rush? What would I grab? After yesterday's news, I couldn't shake the feeling that things were about to get even more complicated. I brainstormed again and this time scratched out a quick list of school essentials before leaving for the day.

Once home I saw a short update from Vickie in Virginia Beach.

Vickie: It was great to talk to you last week. Thanks for forwarding the article about the lockdown in Europe; BBC is always intelligent. I followed your wisdom, went to Costco, and stocked up on a case of wine. Our favorite Italian and Spanish. Good thing I didn't need toilet paper; they were out.

I worked on lesson plans late into the evening because honestly, I felt like a first-year teacher again trying to keep up with all the changes. The army was up late working as well.

US Army Garrison Italy Update

We are following the announcement of the Italian prime minister tonight as many of you are. We are waiting for a copy of the new signed decree so we can understand what our host nation is directing to safeguard the people here. Service members, federal employees, contractors, and host nation professionals should report to work at their designated time. If you are stopped by the *carabinieri* and instructed to return home, please do so immediately and inform your supervisor.

Tuesday, March 10, 2020

The rumor mill continued to churn. The latest gossip was that delivery to the post office on base was going to stop because transportation wasn't available to get the mail from Milan to Vicenza. We heard that gas stations might close down as well, so I made a mental note to fill up at the Agip station on the way home in the afternoon.

Vicenza was now considered a *zona rossa*, a red zone, whatever that meant.

We kept in touch with our teacher friends through a private chat group. It was a good way to stay connected and communicate what was going on in our local schools. It also helped us keep in contact with teachers who had moved to other American schools in Europe.

-- I'm sorry my red-zonian friends. How surreal this all seems. Still having to go into school today? Thinking of you and sending positive vibes from Spain!

-- I came into school early this morning to make sure I could make it in. I wasn't sure what they meant by the "red zone," and I didn't want to get stopped. I actually have a lot of things I could do at home, but I had to get stuff from school.

-- Seriously, good move. As long as you don't get quarantined in the building with admin.

-- OMG, can you imagine?

-- Did anything seem different? Less traffic?

-- Less for me because I'm usually running late, but really it seemed pretty normal. I was able to get gas at the local gas station.

-- We might be late. We are driving around looking for the *carabinieri*, hoping to get pulled over and sent home.

-- When you find them drop a pin.

-- Group photo op

Despite being swallowed up into the red zone, the day started out normally, if normal is the right word for teaching kindergarten from a computer in an empty classroom. We had our morning meeting and I read *The Lorax* to the kids. I kept thinking how excited they would be when they came back to school and saw the colorful Truffula trees lining both sides of the kindergarten hallway. I met with the class again in the afternoon to reconnect and talk about their day.

After my final meeting, an email popped up informing us that beginning tomorrow, we would be teaching from home. Attached to the email was the travel documentation necessary to be on the road in case we needed to leave the house for food or medication. It was in Italian and translated into English, with strict instructions on how to fill it out. As soon as I had printed everything, there was an all call to report to the front office. A flurry of activity was taking place there, consternation and confusion on the faces of most. Old travel documents were tossed out and new documents were printed and distributed. In the time it had taken for them to be translated and sent, the documents had already become obsolete. Hurricane-force changes swirled around us as we scuttled to shelter in place. A new place. We were told to pack up our school computers and go home. Now. Wow. This was really happening.

Is this real or make-believe? That was a question I often posed to my students and now it echoed through my brain. I went back to my classroom and reached for the emergency list I'd scribbled down the day before. I packed my computer, books, files, a white board easel, and a few other items that might come in handy. I packed up everything in two shopping bags and headed for the door. I gave a sad backward glance and felt like the Lorax being lifted away. I stepped back in, picked up the Cat in the Hat, Thing One, and Thing Two, and stuffed them in a shopping bag. Ready or not, I locked the door and left.

When I got home, I dropped the shopping bags inside the front door and tossed my purse on the kitchen table. I plugged the computer in and wondered how long it would take up space there. I pulled my phone out and messaged my sister.

Message to Barbara: Just when you think things can't get any crazier … the entire country of Italy is now in lockdown. We were called to the office this afternoon and told to pack our computers and go home. We were given a travel authorization that allowed us to be on the road. Tomorrow I will be teaching kindergarten from my kitchen. I guess Gene will be teaching physics upstairs. We are only allowed to leave the house to go to the doctor or to get food, but only one person at a time. We have to carry our passports and a travel authorization stating our personal info, date and time, and where we're going. Gene stopped in the commissary on the way home because who knows when we'll go out again. He said it was a zoo! I wonder if the wine store is considered a food store?

Barbara: I saw this on the news. And I would say yes regarding the wine store. You are in Italy.

Me: Or maybe I can just turn on the bathtub.

Barbara: Even better, the price is right!

Me: And I won't have to leave the house. No travel documents needed.

Teacher chat:

-- What ended up happening at school? Do you all have to stay at school or work from home? It would be so tragic not to get to be at school because I know how you love all those professional development meetings. Haha!

-- We just got sent home for three days.

-- You all ok?

-- We've been sent to time-out. Working time-out.

The stock market seemed to be in free fall. We watched in horror as our precious retirement slipped farther and farther from our grasp. At this rate there would be no house this summer.

"Don't look," Gene reminded me grimly.

I tried to look away and prepared to hold on for the bumpy ride.

Wednesday, March 11, 2020

It finally happened; we were teaching from home. Remote, virtual, digital, online, or whatever the buzzword was—we were doing it. Gene, who actually worked in IT at one point, was a technology pro and got right to work on his computer upstairs. I, on the other hand, was a technology toddler and had just been bumbling along and relying on Mrs. Dee and other colleagues to help keep my head above water.

Not only was I at a loss with my computer, but I also wasn't sure how to create a functional space in the house that would serve as a makeshift classroom. My laptop was on a buffet in the kitchen so I could do schoolwork and cook at the same time. The kitchen table became my teacher desk, and with the addition of a couple of standing trays and crates of books, I had a practical workstation. I placed a chair in front of the computer and set my ironing board up behind the chair. I positioned the whiteboard easel behind me on the ironing board. That would have to do. It was conveniently close to the coffeepot and a bathroom, so I thought this could actually work out quite well.

I scavenged an old desk lamp from one of the boys' bedrooms and looked for an outlet. Why this house had three different sized outlets never made sense to me. I fetched an adapter so I could use the plug closest to the computer, then fiddled with the lighting until the kitchen was ready for a broadcast. The Cat in the Hat, Thing One, and Thing Two joined me on the sides of the easel and we started the first virtual meeting of the day. My schedule showed seven individual meetings, two group meetings, and two planning meetings with Mrs. Dee. I was positive we could do this.

The day was busy, productive, and surprisingly snag-free. The kids were very curious about where I was, so we spent considerable time having a virtual tour of my kitchen. During the morning, teachers received an email requesting online assignment completion percentage rates for all students. Today. By one o'clock. Nothing like a last-minute research project—obviously assigned by someone who was not a classroom teacher and perhaps didn't have enough to do.

~

We had a video call with Will in Miami. He was soon to register for his summer session classes, the last before graduating. We were grateful for a summer ceremony after almost missing Ian's at FSU. It was a relief not to squeeze another graduation into a long weekend with international flights at either end.

In January we had taken Will to the Venice airport to board his final flight back to school. I remembered watching him confidently stride toward the security gate, the neck of his ukulele peeking out from the top of his backpack.

"Finish strong," Gene called as Will merged and surged into the line of travelers.

He turned and gave us a thumbs up.

"See you in Miami!"

I managed a wave and a smile. Putting him on the airplane never got any easier. I would spend the entire day on my phone, checking to make sure flights landed and took off on time, praying connections were made without issue. These were things I had no control over but felt the need to worry about. My mom worry cup tended to overflow on those days.

Understand that my mom worry never ends. When bridges and buildings in Miami collapsed, I worried. When hurricanes came and went, I worried. I should've been done worrying, but I wasn't. I guess I never will be.

And now COVID-19.

"Are you ready to switch to online classes?" I asked Will.

He didn't think that would happen anytime soon. Maybe he hadn't been watching the news compulsively, like me. Maybe that was a good thing.

"You should make a trip to the grocery store to stock up on food and supplies," I suggested. "Things are happening very quickly."

Will said he would when he had time, that he needed to study.

No time like the present, I thought, not wanting to sound like I was nagging. Perhaps FIU would somehow escape the madness.

I felt a little better after talking with Will, so now it was time to worry about my parents.

Message to Mom: I hope your company arrived safely and please know I still disapprove of your traveling plans. Love you.

Mom: She did arrive last night. All is well. I stayed in the car and your dad went in the airport to get her. And look what she brought us!

A picture of a thirty-year-old bottle of French wine appeared on my screen. Nice, I thought, as I zoomed in on the label.

Me: Very nice. You should drink it all tonight. (*Before you all get sick, I thought.*)

Mom: We're going to. In our Italian glasses.

Ten years ago, my parents celebrated their fiftieth wedding anniversary with us in Italy, Barbara accompanying them on the trip. Bill called in from his ship, in port in Greece at the time. Barbara and I found a perfect anniversary gift in a local artisan's shop, a unique pair of wine glasses fashioned with pewter grapevines entwining the stems.

It was a joyful and memorable visit capped off by the cancelation of their flight home when the Icelandic volcano Eyjafjallajökull erupted. Ash spewed into the sky, so much so that airlines were forced to cancel flights for weeks. It was the biggest disruption to European air travel since World War II. Until now.

~

The World Health Organization finally called it. Officially, we were in the midst of a global pandemic. An ambiguous voice across the ocean tried to mollify US citizens that everything was under control, this was all going away, stay calm. Here in Italy, we could stay calm, but we didn't think it was just going away, and it definitely wasn't under control. Later, it was announced that all travel from the European Union to the United States would be suspended for the next thirty days. Italy was in time-out.

~

From Miami, we heard from FIU that this would be the last day of in-person instruction; all classes would be moving online immediately until April 4. On-campus residents who were able to go home were encouraged to do so as soon as possible. Students who needed to remain on campus would be allowed to stay during this period. Thank goodness, because Will's options were limited. The university planned to remain fully operational, updates promised. It was noted that there were no confirmed cases of coronavirus in the FIU community at that time.

~

In the evening Gene made a confession, "I'm not feeling so good today, tired and a little short of breath."

"Just today, or has it been longer?" I asked with trepidation.

"A few days now, I guess. It's probably just my annual winter bug. I didn't want to worry you but just in case ..."

"Just in case WHAT?"

I noticed that he sounded a bit congested. Every winter he seemed to come down with a cold that would progress to a sinus infection or bronchitis. When he turned down wine with his dinner, I knew he was serious. That night I woke up and heard him wheezing in his sleep. Commence wife worry.

Lying in the darkness, I tried to remember what the base protocol was for coronavirus symptoms. Were we supposed to stay home or go to the clinic? Or call the clinic first? Or go to the emergency room at the Italian hospital downtown? The hospital beds were at capacity, so would he be left in the hall like we had seen on the news? Was the hospital even safe? If he didn't have coronavirus now, would he catch it at the hospital? The briefing at school seemed a lifetime ago and things were changing minute by minute.

Thursday, March 12, 2020

Day Two of Kindergarten in the Kitchen went decidedly well. With lighting issues and virtual kitchen tour behind us, the morning meeting went off without a hitch.

~

Our landlord, Flavio, lived alone in a small apartment attached to our house. Some Americans preferred not to have their landlords nearby, but for us it was a bonus. He was an on-premises gardener and security guard. A non-English speaker, he had graciously adopted our boisterous family. He had been a good friend and an Italian *nonno,* a grandfather of sorts, to our boys. One spring morning, soon after moving into our house, I woke and glanced out the bedroom window, catching sight of him pedaling his bike out to the garden. Ian was balanced precariously on the handlebars with an umbrella, shielding them both from the rain. It made me happy to think they could connect in that way, teaching each other about language and life.

Flavio took the boys fishing, showed them where to find the best cherries, and pointed out the secret crayfish ditch. He taught me to make risotto and minestrone. He played *dama,* the Italian version of checkers, with Gene late into the night. He brought over special meals when my parents visited. My dad will never forget the *uccelli,* little roasted birds on a stick, a local delicacy.

An octogenarian and an avid gardener, he was out and about most of the day, working in the garden or checking on his new duck pond. He understood the new and complicated risks of being around other people, especially at his age. He came by to check on our situation and I noticed he was carrying one of the long bamboo stakes used to support the tomatoes in the garden. When conversing, he'd hold his stake out in front to force others to keep their distance. Everyone steered clear of his stick. It really was an ingenious idea.

~

Gene and I quickly found that sitting in front of the computer all day was a draining enterprise. We realized we needed to get out of the house to stretch our legs and get some exercise. By the Italian decree, we weren't allowed to go farther than two hundred meters from the house, and that rule was really meant for people who needed to walk their dogs. We had a pretty long private driveway and figured it would be okay to be out there, dog or no dog.

After school we walked to the road at the end of the driveway and back, then passed the house, continued on a path in the opposite direction out into the cornfields, and returned to the house. It took fifteen minutes and if we did that loop twice, we got a thirty-minute walk in. Woodpile, junkpile, duck pond, hay. Cherry trees, cornfield, walk the other way. I hoped the fresh air and exercise would help Gene feel better, but the nighttime wheezing continued.

Friday, March 13, 2020

There was a stinkbug on my toothbrush, staring up at me with beady little eyes, daring me to flush him down the toilet. We'd been inundated with these nasty creatures for the last few years. Rumor was that this invasive species arrived in a shipment of goods from somewhere outside the EU. I didn't know if that was true, but I did know that every October they would squeeze into the house through every nook and cranny and try to find a snugly bed for winter. They congregated in the curtains, behind picture frames, and between books. We waged a constant battle with them until December, when things seem to wind down until spring.

As the world was waking up, so were the stinkbugs, and the war raged on. All the little stinkers that slipped past us in the fall wanted to make their way out of the house now that spring was in the air. They flew toward the light, constantly buzzing, thrashing, and crashing into the windows trying to escape. Now that I was home in the daytime, I realized how many of them spent the winter hibernating in my house. Disgusting.

~

Any day in kindergarten can be a little wacky, but a full moon seems to make it exponential. On such mornings, the kindergarten team would prepare to meet the day. Our go-to full moon morning dance party song was always "Bad Moon Rising" by Creedence Clearwater Revival. Dana would bring her speaker out into the hall where we danced and sang, "There's a bad moon on the rise."

We would laugh, point to the clock, and greet some of our tardy colleagues who regularly tried to sneak in our back door as the bell was ringing.

"There's a bathroom on the right," Misty would belt out, singing not-quite-right lyrics that a five-year-old might have come up with.

We would continue dancing in the hall until the kids came in from the bus, soldier on through the day, sanity check at lunch, and remind each other that we could do this until three o'clock. At the end of the day, hair sticking up, wide-eyed and exhausted, we would stagger out to the parking lot, dreaming of the sofa and a well-deserved glass of vino.

This full moon morning I was melancholy, missing the comradery of the morning dance party. I blasted "Bad Moon Rising" on my phone and did the slipper shuffle by the ironing board, coffee in hand, just to feel a sliver of connection to my former life.

~

From: Mrs. Wright
To: Mrs. Tramm
Subject: Green Eggs and Ham
    Sorry about missing the meetings. We've had slow to no internet the last two days.

From: Mrs. Tramm
To: Mrs. Wright
Subject: RE: Green Eggs and Ham

No worries. Thanks for the picture—it's so cute and Wren looks so happy. And her green eggs and ham looks delicious! Yesterday I had a lot of parents at my morning session, so we had an impromptu meeting about assignments. I took some notes and included them on the last page of the Kindergarten News that I will send this afternoon. Thanks again for the teamwork and enjoy your weekend!

Teacher chat:

-- Happy Friday the thirteenth! What a week!

-- I know! Today was Friday Fun Day for my kids! When I told them they could share anything they wanted except for video games or electronics, their eyes were as wide as saucers! It really warmed my heart to see their joy. I hope everyone had a great day!

-- I had a TON of fun with my kiddos! We're working on rhyming words and today we sang "Willoughby Walloby Woo" with Gerald, the elephant from the Mo Willems books! They LOVED it! I find it has been very rewarding to try to provide some normalcy in their lives! It's helping me, too, because it gives me a mission each day.

So far, Friday the thirteenth had been okay, except for the stinkbug. I was letting out a sigh of relief when a new notification popped up on my phone that changed my mind:

Schools in Vicenza are now closed to students until further notice.

As a precautionary measure, all schools in Vicenza will be closed to students until further notice. This includes any scheduled programs and events during this time. Digital learning plans and instruction will continue to support our student learning during this period. We will send updates as more information becomes available. Please continue to check for these updates prior to making any decisions regarding future schedules. We continue to work closely with our military and host nation partners to monitor the situation. All decisions will be made with the health of our students, staff, and community in mind.

From: Mrs. Tramm
To: VES Kindergarten 2019-2020
Subject: Kindergarten in the Kitchen News, Friday, March 13, 2020

Dear Kindergarten Families,

First of all, thank you for all your efforts this week with the children. Your hard work is noticed and appreciated. Many of you have been present at our morning meetings and active in facilitating the process. A special thanks to all who are helping me out with the mute function. Together we are doing this!

You should have received information from the school earlier today advising that schools are closed to students until further notice. Next week we will begin transitioning to a new virtual classroom format. It should make things more organized and assignments easier to track. This is new for us too, and I'm still learning, so thanks for your patience as I get it figured out. You will need some additional log-in information that I will send later. On Monday morning, I will be meeting with the other kindergarten teachers at school to get that set up. Instead of a class meeting, there will be a parent meeting, but I will still have a class meeting in the afternoon.

On Thursday, I had several questions about online assignments. If you missed the meeting, click on the link below to see notes regarding:

- where to find reading books
- the daily calendar and the weather graph
- why the math program won't always mark assignments "complete"
- downloading photos

BTW, thanks all who already downloaded photos to the spring journals (or emailed them to me). There is still time to add pictures and text to your slides. When you go into the link you should be able to look at the other slides and see what your friends found on their springtime walks.

I hope everyone had a fabulous day, eating green eggs and ham, and having Dr. Seuss fun.

Have a good weekend, stay safe and healthy, and wash those hands!

Karin Tramm
VES Kindergarten

I folded up the ironing board and stashed it behind the kitchen door. This had been a week to remember, or a week to forget, I hadn't yet decided. I took out my phone and sent an update to my sister.

Message to Barbara: Today we were told that our schools will be closed to students until further notice, so I'll still be teaching kinder in the kitchen for a while longer. I'm so sad.

It looks like the shitstorm has now landed on your side of the world. Like we knew it would. I was horrified when Mom told me they are going to a boat show this weekend and next. I have tried and tried to talk to them about the seriousness of this situation. I just hope the shows are canceled. If they are closing Disney, someone should get a clue about this.

Barbara: Yes, it's here. I still have to go to work but they said, "DON'T TOUCH YOUR FACE!" I'll try to talk to Mom and Dad as well. I'll call them again.

Me: I'm not tasking you with that—sorry if you thought that. I'm just venting and worried sick. They are adamant about going. I just talked to Will, and he texted them yesterday and they told him they're still going. I'm so afraid they are going to get sick, all three of them within the next two weeks. I don't even know what to think and I'm scared.

After our stroll up and down the driveway, we had another video call with Will.

"How was your shopping trip? Did you get everything you needed?" I was anxious but trying not to let it show.

"Yep!" he replied. "Everything! I stocked up on rice, pasta, canned stuff, also some fresh veggies, garbage bags, and batteries."

"Batteries?" I asked. "This isn't a hurricane. What about toilet paper? If you run out, you'll need to talk to your brother about how they handle that in Thailand."

There was a long pause. "I'll have to grab some."

Message from Mom: Had a nice text from Will yesterday. He said he went out to get groceries so he could stay in now that his classes are online. We're now in the RV park. We got takeout from the restaurant across the street for supper so we didn't have to eat out. We have food with us for lunch tomorrow and will get supper from the deli so we can eat in again. I only left today to pick up my pass and am using wipes and hand sanitizer constantly. We're not planning on going to the event next weekend, even if they have it. Most sporting events have been canceled and even Disney, Busch Gardens, and Universal are closed. I think the Florida schools will close at the end of spring break. All for now. Promise to be very careful.

Me: I'm glad you are communicating with Will and that you are all taking this seriously. Dad needs to be very careful and take the same precautions as you, if one of you gets it you all get it. Seriously, no shaking hands or touching others. Wipe down the doorknobs, keys, light switches, and anything else you are touching a lot. Your phones are the worst. Wipe the food containers from the store. I'm glad you are not going next weekend. I honestly can't believe this week's event was not canceled. Any public gathering is dangerous. Florida needs to hold on tight because it's an older population. Get ready because this is the tip of the iceberg for the Sunshine State. You'd think this kind of thing would never happen in America. Well stand by because we're just a week or two ahead of you. Be safe and be smart. Love you!

It was pizza night, but Gioia Pizza was closed. We had leftovers instead, how very disappointing. We watched a movie, but it just wasn't the same. My thoughts were scattered across continents, my mind racing in a hundred different directions. My parents wouldn't stay home. Ian was living in a shed in Thailand. I swiped on my phone and saw Will, on Instagram, having a livestream concert from his bathroom. Now, after three weeks, it finally hit me. The waves of anxiety I had been holding back surged over me and it was the first time I cried. I cried long and hard and it felt really good to let the tears flow. I was emotionally exhausted and I needed to let it out and let it go. It was a terrible, horrible, no good, very bad day. Some days are like that. Even in Italy.

Saturday, March 14, 2020

My parents would both turn eighty over the summer. They were still living in the house I grew up in and were completely independent. My father has a passion for wooden boats and has built and raced them since he was a boy. He retired from building recently, but at seventy-nine years old, he was still racing. Living on the edge had been a constant in his life.

Every summer when we went home to visit, Dad would take the boys out for a joyride on the lake, doing doughnuts and spraying water into the air like a fountain. I would watch anxiously until they returned safely to shore.

"Grandpa's a beast!" the boys would shout. High praise for a grandfather indeed.

Every year my parents attended various boating events where they could catch up with old friends, make new friends, and Dad could rip roar around the racecourse. This time they went to a boat meet with their friend visiting from England. I was relieved that Dad was not racing, but terrified because there were hundreds of people gathered for the event. It seemed to be a recipe for social distancing disaster. I wished I could put them in time-out from this kind of living on the edge.

Message from Mom: Just letting you know I'm still in the motor home. We drove down to the event site and your dad fixed breakfast and then he left to help out. I wiped everything down with wipes. I can see the boats run from here. I'm amazed at how well the Italians are doing with their social distancing. Dad is back now and we have leftovers for lunch. Got to go. Love you.

Me: You're taking a huge risk just by being there, even if you're staying in because THEY are going out. They can bring it back!

Mom: We know and I haven't been out. They're back now and I made them use hand sanitizer.

Message from Vickie: The schools here in Virginia Beach are closing for at least two weeks. I'm aware from what you told me, but teachers have no idea what headaches they're in for. Moms my age were complaining because colleges are closed and kids are coming home. Is Will staying in Miami? Happy hour here; gonna sit in my yard with a spritz.

Me: It's amazing how quickly things are happening here and will for you in the States as well. All stores are closed except food stores … Stock up on your Aperol and prosecco. You're going to need a spritz or two every day. And wash your hands before you make it.

I read on the Italian news that at six in the evening there was a call for everyone to go outside and make music. I wasn't sure if we would catch anything other than cows and church bells, but I hoped we might get lucky. I stepped outside on the balcony at the appointed hour, ears pricked.

"Hear anything?" Gene asked.

"No," I replied with disappointment, "Maybe I should have played my ukulele." I picked up my lovely pink instrument and gave it a little strum. It was horribly out of tune.

"Or not."

I was sorry that all I could hear was a chorus of barking dogs. Friends downtown, however, had a different experience. Some heard singing or piano notes wafting across their courtyards. Some had neighbors who came out and played instruments on their balconies. Later I saw videos of family mini concerts, arias, and impromptu sing-alongs in the high-rise apartment buildings in many Italian cities. Sometimes clamorous, sometimes haunting, but always from *il cuore*.

Sunday, March 15, 2020

Sunday offered an opportunity to power down and let things go. As much as I tried not to think about it, I was worried about my parents' travel plans back home. Barbara felt the same and later messaged me on her latest attempts to put them in time-out.

Barbara: I argued with them both. As you know they are at the boat show again today but finally decided not to go to the second show next weekend. They said they won't go to a restaurant tonight; they'd just get dinner from the grocery store.

Me: Now we have to figure out what to do if they get sick. What hospitals are taking those patients? Is there a special hotline to call before they can go? I know this sounds horrible, but it's happening all around me right now. Every day. And what about their friend? She will be stuck in the States. What then?

Later in the day Barbara sent me a picture of the empty shelves in the grocery store.

Barbara: It's happening.

Me: Yup! Don't worry, after the initial panic they will restock. Just try to limit your trips and BOGO your wine.

From: Bill
To: Karin
Subject: Coronavirus in Italy

Karin,

I've been keeping an eye on the cases in Italy and see it's getting quite bad. Northern Italy has now been declared the epicenter since things are looking up in China. I understand you are all on lockdown and all businesses in Italy have been ordered closed, except grocery stores and pharmacies. All of Europe is now considered a Level 3 travel risk by CDC, and your area a Level 4. Travel to and from Diego Garcia is getting quite challenging with the European flight ban. I expect all flights to and from DG to be canceled this week as the military has travel restrictions for high-risk countries.

I need to check in with Mom and Dad to see if they are behaving. You are right, they are the most at-risk demographic due to their age AND Mom's Sjogren's syndrome AND lymphoma. They were supposed to go to a boat show this weekend, but I wouldn't be surprised if it's canceled. Also, wouldn't be surprised if their company gets stuck in the US since cases in the UK are on the rise too. I'm due to go home in two weeks, but I'm not holding my breath. I have a feeling that in two weeks, the US will be in the same situation Europe is in today.

Anyway, tell Gene I said hello and you all be safe.

Bill

From: Karin
To: Bill
Subject: RE: Coronavirus in Italy

Ummm … I hate to tell you this, but Mom and Dad are at the boat show. Barbara and I both tried to talk them out of it. I'm afraid that in America many people still don't understand the severity of the situation nor the consequences of their actions. The show must go on. The only thing we can do now is be prepared in case they get sick. I've already researched the Manatee County emergency numbers to call and sent them to Barb.

We are confined to our house but are continuing to work. I'm still teaching kinder downstairs in the kitchen, and I just have to make sure Gene doesn't stroll through the kitchen in his underwear to refill his coffee cup when I'm doing my virtual meetings.

We are both well although Gene has had a wheezy cold for a couple of weeks, chills but no fever. He has not been tested. The one good thing about being locked down is we can get some extra rest in case we have been exposed so we can be more resilient.

I hope you make it back in a timely manner, but like you said, things don't look that good right now. I'll keep you posted as our situation develops. Thanks for checking in on us.

Love,
Karin

From Miami, Florida International University asked all residents still on campus who had homes within a short distance to make arrangements to vacate no later than noon the following day. International students, like Will, and others who weren't able to secure transportation to go home were able to remain on campus but were expected to practice social distancing and no guests or visitors would be allowed. The libraries, pools, recreational centers, and social gathering spaces on campus were all closed until further notice. The campus would be desolate.

Now Will was in time-out too, but we were lucky the university understood the logistical nightmare of international students trying to find a place to go. Many of our friends who had college students in the States had to scramble to figure out what to do as dormitories suddenly closed. They struggled to find safe places for their children to wait it out, storage for their personal items, and transportation. I was grateful Will was able to stay in his campus apartment but I was scared for his safety and his health.

I pondered the text conversation I'd had with Vickie the day before. She mentioned how some parents of college-age kids were annoyed when the dorms closed and the students returned home. To me they were so lucky; I would have given anything to have my son safe at home.

~

My phone vibrated with another message from my friend, Alison, who was teaching kindergarten in the state of Washington.

Alison: Hi!!! How are you? I hope you guys are safe and doing well. We just shut down our schools here for six weeks. Thursday was our last day together and we found out an hour and a half before school got out. We work tomorrow and kids can come by to pick up materials. How are you making this work?

Me: We started out with video meetings from the classroom, but after a week we were tasked with teaching online from home … It's crazy. I have learned how to hold virtual meetings with Google Meet and make assignments with Google Classroom and so many other things I never thought I'd need to know. It's been a steep learning curve for sure.

Alison: We go tomorrow to hand out packets. We created a six-week packet that goes along with our reading series and math series. Plus, a bag of materials—crayons, scissors, glue, pencils, etc. We plan on doing videos on Monday that go with our book of the week. Then I'm hoping to do some videos of me reading and whatever other fun things I can think of. We were not told to do any of this. Our district hasn't provided much guidance as to what we should be doing. I know kindergarten was the only team in there yesterday making packets. Were you guys given guidance on what you should put out, how often? How many of your kiddos are participating? Sorry for all the questions!

Me: We were brought in for a day of virtual training, then pretty much let go. The first week we were at school, so everyone was helping each other, but now we are stuck in the house, so we do a lot of virtual meets with the team. Each grade has to upload a day of lesson plans every morning by ten o'clock. We are required to meet with each child at least twice a week. The counselors are following up with phone calls if they don't attend the meetings. I only have two out of twenty-one that are AWOL. I have a morning meeting with the class and then the kids have work to do. I do individual meetings during that time. We have an afternoon closing to talk about our day and write about it together. Rumor is that the Italian schools won't go back at all this year, but that is just a rumor. Two weeks ago, I never thought we'd be at this point, but here we are. And in two weeks you will be here too. I hope you are all doing well. Elbow bumps and wash those hands!

Alison: Oh wow!!! Our school has put out no real guidance except for us to update our teacher web pages. I haven't looked at that since the first week of school. That is shocking how much you guys are required to do. Wow!!! Is there a way I can see one of your lesson plans? We were the only grade to put together work packets and many aren't doing an online page. Just putting things on their teacher page. It's wild how different the expectations are in different areas. Elbow bumps to you guys as well!

Me: We'll survive. I'll send you a link to the school virtual page.

WEEK 4: FAMILY AFFAIRS

Monday, March 16, 2020

We were switching to a new virtual classroom format and the kindergarten team wanted to think smarter, not harder. We thought it wise to divide and conquer to get the program organized and functional. That meant leaving the house and driving to school, but it was worth it to tackle this task together. I looked forward to touching base with my colleagues again, as we hadn't seen each other since that crazed afternoon when we had been banished to time-out. Was that really just last week? It seemed like so many things had happened since then.

I printed out my travel authorizations, tucked my passport and computer into my school bag, and made the journey to VES. There were very few cars on the road and for once I relished the fifteen-minute trip. It had only been six days since I'd taken this route, but it was surprisingly different. Springtime flowers had burst into bloom. Brightly blossomed fruit trees and forsythia splashed color along the roadside like a fanciful drive through an impressionist painting. Huge fields, green just last week, were blanketed with bright yellow canola flowers. And there was light, beautiful sunlight, angling through the new grass on each side of the road, the translucent green color reminiscent of my childhood Easter basket.

I continued past farms and fields until I was close to school and approached the ever-dreaded roundabout. Over the past two years local traffic had increased on this stretch of road, and this intersection had become contentiously backed up with early-morning commuters. It usually it added five or even ten sluggish minutes to our morning drive, but this time there were no cars and I joyfully zipped through it.

The school building was just as empty as the roads. Instead of fruit trees, the kindergarten halls were lined with Dr. Seuss's colorful Truffula trees. When I unlocked the door and entered my classroom, I paused and let the emotion roll over me.

This space, once a living, breathing, and laughing- loud place, was now abandoned, a motionless snapshot of time past. The tables were set up with activities for when the kids would come back, because surely, they would be back, right? My easel was still in place, poised for the next virtual meeting. And there was that lousy box of reading tests that surely needed to be put out of sight, out of mind. Or not. Maybe the cleaners would accidentally throw it away. One could only hope.

The worst thing was the sound of silence. Hollow, empty, sad silence. How many times had I reminded my kids to "zip it, lock it, put it in your pocket"? I would go home with my ears ringing from the constant cacophony of voices. Funny, their incessant chatter was exactly what was missing now.

It was our good fortune to have a young colleague on the kindergarten team who was well versed in the new and improved virtual format we would be switching to; her patience with the rest of us was a virtue. We gathered in her classroom, practiced appropriate social distancing, and set it up piece by piece. We put together a presentation for all kindergarten parents, set up a camera, then sent the link. We walked through the program and answered questions. Honestly, when we were finished, I had just as many questions as the parents did and probably more because you don't know what you don't know.

On the way home I swung by the commissary for a few necessities. The cleaning supplies were still wiped out, but most of the other shelves had been restocked. I did notice there had been a run on Pop-Tarts. I cringed thinking about all those sugared-up kids at home.

Back in Bolzano Vicentino, Gene met me on the porch with a canister of wipes and we cleaned every box, package, and bag before it came into the house. I stripped off my clothes, threw them in the laundry, and washed them. It was annoying, but at the time we felt it was necessary.

After dinner, a message from Will lit up my phone. I was feeling a little nervous about his current situation, so I was relieved to hear from him.

Will: Hey, just wanted to check in. *Tutto bene?*

Me: Thanks, Will, *tutto bene*. I hope online classes are going okay. How was your gig last weekend?

Will: It got canceled. Basically, every gig is canceled.

Me: It's for the best right now. You can continue to do virtual concerts from the safety of your bathroom. You could make a backdrop of toilet paper. BTW, did you get any toilet paper? And bathroom acoustics are probably pretty good. Instead of the Hattts, you can be the Bathmattts. Or the Shower Cappps.

Radio silence from Will. Apparently, he didn't think my mom joke was very funny.

Ian called to share the dreadful news that the Peace Corps would be temporarily suspending operations globally and evacuating the volunteers. As COVID-19 continued to spread and international travel became more and more problematic, they felt it prudent to prevent a situation where volunteers would be unable to leave their host countries. Ian would leave Thailand within a few days and he was devastated.

Tuesday, March 17, 2020

I returned to my classroom for a second day. Mrs. Dee arrived soon after and we worked together to assemble another snail mail package for the kids. We added new pictures to our Welcome Back bulletin board so it would be ready when the kids came back after spring break. Surely in another month all of this would be over.

I traded out books and collected other supplies that I could use in my kitchen classroom at home. Finally, there was just one more thing to do before leaving for the day. I stood on a chair and reached up for Stella, our Christmas Elf on a Shelf. She was perched on her observation post— on top of the whiteboard at the front of the classroom. She came to us one Christmas a few years ago and after Christmas she told me that she wanted to stay at school to learn to read and count to one hundred. So, Stella stayed on, learning to read, write, and spell, and, of course, keeping an eye out for who was naughty and nice. She had an old rotary phone by her side, receiver to her ear, just in case she needed to call the North Pole.

When I got home, Stella and her phone found a new vantage point, atop a kitchen cabinet directly behind the ironing board. She had a fine view of the computer screen and the kids had a fine view of her.

To: VES Staff
Subject: NEW Declaration Form
Please use the attached NEW form to declare the purpose of your travel if you are on the road in Italy. It contains an additional statement confirming that the person is not under quarantine nor has tested positive for COVID-19. Fill in the Italian form and print it and be prepared to present it to the police upon request. Have it with you, even when walking in the vicinity of your home. You should make several copies.

We were told that many people who had tested positive and were supposed to be in isolation were actually going out and about and potentially spreading the virus. The penalty was stiff, up to twelve years in jail for violating the measure. Hence, the new form. Italy was not messing around, and we were glad.

We printed new travel forms for our driveway walk but I left the passports home. Passing the duck pond, I got a message from Mom.

Mom: We enjoyed our weekend; I never left the motor home. At night we parked in the RV park and then we drove over to the show in the morning and your dad cooked breakfast there. He parked in a place where I had a great view of the racecourse.

The boating events for the rest of the month are canceled. Our friend is keeping in touch with her travel agent and, as of a few minutes ago, her flight on the 27th is still confirmed.

Later that day I got another message from my friend Alison:

Alison: My home office is the couch. Day one of homeschooling and ZERO has been done.

Me: Happy Wednesday, my friend. You can do this! I have been working in my classroom the last two days trying to get a packet put together and get the virtual classroom organized and launched. I try to deal with 400 confused parent emails every day that I can't even answer because I'm still learning! Today I had to check in by 7:55 and my meetings started at 8:30. I had six individual meetings, one large group, one small group, and two meetings with my aide. Tomorrow, we have to have our K team meeting virtually, followed by a virtual faculty meeting. No rest for the weary. But at least I can pee when I need to—if I can be quick between meetings.

Alison: OMG that's crazy. Great on one hand but also extreme. We've had no guidance. I feel like we are all just flapping in the wind.

In Thailand, Ian moved back in with his host family to prepare for departure. He was sick at heart. This was not the way things were supposed to happen, not the plan. He had gone from the most secure and purposeful situation of his adult life to having the rug pulled out from under him in just a few short days. It would take some time for him to slow his descent and re-enter his old but new reality.

Wednesday, March 18, 2020

Gene tossed and turned throughout the night with chills and chattering teeth. In the morning he got up, showered, checked in, and put on his teacher face. One good thing about working from home was that you didn't have to call in sick or write sub plans. As all teachers know, preparing for, and recovering from, being absent is much more painful than just plowing through the day. Gene championed on.

Symptomatic civilians had been advised to stay home unless encountering severe respiratory distress. I wished Gene could be tested but the risk of exposure at the hospital outweighed the benefits of knowing for sure if he was positive or negative. He had not lost his sense of smell. If only we had a home test, it would put our minds at ease. Or allow us to plan for what came next.

Fortunately, I was feeling fine and showing no symptoms.

~

When the Vicenza schools closed to students, they were soon followed by the schools in Aviano. By now the rest of the American schools in Italy—Livorno, Naples, and Sigonella—were operating virtually. Teachers reached out to support one another as best we could.

Message from Misty (in Sicily): Hey! I hope you are hanging in there. This is only day five for us and it's the pits! I miss my kids!!

Me: Thanks for sharing your lesson plans. It's good to mix and match— it saves some time and that's a good thing. We still have required team meetings and virtual faculty meetings, although the faculty meetings have been blessedly short. I think I spend over two hours a day answering emails. My parents have been exceptional, so supportive and patient, but it seems like every day there is a new snag, a new expectation from admin, or a new piece of tech we are required to learn. So much more on the plate and less time to do it. My eye won't stop twitching!

Misty: Is the virtual classroom easy to set up?

Me: Mixed thoughts. It was easy but time consuming to get going. It's easier for the parents for sure because everything is now in one place. Also, it's another open route of communication, which is so very important right now. I love the chat feature. It can be hilarious.

Misty: I tried my first virtual meeting with my kindergartners yesterday, uhhhh, CHAOS!!

Me: I can help you if you want. I have a lot of meetings today. I'll be done around 3:00. First thing to do, this is VERY important, is teach the kids how to MUTE THE MICROPHONE. I let them talk for a few minutes before the meeting starts, then we sing the "Hello Song" and everyone mutes. They're good at it now. They raise their hand by typing an X in the chat box. When it's their turn they can unmute and read. It's working very well and the parents are awesome on their end. I'm so lucky with this group.

I'll send a private video link for the two of us to talk. Put it on your desktop so we can use the same one every time.

~

Will's band, the Hattts, performed a remote livestream concert. I hoped playing music would be a good outlet for him to alleviate some stress and help him feel connected to his friends and the outside world. His roommate had moved back home with his parents and I knew it was going to be hard for Will to be there in the apartment all alone, all the time. I felt awful that we couldn't be there as a safety net. Mom guilt and worry consumed me.

Another message came through from the States:

Bob: Tramms are you doing OK?! Thinking of you.

Me: We're alive and well and going into the fourth week of online instruction from Casa Tramm.

Bob: Fortunately, you are Tramms, so you will not only survive, you will thrive. Are you down to your last few quarts of last year's glühwein?

Me: We are still well stocked.

Bob: I heard that Ian might be making his way here. Poor kid. Good news is that I have a bike he can ride.

Gene: Thanks, my friend! Can you tutor him through med school so he can get a job?

Thursday, March 19, 2020

Thursdays were always meeting days at VES. First, we met as a grade-level team, followed by a faculty meeting, a data meeting, or some other meeting to have a meeting. It looked as if our meeting schedule would continue during virtual school with meetings and more meetings. We were sent a link and instructed to log in at two thirty. On one hand, it was good to experience the other side of a virtual meeting. Not being the presenter allowed me to see the session from the perspective of a student. On the other hand, couldn't this have just as easily been an email?

I dutifully logged in to the meeting, typed "present" in the chat box, and muted my microphone. It was strange to see my colleagues' faces all in their own little boxes, peering out from their dens and dining rooms. It was reminiscent of the old TV game show, *Hollywood Squares*, but in this game, there were more than seventy people. Then, I did something I always wanted to do—I poured myself a glass of wine and enjoyed it during the faculty meeting, making double sure that my camera had been turned off. Bucket list checkmark! I hope Stella did not call Santa.

Message from Misty: I tried the meeting today with the "Hello Song" and muting. It was better. I practiced sharing my screen and reading a story.

Me: Yay! Just try to do one new thing a day so you don't go crazy.

Friday, March 20, 2020

An old family friend in South Carolina passed away. Following a stroke, he had been hospitalized for a few days. We all knew what was about to happen and mom called to break the news.

"We just heard. Your dad really feels like he needs to be there. He wants to drive up."

I took a big breath and processed this. "I'm so sorry, Mom, I know this is hard for both of you, but please don't let Dad drive up there." I tried to remain calm. "There's nothing he can do and there won't be a funeral because public gatherings have been banned. Please, both of you just need to stay home."

"I know, we know," she replied, frustrated. "We're staying here. Maybe there'll be a memorial service later that we can attend. We're not going."

"Okay, good, that makes me feel better." I was relieved there was not more of a push back about that. "And don't let him change his mind."

"We're doing our best to stay put. My doctor called and said I shouldn't come in to get my allergy shots today, so I didn't go."

I could hear the TV on in the background, not at all normal for my parents at that time of the day.

"Why's the TV on?" I asked.

"We're watching the news. They're showing a hospital in Italy, somewhere near Bergamo, I think. They're talking about how they're making life and death decisions about who will get treatment and who won't."

"I know, it's awful," I said. "That's been going on for a couple of weeks now; things are getting desperate here. People are dying in the halls at the hospitals. That's why you have to stay put. It's going to be so much worse in the States because no one is listening. People think it can't happen in America but here it comes. Stay home!"

I was sure she was sick of hearing this.

"Everything here is being closed," she went on with annoyance. "The beaches are closed and some restaurants are closed, others are for take-out only. The malls are closed, the tourist destinations are closed, so like it or not you might as well stay home because there's nowhere to go."

"Finally, and thank goodness," I responded. "This should've happened two weeks ago."

From Thailand came a soul crushing message from Ian:

Ian: I had to say goodbye today. My five-year-old host sister thinks that my leaving means I don't love her. I'm hurting so much, Mom.

Me: I know it's so hard. I'm so very sorry. Just think of the positive impact you've had on her life. She needs time and so do you. And remember, your feelings are valid. You're sad and angry and scared. And horribly disappointed. Don't try to hold all that back. Talk to people, ask for help, and cry hard. That's all okay. And write about it.

From Miami, FIU News reported that as the number of the COVID-19 cases continued to rise in South Florida, they would remain vigilant in monitoring the impact on the university community. They reiterated their commitment to keeping students, families, and colleagues healthy and feeling supported. They noted that the cancelation of all on- and off-campus events was now extended through May 10.

What a day. Everyone was in turmoil and there was nothing we could do. It was Friday, pizza night again, but it wasn't, because Gioia Pizza was still closed. I wondered what treasures I could discover in the back of the fridge. I paused from writing my class newsletter and picked up my phone to scan the news. A message from my friend Misty awaited.

Misty: Do we need a virtual happy hour on our personal link?

Me: Please YES! When?

Misty: Let us know when y'all are finished with work. We can enjoy a quarantini together.

Me: OK, just trying to get my parent newsletter out.

Misty: Don't rush, we're not going anywhere—LOL.

From: Mrs. Tramm
To: VES Kindergarten 2019-2020
Subject: Kindergarten in the Kitchen News. Friday, March 20, 2020

Dear Kindergarten Families,

This week we began our unit on weather. I hope everyone has been able to enjoy the sunny days and watch the trees budding and blooming in your yard.

A big thanks to Mrs. Dee for all her tech help this week and for organizing the links at the top of the virtual classroom. She has been finding websites for some of our optional online activities and she sorted out the Digital Learning Scrapbook photos and created a link to the slide show.

This afternoon at our group meeting we came up with some ideas for Spirit Week. We decided on PJ Day for Monday, Tie-dye Day for Tuesday, Hat Day for Wednesday, Costume Day for Thursday, and Talent Day on Friday. That's right, we will have a short Virtual Talent Show for those who would like to participate. Let me know if your child has a song, dance, painting, or anything else they are proud of and would like to share. We already have a Hula-Hoop act lined up. We will keep the acts short, a minute or less. We will talk more about this next week.

Have a great weekend!

Karin Tramm
VES Kindergarten

I put the ironing board away, replaced it with two chairs and two glasses. There was no pizza tonight, but Virtual Happy Hour was the best idea ever.

"*Prost!*"

"*Cin! Cin!*"

"*Salute!*"

"Cheers!"

The language didn't matter. It was emotional balm to see Misty and her husband, Andy, and step away from our fraying daily existence. We had a virtual tour of their new house and hoped that someday soon we could go down to Sicily for a visit. Even Gene had a splash of vino.

As we said goodbye, we gave our friends a big virtual hug. It was a grand idea and a great end to another surreal day.

Before going to bed I checked my phone for word from Ian and found nothing. I was sure he was somewhere over the Pacific Ocean. I didn't know his route so I couldn't continuously check his flight, which was probably a good thing. I didn't mute my phone before turning off the light.

Saturday, March 21, 2020

I tossed and turned all night, half-awake listening for the ping of a message. How could all of this have happened so quickly? In the morning there was still no word, so I went into mom worry mode and texted.

Message to Ian: How are you doing? Where are you? When are you flying?

Ian: I'm alive. I'm in Chicago now.

Me: What's your story?

Ian: Flew Bangkok to Tokyo, Tokyo to Chicago. Now I fly to Philly. It's cold.

Me: Do you have warm clothes? I'm glad your phone works.

Ian: There's Wi-Fi in the airport. And I have a hoodie in my suitcase.

Me: Is the airport crazy? We saw a video of O'Hare the other day and it was madness. How long is your layover? When is the Philly flight?

Ian: It's not bad here. It was actually quite painless. We already made it through Customs and Immigration and have rechecked our bags. We're going through security now.

Me: Did they take your temp?

Ian: They did not. Never once. Not at any of the airports.

Message from Barbara: We went by Mom and Dad's and visited for a minute from outside the door. Dad has given up on making the trip to South Carolina.

Me: Thank goodness. Are they convinced they need to stay in the house now? How long has it been since one of them has been out and about? It would be good if they could make it to fourteen days so we would know they were okay.

Barbara: It's only been three days since Dad's been out. They are in now except for taking walks.

Me: Okay, eleven days to go. We're not even allowed to go outside to walk right now, but who is going to check if we're walking up and down our driveway? The rule is that you can only be two hundred meters away from your house. That's just to walk your dog. And then you have to have your travel authorization papers and your passport with you. Imagine having to carry your passport just to walk in the driveway. In Italy there were 5,322 new cases yesterday, 427 deaths. The totals are 47,021 cases and 4,032 deaths. Those numbers are horrific for a relatively small country.

Barbara: The US had 19,624 confirmed cases and 260 deaths. On Monday, the news said our counts were where Italy was two weeks ago. We're buckling up.

Me: And Italy's a little bit bigger than Florida. Think how big the US is in comparison, so the potential to be exponential is mind boggling. And the fact that not everyone is taking it seriously puts everyone else at increased risk.

Barbara: I know. Things are getting very real today.

Police cars began to drive through the streets of our *comune*. We could hear the loudspeaker cautioning people to stay inside their homes. The apocalyptic broadcast carried across the fields and through the windows of our house. The thump thump thump of helicopters overhead often broke the afternoon stillness. It was like a movie. A horror movie. In the evening, across the cornfield, we could see the flashing lights of the ambulances on the highway, rushing from one emergency to another. The death rate, almost eight hundred, had doubled from the day before. Every time I heard the sirens, my heart plunged.

In retrospect, these chilling numbers were nothing compared to what would go on later in Italy and in the States. At the time, we watched stunned as the tallies rose. We couldn't imagine that things could get any worse. Of course, that's the problem with thinking things can't be worse, because the world has a way of showing you that yes, indeed, they can.

~

My niece, Morgan, a special needs teacher, worked at a DoDEA preschool at Fort Bragg, North Carolina. She was a godsend when Ian needed a place to live before leaving for his Peace Corps work in Thailand. Barbara and I marveled that those two could actually live together under the same roof without issue. Two peas in a pod, Morgan and Ian always bickered like sister and brother, but they also propped each other up as siblings do. We referred to them collectively as the Morg-Ian.

In the evening, I saw Morgan's video post of a virtual karaoke party. True to herself, she was making the best of her situation. I texted and chided her for not wearing the banana suit I'd sent last year when she and Ian attended their first Jimmy Buffet concert. Ian already owned a banana suit and had worn it proudly to beaches, bars, and ski slopes. After getting the concert tickets, we ordered his cousin a suit to match.

Message to Morgan: I saw your hilarious karaoke video. You should have worn your banana suit! I hope you're surviving virtual school. We're starting week five and I'm still trying to figure it out. Ian was just evacuated from Thailand—I don't know if he had a chance to tell you. He just landed in Chicago about an hour ago and is flying on to Philadelphia. He's going to quarantine there with a coworker. Stay safe and wash your hands.

Morgan: Oh no, that's intense. We just started virtual teaching this week but I'm still trying to figure it out. It's a lot. And no, I didn't know about Ian. I hope he's OK. I need to call him soon and you, too! Want to chat tomorrow morning (my time)? Also, I totally should have worn my banana suit! Next time!

Me: I'd love to chat. I'll be home all day—haha! Call me after you've had your coffee.

Sunday, March 22, 2020

I tried not to work on weekends, but it was easy to get a lot done when I was fresh in the morning. After a cup of coffee, I focused and finalized the next week's schedule for individual virtual meetings with my students. The parents had provided input to assist me in working around the schedules of older siblings. I also needed to coordinate with the English as a Second Language specialist and the speech teacher so they could attend some of the meetings with me. It was like piecing together a thousand-piece jigsaw puzzle, complicated but satisfying when completed.

During our afternoon driveway walk we had a video call with Morgan. She was doing well but feeling overwhelmed with the challenges of virtual teaching with three- and four-year-old students with special needs.

"It'll get easier over time," I assured her, "just be patient and teach the kids how to use the mute function right away. Parents can help with this."

Then Morgan chided us for walking up and down our driveway.

"You're like a couple of boring old people out for a Sunday stroll," she teased.

Yes, I guess we were. Maybe we should liven it up a bit and order some banana suits.

~

I called Mom while I was cooking dinner.

"What's your plan for getting groceries?" I asked. "Even if the stores have special senior hours, I still don't think you should go. Do you know of any places that deliver?"

"Publix has delivery but I'm not sure if the store here in Palmetto does. You can send them an order and pick it up curbside. Barb brought us fresh lettuce from the garden yesterday. She and Brian stayed on the porch. No one else has been here and your dad has been walking in the neighborhood every day after lunch."

"I'm happy to hear about the delivery service. Let's check to see if they're delivering in Palmetto and then please start using it," I encouraged. "I'm glad Barb can bring you fresh lettuce. Flavio brought some over yesterday. A lot."

"How's he doing?" she asked. "I hope he's well."

"He's good," I answered. "He's walking around with a bamboo stick to keep people from getting too close to him."

Mom laughed. "Is Gene feeling better?"

"He's so-so, getting better" I replied. "He's still exhausted but no more relapses so I think he is on the road to recovery."

"Okay, that's good. So, what's going on with Ian?"

I took a big breath. "Ian is not so good. He has been evacuated from Thailand," I told her. "He's going to quarantine with a Peace Corps colleague near Philadelphia."

"Should I try to call him?" she asked, concerned. "Does he need anything?"

"Not right now, Mom. He is still processing and understandably upset. He needs some time. He's not sick, don't worry, but I don't think he's ready to talk about it yet. He won't be coming to Florida anytime soon because he has to stay there at least fourteen days. I'll update you on his situation when I know more. Last we heard from him he was in Chicago waiting for his next flight. I assume he made it okay; we haven't heard from him since then. His phone may not work or it might need a charge."

"Well, let me know if we can help. You know your dad and I will do whatever we can."

"I know, thanks. We don't know what he needs yet. I'm not sure that he even knows yet."

I forwarded Mom the information on two different grocery deliveries in their area. She would have a hard time giving up grocery shopping. She watched the newspaper flyers, got her coupons ready, and crisscrossed town looking for the best bargains. Dad would go along to drive and carry the bags.

Grocery shopping was a social event in their small town, depending on whose car was in the parking lot. Mom was also acquainted with many of the store employees, and I was concerned that giving up this piece of hometown networking might prove difficult for her. However, a delivery service made sense. It was safer and one less thing for them to worry about. I hoped they would find it convenient and it would encourage them to stay home. I forwarded a sign for them to print and put on the front door asking that deliveries just be left outside on the porch.

I heard the ping. Glancing at my phone, my heart skipped a beat and I unplugged it from the charger. The message was from Ian.

Ian: Hey, sorry you haven't heard from me, I just got Wi-Fi. I've been off the grid, but I am alive and cold.

Me: Where are you?

Ian: In a tiny house near Allentown, Pennsylvania.

Me: It is very cool for this family to take you in. So, what can we do to support you and help this family that inherited you?

Ian: I dunno yet. I'll think about it and let you know. I'm just trying to figure out my phone situation and then go from there.

Me: Right. Rest and phone first. Maybe we can link you to your brother's account.

From: Bill
To: Karin
Subject: Checking in

Karin & Gene,

Just checking in to see if everyone is OK. We have been restricted to the ship now, can't even go ashore. All passenger flights have stopped and there is one plane a week that brings stores, provisions, mail, etc. but NO passengers. I'm not even sure if we could get a medivac flight if it were needed. Thank goodness everyone is taking it pretty well so far. We can get mail if it comes in. The weather is perfect, but we can't get off the ship. Let me know how you're doing.

Bill

From: Karin
To: Bill
Subject: RE: Checking in

We're both doing fine, going on week five now and things are not getting any better yet here in Italy. From time to time, we can hear the police broadcasting over their loudspeakers telling everyone to stay in their houses. It gives me chills. We're just trying to stay home … just walking in the driveway.

I'm most worried about Mom and Dad. I think Dr. A called them and told them to stay home. I'm hoping they're listening to him. I sent them links for grocery delivery.

Ian was evacuated from Thailand on Friday and is now in self-quarantine with a coworker in Pennsylvania. Not sure what comes next for him.

Will's campus was closed but he is one of a few international students they let stay on in his apartment because obviously he can't come here to Italy and he can't go to Mom and Dad's either. He is okay, just has cabin fever, and every now and then livestreams guitar concerts from his bathroom.

Glad you are safe and hope you stay sane.

Love,
Karin

PART 2

THE MIDDLE OF THE BEGINNING

"Soon the seed flowered into the bright,
delicate dandelion it was meant to be."

The Dandelion Seed, Joseph Anthony

WEEK 5: SPIRIT WEEK

Monday, March 23, 2020

I don't know any teacher who looks forward to getting up on Monday morning, but Pajama Day made this Monday a little bit easier. I put the ironing board back up, made coffee, and signed in. I skipped the shower and stayed in my pajamas. Maybe just a tad of makeup.

Our new virtual classroom offered a practical feature, a chat where the class was able to post pictures, ask questions, and make comments. I appreciated this component of the platform because it helped the kids retain a sense of community and allowed us to stay a little more connected. I was encouraged to see the parents helping their kids post pictures and add to the conversations. I threw a little something out each morning to get the conversation going. Their conversations cheered me up almost as much as a morning dance party.

Kindergarten chat:

Good morning, friends, and Happy Monday! Are you wearing your PJs today? My PJs are white with black polka dots. Send us some pictures of your PJs!

Photos and comments filled the stream. I scrolled down to read and could feel their excitement.

-- I have my Sonic PJs on today!

-- Happy Pajama Day!

-- I have feet in my pajamas.

-- Me, too!

-- I like your soldier pajamas.

-- Your Pokémon PJs are awesome!

-- Here are my football pajamas.

-- I like football, it's my favorite sport.

-- We are having pancakes for breakfast! And my mom is wearing her pajamas, too.

A photo of mom and daughter in matching jammies popped up.

Ahh! Happiness is Pajama Day. It added a bit of balance to my Monday.

I felt like I was getting a handle on the technology, most days, but there were still times when I just wanted to power down in disgust. My internet hiccupped. My data ran out in the middle of meetings, forcing me to set up a hot spot with my phone. I longed for real books, puzzles, math games, and singing. The parents felt the same and I'm sure the kids did, too. These were digital times, however, and we would adapt. We had to.

Teacher chat:

-- This has been so hard on some families. A sweet mom was crying yesterday saying her girls are so difficult, and she's having to help them with online assignments and breakdowns. Technology is not her thing.

-- Although I do find it interesting that some parents are saying that they can't manage two kids on computers. I want to invite them into a computer lab when we have to help twenty-one or more children get logged on, stay on task, and troubleshoot all their tech problems! I do understand, though, but I'm a little glad that some parents are gaining some much-needed perspective!

-- I think some good will come out of this too, understanding for what teachers deal with every day. I miss you guys so much. Hang in there. The numbers looked so horrible yesterday.

Message from Misty: Hey! I was trying to look at your digital learning plan and it said I didn't have access. I just wanted to see how you set up your weeks again.

Me: Sorry, I know. A parent told me the same thing this morning. It looks like someone stormed the gates of our site over the weekend and all the sudden we had seventy-six editors instead of just the kinder team, UGH!! It's all messed up and we're trying to figure out what happened. I'll let you know when we get it up and running again.

This was one of those times I wanted to power down in disgust. Our team had worked so hard to create a perfect virtual lesson plan for the entire week, but someone had left the back door unlocked. Twice now it seemed. I hoped it wasn't me.

To: Vicenza Elementary School Staff
Subject: BREAKING NEWS! Professional Development has been scheduled for this Wednesday. Please read this message.
Importance: High
  Good Morning! The District is giving us an opportunity for digital Professional Development this Wednesday. I apologize to those of you who have already scheduled virtual meetings for that day. Please see if you can reschedule them for another day this week. Additional information will be forthcoming as we receive it. We appreciate all the flexibility you have shown. You are the best!

I had conflicted feelings about this news. On one hand, I welcomed time to dig in and explore our new resources, and I was thrilled that this was one training for which no sub plans were required. Learning on the fly hadn't been optimal for any of us but we had done it with flying colors.

On the other hand, the word "opportunity" was an admin red flag that indicated something we might not want to do. I wondered if I would be able to delve in and explore the things I needed for kindergarten or if I'd be tasked with someone else's agenda. It's hard not to feel annoyed when we're asked to do third grade lesson plans, which happened frequently in our trainings because it's deemed to be middle ground for all the grades. So much of our PD fell short in this regard. Frankly, most teachers find PD a bitter pill to swallow for this very reason. We feel frustrated when we're not treated as professionals and it makes us wary of anything that contains the words "initiative," "rigor," or "unpacking." There's really just one thing I wanted to be packing and unpacking: a suitcase.

The virtual meeting schedule I had delicately pieced together the day before toppled like a house of cards. There would be a lot of rearranging.

I think I CAN. I think I CAN. I think I CAN. I think I CAN.

Tuesday, March 24, 2020

An email from Ian was waiting in my inbox. I was glad he was writing about his experience and hoped it would help him process his current situation. He wrote periodically for the online Peace Corps Thailand magazine, *Sticky Rice*, and had prepared a submission.

exodus pandemia
by Ian Tramm
Peace Corps Youth in Development Program 131

for months all i'd seen were bright lights
foreign colors rich and vibrant
exciting in their novelty and
future promise,
woefully all it takes is the volant
gust of a hurriedly worded email to dim
the glimmering candlelit lull of
rested assurance,
with clarity's glow dulled
i don't know where to go
i only know i feel i'm falling into
an abyssal and unknown below
a cough-sneeze-greeting meeting me as
i retreat seemingly deeper into quarantine
my return to the land of the free
less freely chosen than mandated
my land of smiles fast faded and left behind
as i quick pack clothes and medical supplies
go to say my last goodbyes
eyes wet with tears i'm crying
i can't stop
this is my land of frowning
wait
hold on
slow down
i'm drowning
i'm not supposed to be there
i'm scared
let go of me
i'm not ready
what's happening
please stop.
i need to hug them.
we were meant to have more time.

His poem was published a week later. I was glad he was writing, but my mom heart broke when I read it.

~

From Miami, FIU reported that a student had tested positive for COVID-19. It had been more than two weeks since the student had been on campus, so it wasn't likely that anyone in residence was exposed. Thank goodness the FIU Health Clinic remained open. Thank goodness Will had a place to live and was staying home. As far as I knew.

Wednesday, March 25, 2020

I would have much rather spent the day with my students but committed myself to stay focused and positive for the professional development. I put on my happy face and made myself some "I think I CAN" statements:

I CAN write a digital lesson plan.

I CAN set up a virtual classroom.

I CAN make an instructional video.

I CAN make it through this day.

Teacher chat:

-- Can you believe we have to sit through this? All day.

-- At least we're at home. And we're getting paid. And no sub plans.

-- True.

-- I think they're just trying to help, but really, we've done all this on our own already. I wish they would just let me work on what I need to get done.

-- Seriously, people, we need to be getting some recertification credits for this. I've been working my butt off and the demands from admin just keep coming.

-- Maybe we all get a FIVE on our end of year evaluation. You know we deserve it.

-- Bahahaha!!

Many of us had been collaborating with teachers in other schools. Our team had shared the "Vicenza Model" with colleagues in Italy as well as in England, Japan, and Germany. We had answered questions and shared lesson plans with stateside schools in various locations. We were constantly reminded that collaboration with peers was one of the most powerful factors in continuous school improvement. What a collaborative effort the last month had been. While we agreed that every teacher deserved a professional rating of FIVE (the highest) for their end-of-year evaluation, that would remain to be seen.

Message from Misty: OK, so you have to sit logged in to a PD all day?

Me: Yes, I'm in Session One right now, but since my classroom is in my kitchen, I CAN also make soup. Multitasking is my forte.

Misty: Are you smarter now?

Me: Of course, but also a raging headache from some of the blather. At least I have dinner in the slow cooker. You will probably be getting this training next week. With little or no notice. Be prepared to make a video of yourself, write virtual lesson plans, then submit it all via the Google Classroom. I'll forward the agenda to you.

Misty: Why don't we do some real professional development and have a collaboration meeting each Friday? Just us. We can put it in our schedules and share some real lessons and ideas.

Me: I love it—that would be perfect. Friday is my make-up day when I reschedule missed meetings and try to get my lesson plans for the next week organized. We can just make it a standing appointment, collaboration and counseling combined. Except I can't start this Friday … because I had to reschedule all my Wednesday meetings.

At long last we had a video chat from Ian from his quarantine location in Pennsylvania. He hadn't been able to get a new phone plan yet and was still relying on his plan from Thailand. For this call he was outside a neighboring house riding their Wi-Fi. It was great to talk to him, but I could tell when I saw him that things were not good. He was cold and miserable, shivering, with his hoodie pulled up over his head. It had been quite a shock to go from the balmy tropical weather of Thailand to the overcast dreariness of a northeastern winter.

"Can I send you a coat? You still have a few here. Or I can order one and have it delivered to you in Pennsylvania."

"No, no, I'm okay," he tried to reassure me.

I knew that voice and I most certainly knew he wasn't okay. To make matters worse, his ATM card had expired a few days before he left Thailand, so he had no access to his money. The bank had sent the new ATM card to my parents' home in Florida, that being his permanent stateside address. My parents sent it to us in Italy and we forwarded it on to his Thai address, never imagining the chain of events that had led to his evacuation. Unfortunately, it didn't reach him before he left, and his card was somewhere out there in snail mail limbo between Italy and Thailand. He was able to get online and order another one, but it was being sent to Florida. Again.

Later, Ian confided in me that during these initial days of quarantine he felt untethered, disconnected from reality. I was glad he was safe and staying with his coworker as they had shared this experience and could grieve their loss together. I was still concerned about his wellbeing, but I knew I needed to give him some space. Moms want to fix everything, but moms also know when they have to let their boys be men.

Then I thought about my day of professional development and how annoyed I was when my schedule was rearranged. Ian's situation really put that into perspective. Yes, my entire day got hijacked, but not my entire life.

Mom and Dad wanted to do something to help the boys, but their situation made it a challenge. Now I had a task only they could manage. From home. And it would be easy.

Message to Mom: Ian's ATM card is being sent to you again. I'm sorry to involve you in this. They wouldn't send it to Pennsylvania, only to his permanent address, which is your house. I sent you an email with his quarantine address.

Mom: OK we'll send it to him. I'll let you know when that happens.

Me: Thanks. If they make you sign for it, please use your own pen. I hope they'll just leave it on the porch.

Mom: We'll watch for it on the porch. They make you sign for things with your finger now. I'll wash well after.

Thursday, March 26, 2020

After the morning meeting with my students, I logged on to our virtual classroom and sent them a reminder about our upcoming special event.

Kindergarten chat:

-- Hello friends! It was fun to see you in your costumes this morning. Don't forget that tomorrow is our Virtual Talent Show! If you have something special to share, please let me know so I can put you on the Talent Show program. Since we are such a talented class, we will need to keep the presentations short so everyone (who wants to) gets a chance to shine.

I couldn't wait to see what they came up with.

Just two days earlier, we had received updated travel documents and now we were given yet another set, an English translation of the Italian original. I couldn't even remember how many updates this made, maybe five or six so far, and I didn't really understand what was new and different about this particular one. I just put the old ones in the fireplace so I could get rid of them and not run the risk of producing the wrong paperwork if asked. We'd heard that if you were stopped by the police and didn't have the latest version that you could be fined up to three thousand euro. Of course, this was just another rumor, but not one I wanted to find out about firsthand while I was getting groceries.

Thinking about groceries brought my mind back to Walmart. I sent a message to my sister to update her on the latest plan for our parents.

Message to Barbara: I set up a Walmart grocery account for Mom and Dad. As soon as I get their credit card added they're good to go. They'll miss grocery shopping but it's for their own good. Grocery shopping will come back for them, and before they know it they'll be chatting with their friends in the produce section again.

Friday, March 27, 2020

Because of Wednesday's professional development, I was behind on lesson planning. Still, I was able to meet my goal of doing individual work with every child. After the make-up lessons came the best part of the day—the much-anticipated Virtual Talent Show. Most of the class joined the meeting to participate or just to watch.

The extravaganza opened with dog tricks: sitting, fetching, rolling over. This was followed by break dancing and a Hula-Hoop demonstration. There were three Lego creations and a few paintings. Late musical entries included a drum solo and a harmonica player. I don't remember how we thought of the talent show idea, but it was hands-down one of the best meetings we ever had. We laughed and clapped and almost felt real again.

I couldn't wait to tell Misty about it so she could try it with her kids.

Message to Misty: This afternoon we had a virtual talent show and it was hilarious!! We had dog tricks, break dancing, drums, a Hula-Hoop act, harmonica, and more! OMG you have to do it!

Misty: Sounds awesome—maybe I can do it next Thursday! I had a great day, too. I just had a parent email me apologizing for her daughter missing the morning meeting, but she was really sad, too, because SHE missed the next chapter of Junie B. Jones. So … I just finished reading it to both of them!

Me: You're a FIVE!

Misty: To my students. That's what I really care about.

Me: And to me.

From: Mrs. Tramm
To: VES Kindergarten 2019-2020
Subject: Kindergarten in the Kitchen News, Friday, March 27, 2020

Dear Kindergarten Families,

It was good to meet with the kids this week and listen to them read, rhyme, count, and share with us. Thanks for being flexible and shifting your Wednesday meetings; I really appreciate it.

What a great Virtual Talent Show today! It was such a fabulous event and I think we should do it again. Thank you for keeping the acts short and simple; it was just right! We enjoyed the dog tricks, Hula-Hoop demonstration, and the break dancer. The paintings were beautiful and the Lego creations were very original. We even had a musical portion featuring a harmonica player and a drum solo. The kids did a great job with their virtual audience behavior, keeping the microphones off, waiting their turns, and using the pin to watch the acts. We are a talented and gifted group for sure!

As always, if you encounter any issues with the assignments, let me know as soon as possible so we can try to get them fixed. Thanks for all you are doing for the kids—above and beyond! Have a great weekend!

Karin Tramm
VES Kindergarten

As soon as I put the ironing board away, I felt a warm sense of relief wash over me. The weekend was here and I could breathe again. My ironing board had not seen this much action in the past thirty years. I hate ironing, but I always knew there would be a good reason to keep the ironing board.

I poured wine, emptying the last garnet drops of the two-liter bottle into my glass. I checked my stash in the cabinet and frowned, realizing it was the last bottle. Outside in the fading sun, I sat on a dusty porch chair and messaged my mom.

Message to Mom: I hope you and Dad were able to figure out the Walmart shopping app. Soon you will be enjoying home delivery. Barb told me that Dad's going to the airport.

DAD, please stay in the car at the airport. You should get her bag out of the trunk only if no one else is there at the curbside. If there is curbside assistance, just pop the trunk and let them do it. And wipe the trunk down when you get home.

We love you so much and care about your safety. This is going to be a hard time for everyone in our family. Please bear with us if we sound bossy but know it's the voice of love and concern.

Mom: They are just leaving. I have successfully made our first order from Walmart. It will be delivered tomorrow between one and two in the afternoon. Thanks so much for setting that up for us.

Me: I'm glad you've figured out the app and have used it already. The emails will come to me, but I don't care—I'll always just forward them to you as soon as they come. I'm so glad this is working out.

Mom: Thank you!!

Me: *Prego!*

Check and check. I was relieved that their company was gone. I was even more relieved that they had a safe plan for getting food. This Friday was definitely an improvement over last Friday. If only there were pizza.

I saw that I also had a message from Vickie to answer.

Vickie: I'm already bored with my self-quarantine. I caused panic when I tried to go to work this week. I didn't know I was supposed to stay home after my trip. I know you have been doing this for weeks already!! Guess I'll go make a spritz as you suggested.

Last we talked you were overwhelmed with online school. Hope you get a Friday break soon and are still allowed to get your pizza and wine. I'm doing well, thank you for the warnings, because I knew what was coming from our talks starting back in February while I was on Guam. Things are not a surprise to me. I hope you and Gene are both ok. I miss all my boys. No one's at home so we video chat but it's not the same as a visit. Again, thinking of you and your faraway boys. If you do have time for a chat, virtual happy hours are popular now. Let me know. We can keep it lighthearted. I have a funny story.

Me: I need a funny story. Things are still dismal here. 900 dead yesterday, 919 today. We're on week five of lockdown. Brace yourself.

The Peace Corps evacuated Ian from Thailand. He is in quarantine in Pennsylvania with no money, no phone plan, and no warm clothes. Will is in Miami still in his apartment. He just found out the last class he needed to graduate, to be taken this summer, has been delayed until fall. But WTH, there probably won't be a graduation in July anyway so whatever at this point. He has a place to live, money, and a phone, so he is the least of my worries today. Trying to keep my parents in the house has been a nightmare. Maybe we can chat tomorrow. *Ciao* for now!

One of the many blessings of our little *comune* was the wine store. Although there were countless bottles of wine available in the local grocery, the *enoteca,* or the *vinoteca,* as we liked to call it, was our favorite place to go.

The shelves were stocked with a myriad of wine choices, displays of local artisanal food, and craft beer. The owner was quick to offer an impromptu wine tasting and some snacks. Often there was cake, baked and sent in by his mother. Lately there had been the crunchy and sugar coated *chiacchiere*, the sweet fried dough Italians enjoyed during *Carnevale*.

The owner was also an artist of wine corks and bottles. His many creations, from planters to light fixtures, graced the store. My favorite went out on display every December, the wine cork nativity scene. His barrel planters out front brimmed with fresh flowers throughout the year. I asked him once how he kept them so healthy and he explained that after he rinsed out the wine bottles, he saved the water for the plants.

"They like the grape," he confided to me in Italian.

We lovingly referred to the *enoteca* as the "wine gas station". The wall behind the cash register was lined with taps for the bulk wines, or *vini sfusi*, as the Italians call them. This meant for two euro a liter (two fifty for *prosecco*) we could take our own bottles and have them filled up with local wine. Fill 'er up, I'd think, as I watched the deep red liquid flow. The cabernet was our favorite and we always took all four of our two-liter bottles in for a refill so we would be stocked up for a couple of weeks. The vino was Italian table wine, so not top of the line, but pretty good when paired with pizza. Conveniently, it was right across the street from Gioia so we could make it one-stop shopping on Friday night.

Much to our distress, this Friday night the pizzeria was still *chiuso*, closed, and then, to make matters worse, I finished the *vino sfuso*.

Message to Will: Happy Friday!

Will: Thanks, you too! We did a Hattts livestream on Wednesday. It went really well. How are you guys doing?

Me: We're out of sfuso wine.

Will: But you have bottles in the basement, right?

Me: Yes, we're going to have to break into the good stuff.

A photo from Will popped up next, a plant in his windowsill.

Will: Look! My spiderwort is starting to bloom!!

Me: Congratulations. Life finds a way, even in the midst of this craziness.

I was glad Will was smart enough to have a plant friend living with him in his campus apartment.

Saturday, March 28, 2020

As soon as I woke up, I checked for any news from Ian. Even though he didn't have Wi-Fi or a phone plan, anything was possible, so I could hope. There was nothing from him this morning, but there was a voicemail from our North Carolina friends.

"Good morning, Tramms! I hope everything is well in your world. We are lying in bed having our morning coffee—we're one meter apart per the social distancing requirement. We are thinking about you and hoping all is well and you have all the supplies you need and you are happy and healthy. Hopefully Ian has found his way out of Thailand and is safe and sound. I'm thinking he may cross our path at some point. We are experimenting with the technology so hopefully this voice message goes through. You know we love you guys. Be happy, be safe."

Message to Mari: Oh, so good to hear your voice. We just survived the fifth week of lockdown. Thanks for checking in with us. I don't know what to say about Ian. I wish he were still in Thailand. But he's not, so we are trying to help him land on his feet, set up a phone plan, etc. He has no Wi-Fi, so he has to stand outside someone's house and try to ride theirs. We have only been able to talk to him once. He's still processing his situation and trying to figure out what comes next. You will see him before we do. I would say to give him a big hug from us, but no, don't do that, an elbow bump will be safer. Stay well and wash your hands.

Mari: Karin, you know we will do anything to help Ian. I will reach out to him again and let him know. Hang in there. We love you guys!!

Me: Many thanks, friends! Love you, too!

Vickie called later and we talked for an hour. We chatted a bit more about the latest Guam gossip, old friends, and new restaurants.

"Last time we talked, I forgot to ask you—did you ever get to have Shirley's fried rice?"

Shirley's was one of my favorite breakfast places. They had the best breakfast fried rice on the island, topped with an egg, sunny side up. On a sleepy Sunday morning, it didn't get much better than that. I've tried to recreate Shirley's recipe in my own kitchen and it's come closer over the years, but maybe only the passage of time and my fading memory made it so. Shirley also served up a mean Spam and eggs plate, not my favorite, but a local specialty to be sure.

Vickie and I talked about the crazy happenings in our lives. We traded stories about our boys and how they were managing their new apartments and their new lives. Later she messaged.

Vickie: It's always good to talk with you, especially right now so I know where things are going and also realize things could be a whole lot worse. You are calm! Last time I was at the commissary, I stocked up on chocolate gelato, an essential supply—for me anyway. Truly if you think of anything we can do for Ian to help on his latest adventure, very glad to help. *Ciao amica!*

I was surprised and happy she thought I was calm. With Gene's illness, Ian's evacuation, Will's isolation, school in unknown territory, and things spiraling out of control around the world, I felt anything but calm. However, talking with a lifelong friend, even about the mundane, gave my mind a rest and let me put things in perspective.

Although Vicenza is primarily an army community, there was a small group of retired navy folks living in the area. Some worked as teachers, some as contractors, and some as government civil service employees. We tried to get together from time to time to celebrate the navy's birthday or to watch the Army/Navy football game.

It was good for Gene to maintain a connection to his long-ago other life. As our real life continued to sail into uncharted waters, this bond became more and more significant with the passing of each day, a life buoy of sorts. Someone floated the idea to connect on Saturday evening for adult beverages.

Navy chat:

-- Hello navy friends! Let's meet for a virtual happy hour tonight at six in the evening. All you need is a drink of choice, and we can share some together time!!

-- Great idea! We're ready!

-- Anchors aweigh my friends! See you then.

Thus, the Navy Happy Hour was established, a tradition that continued every Saturday throughout the first lockdown. Gene's adult beverage of choice for the first gathering was orange juice, with a shot of vitamin C, to keep the scurvy at bay. It was good to reach out, catch up, and talk about the world gone mad.

Sunday, March 29, 2020

Several emails from Walmart appeared in my inbox. I was surprised by the number but didn't mind and forwarded everything to Mom and Dad. I messaged to make sure the process went smoothly for them.

Message to Mom: I hope your grocery delivery came without a problem. I forwarded the order summary to you. FYI, we had daylight savings this weekend. Have a great Sunday!

Mom: We got everything I ordered, except the potatoes and eggs, but we have a dozen eggs from Barbara so we're good. He was here right at one o'clock. Your dad gave him a tip.

Me: Right, I had another email from Walmart about that. I'll forward it. I just got the delivery confirmation email, too, so I'll send that as well.

Mom: We used gloves, unloaded the bags on the porch, wiped everything down before bringing it in. Then we loaded their plastic bags into another bag we had, added our gloves and wipes to it, and put all in the outside trash. Thank you again for setting it up. Love you!

Me: Welcome! I forwarded another email with the tip receipt and another one asking you to rate the service. Love you too!

Message from Vickie: I'm trying to remember our phone conversation and verifying facts telling friends here what to expect. Have you been locked in for ten days with Gene only? You don't get to go visit with friends or coworkers, only online, correct? Two hundred meters walk only from house. Is the commissary still open? Still thinking of your boys and the crazy situation for Ian. I talked with my Miami guys this morning, so this is on my mind. Always sending good thoughts and well wishes.

Me: Yes, all of that. Commissary is open but don't know for how much longer or if we're allowed to go to the base. Rumors, rumors. I can't even remember how long we've been in the house … we're going on week six of virtual school.

Vickie: I'm just telling some of your story instead of saying what I really want to say to them: to SHUT UP and quit whining because some people have it so much worse than others!! You know the biggest whiners are the ones giving up the least.

Me: Right? If any of them have gel nails, advise them to get them taken off right now while they still can or they will start ripping off later. And look awful, just like mine. COVID nails are the worst! Tell them to hurry while their nail salon is still open. LOL.

Vickie: And their hair is going gray, and some people are worried about their dog grooming being shut down, but you and I don't have to worry about that thankfully.

Me: That's right. Another reason to love the pet-free existence.

From: Bill
To: Karin
Subject: Another week

Karin,

How are things with you? No change here; we are still restricted to the ship. The good news is that there were three people with symptoms, and they all tested negative. There are fifteen people still in quarantine on the island—people who came in contact with them before they were tested. Not sure why the fifteen people are still being quarantined, but the good news is that we APPEAR to be COVID-free.

I see the number of new cases in Italy has seemed to plateau around five thousand per day. I hope they start to go down soon. I have been in touch with Mom and Dad and they're staying home which is good. Their company is gone, too. (I think that might be good, too.) I've emailed Barbara twice but she hasn't responded. I think my emails are going into her junk folder.

All for now,
Bill

From: Karin
To: Bill
Subject: RE: Another week

I'll tell Barb to look in her junk folder. She and I have been keeping in touch regularly, trying to keep Mom and Dad under control. I got them set up with a Walmart grocery account and they successfully received their first delivery yesterday. I think everything went smoothly.

We're entering week six of virtual school. We're out of milk, cheese, juice, fresh veggies, and cheap wine. But we're trying to stay in for the next week or so just to make sure we're okay. Gene still is not 100 percent so I just want to be cautious.

Our spring break is next week. We will be visiting the front porch, back porch, and driveway. I hope the fam is all well in FL.

Love, K

From: Bill
To: Karin
Subject: RE: Another week

Karin,

Thanks for the update. I'm glad to hear you're doing okay, except being out of wine. We don't have any wine here, but there is plenty of WHINE that's for sure. Actually, everyone is really taking things in stride.

I can relate to your spring break. On here, we visit the bridge, engine room, galley, and take long walks to the bow. But I'm just happy to have a job and to be in a safe part of the world.

I'm expecting my weekly phone call from home tonight. Tell Gene to get well or else!

Be safe,
Bill

From: Karin
To: Bill
Subject: RE: Another week
Thank goodness I am not completely out of wine, just the *sfusi*. Now we're raiding the basement and breaking into the good stuff …
Tell the girls I said hello, stay safe, stay home, and wash their hands!

Later we virtually hopscotched across time zones from Italy, to Florida, to Pennsylvania. After multiple phone calls, emails, and texts, we were finally able to link Ian's phone with his brother's plan. It was a sigh of relief to finally have better communication with him, especially in the midst of this colossal disruption. Not that he had much to tell us right now other than that in Pennsylvania the gun stores were still open, but the liquor stores were closed. Still, knowing he could connect when he needed to was a load off our minds.

WEEK 6: PREDICTABILITY AND ROUTINE

Monday, March 30, 2020

I strive for predictability and routine for my students. As military kids, their lives are a series of upheavals as a result of moving out, moving in, deployments, and living in a foreign country. Strangers boxing up favorite things, living on loaner furniture, and heartbreaking goodbyes are hard enough on adults; on children it can be exponentially more difficult. It makes me happy that school is a safe place where they know what to expect when things at home are unraveling or unpredictable. Our school year had been predictable and routine—for one hundred days.

With over a month of virtual school under our belts, I hoped I was providing a new kind of predictability and routine as we moved through the current upheaval. Gene and I had settled into a familiar workday routine as well. It was nice not to wake up in the dark and to have a few extra minutes of sleep. We made the bed, showered, and got ready just as if we were leaving the house. I put on my school clothes, earrings, and makeup, and fixed my hair. Morning meetings, lunch, afternoon meetings, a driveway walk, check in on the family, dinner, and bed. It wasn't exciting but it was oh-so predictable.

As the temperatures outside began to rise, we turned the heat off inside. It was invigorating to open the windows and let the fresh air sweep through. I slept better in spring and fall, tucked under the duvet, with the cool night air flowing in.

This morning, however, when I woke up it felt like someone was pinching my nose. Peering out the window, I noticed the screen was covered with linty fluff. The cottonwood trees were blooming and the seeds were everywhere. Puffballs filled the air and tumbleweeds of white cotton candy blew across the terrace. My allergies were in full swing and now was definitely not the time to be coughing, wheezing, or sneezing.

It had been a couple of weeks since Gene had been feeling poorly. With all the spring flowers and grasses in bloom, and now the cottonwood too, we couldn't be sure if his symptoms were allergies or something more sinister. Just when Gene seemed to improve, he would relapse with more chills but no fever. Current guidance for our community maintained to stay at home unless there was a need for emergency medical attention. Teachers were also told to inform the school if they were experiencing any COVID-related symptoms. He self-reported to his principal and was told to stay home unless his condition deteriorated.

Gene rallied through the day and pressed on for our afternoon walk.

"It's like a snowstorm," I said, noting the cottonwood seeds spewing forth from the trees at the end of the driveway.

We finished our laps and came back for a break before dinner. I called Mom to check in and she was happy to report that Ian's ATM card had just arrived.

"That's great news, I'm so glad." I was relieved, this was another problem solved, or almost.

"Your dad thinks he should go to the post office and send it overnight, or should he just put it in the mailbox?"

"Tell Dad not to go to the post office. It's okay to just put it in the mailbox. Ian's still in quarantine and he's not going anywhere right now."

"OK, done. And I didn't have to sign for it."

"You did have the Pennsylvania address, right?" I asked, making sure. "Was it just a regular envelope? Just a regular stamp?"

"Yes, I had the Pennsylvania address. Regular envelope and regular stamp. I bought a lot of Forever stamps at forty-five cents and they're fifty-five cents now. Glad I did that."

"Me too. Thanks for helping us with this. I can't tell you how frustrating and scary this is. Everything is unraveling so quickly, and we're stuck here and the boys are stuck there." I was starting to spiral. "I feel helpless, like we can't do anything from over here. I'm just so grateful you're there when all this stuff comes up."

"You're welcome. You know we'll do anything we can to help," Mom said. "We're family. That's what we do."

Tuesday, March 31, 2020

Beams of early daybreak streamed in, red sunlight reflecting off the bathroom mirror. When I opened the window and looked out on that all-too-familiar landscape, I noticed Flavio had raised an Italian flag on the fence by the cornfield, a symbolic gesture of *forza*, strength, in the midst of this crisis. The red, white, and green banner fluttered in the breeze with the pink sunrise as a backdrop. The scene gave me pause and I went from window to window upstairs to soak up the silent morning.

From the bedroom, the front yard was still a little frosty and crisp, cherry blossoms blushing from the tree below the window. Looking out from the office, now Gene's classroom, I could see bright yellow daffodils lining either side of the stone walkway. As I moved downstairs, the living room window showcased apple trees in bloom, newly plowed fields, and the Dolomiti blanketed in a fresh sparkle of snow. From the kitchen, a shimmery vista across the hayfield all the way to the blue Berici hills in the distance. Lockdown was certainly confining, but I appreciated my morning commute, be it simply from upstairs to downstairs.

We had coffee, fruit, and toast while checking in, the ironing board doing double duty as a coffee bar every morning. While I was required to fill in an online form each day, Gene had to join a virtual meeting with his principal. The school nurse was present to talk to him about his condition and he reported it was about the same. He hadn't left the house for twenty-one days and the only person he had been around was me. I had experienced no symptoms and that was a good sign—and we both could still smell the coffee. Another good sign. We hoped for the best.

Wednesday, April 1, 2020

Rain, rain, go away. Come again another day.

Rainclouds on the horizon, bringing thoughts of inside recess, instill dread in the heart of a kindergarten teacher. Twenty or more bouncing bodies with no time to run and play make for a difficult day, not to mention coming up with a plan to entertain them and to squeeze in a pee break for myself during the day. It was almost enough to consider calling in sick, except for the thought of having to write sub plans.

Another silver lining, I thought: inside recess was something I didn't have to worry about while in virtual school. It only sprinkled a little and then stopped; if I'd been at school, I probably would've sent them out anyway. It was just enough to tamp down the dust in the driveway, and it was sunny by the time Gene and I went out for our afternoon walk.

With my kitchen table subbing as my teacher desk, Gene and I had fallen into the bad habit of eating dinner in the living room, something we rarely let the boys do except for a treat or for pizza night, of course. We'd binged more than our fair share of Netflix over the past few weeks and had just finished the latest season of *Chef's Table*. We asked around for some recommendations, something interesting, something funny, something to take our minds off everything. Appropriately, it was April Fools' Day that someone told us about a bizarre new show on Netflix called *Tiger King*.

Message from Ian: Wouldn't it be nice if this was all just a big April Fools' joke? Haha!

Me: I know. I'm just happy your phone is working and we can talk to you. That's no joke.

Ian: Me, too. Hopefully, my ATM card will come today.

Me: Crossing my fingers but Grandma just forwarded it yesterday. I don't think the snail mail will deliver that fast. But don't worry—it's on the way.

It was good to hear from Ian and it sounded like his mood was starting to pick up again. He wasn't out of the woods yet, but getting the phone plan in place and the ATM card replaced were giant steps in the right direction. Gene and I continued to struggle with the fact that the boys were stuck in the States, while we were stuck in Italy. At least the continent count had decreased from three to two, although we hoped Ian would be on his way back to Thailand shortly.

We're so proud that we created these fiercely independent human beings, but our parental instinct to protect them never diminishes. A couple of years back, Florida State and Florida International spring breaks coincided and the boys planned a big adventure together. They threw around ideas and finally Will called to fill us in on the details.

"Soooo ... did Ian tell you what we're doing for spring break?"

I felt my mom prickles start to rise. I took a big breath and braced myself.

"Ummm, no, he didn't. I guess you're gonna tell me now."

"Well," a little hesitation, and then, "we're going to Cuba."

"What?!" I asked, in shock and exasperation. "You can't just do that! You know you have to have a visa?! You can't just go there!"

"Yeah, I know, I know. Ian applied for a journalism visa. He's gonna write an article about Airbnb rentals in Cuba. It was approved and I'm going as his assistant. We're flying out of Miami to Havana. We've got an Airbnb set up; it's all good. No worries."

No worries? Seriously? I didn't even know what to say. Will was probably glad there was an entire ocean between us.

They were so thrilled to be going somewhere their parents had never been, independent military kids, those two. I drank a lot of wine that week when they were offline and out of touch. They had a few misadventures but arrived back in Miami safe, sunburned, and with stories to tell.

These were the boys I had to now trust to navigate this COVID-19 mess on the other side of the world without us.

TALLAHASSEE, Fla.—The Governor announced Wednesday afternoon that the state of Florida is being shut down amid the coronavirus pandemic.

Finally. I was relieved when Florida at long last shut down. As soon as I heard the news, I picked up my phone and called Mom.

"Finally! I'm so glad. It's the right move. I wish it'd been two weeks ago."

"Me, too," she agreed. "But better late than never, I guess."

"But at least you're safe because you've been in the house this whole time. Because you knew. And because you have Walmart."

That conversation must have jogged her memory because right after I hung up, another email arrived from Walmart:

Walmart Grocery Order Summary
2 Riunite Emilia Lambrusco Wine 1.5 L $19.92

Message to Barbara: They certainly are enjoying their Walmart grocery delivery service.

Barbara: She told me yesterday she placed a new BIGGER order. I hope they don't go bankrupt. I did remind them that everything that comes into the house is an added risk.

Me: And for every order, I get seven associated emails outlining the order, order summary, changes they make, substitutions the store makes, out-for-delivery notice, delivery confirmation, tip receipt, etc. Mamma mia! But really, I don't mind; I actually welcome this. I'm glad they are staying home, and this makes me very happy, even if it's for Riunite. I just forward all the emails on to them.

Navy chat:

-- How's Gene? Feeling better, I hope?

-- He's doing ok, about the same. I think he's having some allergies but we're watching carefully. I'll know he's back on track when I see him with a glass of wine. Thanks for checking up on him.

Thursday, April 2, 2020

Message from Misty: OMG! The talent show was a FABULOUS idea! I had a break-dancer, too!
Me: Didn't it make your heart happy? That's one of our best days so far.

Another Thursday, another meeting. After the kindergarten team meeting, we were given a link to another meeting for the entire faculty to attend. We were directed to make sure all microphones were muted and all cameras were ON. Maybe Stella called the principal, instead of calling Santa. Okay, fine, I thought wearily and joined the Hollywood Squares. I made sure my wine glass was out of sight.

Our faculty meetings usually highlighted someone's "best practices," and this continued even when we gathered virtually. Some of my younger tech-savvy colleagues had some great ideas and were asked to share them. I was genuinely happy this shift had been easy for them, I was, really. I wanted to learn from them, to be a better robo-teacher. But honestly, hearing it at the end of a long day made me feel like a total failure. I was so happy when that meeting was over and I could switch to the *après* meeting. But first my parent newsletter.

From: Mrs. Tramm
To: VES Kindergarten 2019-2020
Subject: Kindergarten in the Kitchen News, Thursday, April 2, 2020

Dear Kindergarten Families,
    I can't believe it's the end of the third quarter already. I will be working on progress reports tomorrow so there will be no meetings. Instruction will resume on Monday, April 13th. There will be no assignments over the spring break, but I will post some virtual field trips to enjoy. I hope everyone has some relaxing family time over your staycation!

Karin Tramm
VES Kindergarten

I clicked SEND and refilled my wine glass. I picked up my phone and checked the news for the hundredth time. I never checked the weather anymore; rain didn't matter. A message from my sister was waiting.

Barbara: We're in the house arrest club now. They don't expect our numbers to peak for two to four more weeks.

Me: You're in it now. So glad you're staying home. I hope things pass quickly in Florida.

As much as I wanted to go back home, as much as I needed to go home, the boys both continued to tell us they were glad we were still in Italy. I wondered if they worried about us like I worried about my parents.

"People here aren't listening, Mom. They won't wear masks; they don't think COVID is a thing."

I was heartened when we were finally able to have a video chat with both boys at the same time. It was the first time we had talked together, all four of us, in what seemed like forever. It recharged my soul to hear their voices and listen to them laugh and banter with each other, just as if we were all home at the dinner table. At the same time, it was hard to take in what they were going through, Ian with his evacuation and quarantine, and Will with his isolation and switch to online classes. Always the mom, I wanted to jump in and make it all better, but this time I couldn't. I had to continue to step back and let things play out.

Health Alert: US Embassy Rome, 2 April 2020

Location: Italy

Event: The Italian government has confirmed cases of COVID-19 throughout the country. The Department of State has issued a Global Level 4 Health Advisory for COVID-19. US citizens, lawful permanent residents, and qualifying family members who normally reside in the United States should arrange for immediate return home or be prepared to remain abroad for an indefinite period.

Friday, April 3, 2020

It was the end of the third quarter and a teacher workday. I prepared report cards and submitted them to my supervisor for approval. It was hard to believe we'd been having virtual school for six weeks already.

We were notified later in the morning that voluntary evacuation had become an option for Department of Defense teachers. If we chose to leave, we would be required to continue to work from a safe haven in Arlington, Virginia. Our working hours would be based on Italian time, which meant we would have to be awake, online, and ready for kids at two in the morning East Coast time.

Thanks, but no thanks, Gene and I both agreed. We knew we were better off here in our isolated farmhouse in Bolzano Vicentino than passing through numerous airports and living in some kind of safe haven, probably military barracks. The way things were starting to look in the States, we felt much safer staying put. How I wished we could bring the boys home to Italy, but it was impossible with the travel restrictions.

Message from Barbara: I agree with staying put, as long as you can safely get food. And wine.

Me: Yes, and yes. I'm well stocked and not going out until I absolutely have to. Gene had a relapse this week but worked through it and now is doing better. He's still not drinking wine yet. We had a group chat with the boys last night. That made me so happy.

Barbara: Hate to hear about Gene. Have you been sick? How are the boys?

Me: I'm fine and Gene is better. Maybe it's just allergies but he doesn't usually get them. He did self-report to his principal and the school has to follow up with the district superintendent's office. Then they have to follow up with the base to report that he was showing symptoms. I don't know if there's any more follow up with him unless he ends up in the hospital. He's been in the house for almost three weeks and continues to isolate here. I wish we could get him tested so we'd know for certain. If he's had it already, then he's the one who gets to go to the grocery store next time. LOL

I have to say that even though I haven't left the house for two weeks I'm not feeling that isolated. I love that I can see my students every day, even if it's just on the computer screen. I know that helps a lot. And I especially love that I can mute them.

~

We decided to try to watch TV together as a family. I thought it would help us all feel connected and bring some levity to our situation. Will could tune in from Miami, Ian from Pennsylvania, and Gene and I from Italy. It turned out to be a bit more complicated than we thought. First, we had to agree on what to watch, Will staunchly refused to watch *Tiger King*, while Ian loved the absurdity of it. It took some maneuvering to agree on the show and to make the technology play nicely, but we were finally able to sync up, minimize the feedback, and watch together.

"Are you there?" we shouted at the phone. "Will, can you hear us? Ian, are you there?"

When the boys were little, we used to watch the old claymation version of Arnold Lobel's classic *Frog and Toad* before bedtime. Once upon a time, we owned the VHS collection of short stories about the two mismatched amphibian friends. "A Swim," "The Lost Button," or "The Garden," it was hard to choose my favorite tale. However, Will's favorite was definitely "The Story."

When Frog was sick, his friend Toad tried to help him feel better. Three-year-old Will would belly laugh as Toad poured water over his head, stood upside down, and banged his head against the wall trying to think of a good story to tell his friend Frog. When Frog felt better, he became the storyteller and regaled Toad until he fell asleep, just in time for the boys to doze off. We thought *Frog and Toad* was the perfect thing to watch to lighten everyone's mood. It felt good to belly laugh again.

Health Alert: US Embassy Rome, 3 April 2020

Location: Italy

Event: International commercial flight options currently exist in Italy. US citizens who wish to return to the United States should make commercial arrangements as soon as possible unless they are prepared to remain abroad for an indefinite period. The US government has no plans to arrange repatriation flights in Italy at this time.

Yes, a very long and indefinite period as things turned out.

Saturday, April 4, 2020

The first day of spring break arrived. It was time to step away from school and focus on something else, anything else. We had nine glorious days off, but what to do? Gene and I lounged a bit and had coffee in bed, relishing the fact that we didn't have to check in to school.

The weather had been beautiful and now we hoped to spend some time reading, relaxing, and enjoying our meals *al fresco*. Outside, the porches were a disaster, covered with farm dust, leaves, and cottonwood seeds. We moved the furniture from the front porch, hosed everything down, and beat the dust out of the pads. We squeegeed the tile. We cleared cobwebs and dead stinkbugs from the windows. The plants that had been wintering inside the greenhouse were brought back outside, watered, and pruned.

"So glad the peacocks are gone," Gene mused.

I had to agree. Cleaning up was so much easier without them. I loved those majestic birds, but they were nasty. When they first came to live on the farm we were fascinated. There was a huge male and a white female. Every year there was a brood of chicks, a few of which stayed and roamed around the property like watchdogs. They knew us and would greet us with their familiar calls whenever we went outside or when we arrived home from school.

The peacocks settled into their farm routine just as we had. They liked to perch in the windows in winter to catch the heat flowing out through the leaks. In summer they hung out there to enjoy the air conditioning. They liked to watch TV too, and would often curl up in the living room window on pizza night and watch movies with us through the glass. One of them would peer through the kitchen window in the evenings to watch me cook.

They were charming but they were foul fowl. They would poop in the most inconvenient places, all over the porch, front doorstep, tile table, and top of the car. Maybe they were trying to tell us something or maybe they thought they were being nice, like our cats, who brought mice, snakes, and even an owl to us as gifts.

One summer we went home to Florida and came back to find the last of the peacocks gone. We were never sure what happened to our filthy friends.

We finished cleaning the front porch and continued on around the corner to the side terrace, scrubbing the mosaic tile table and the floor. The kiwis and grapevines were beginning to sprout leaves and spread out on the pergola overhead. The only thing missing was the geraniums for the flower boxes. They would have to wait until we could get to the garden store.

It was a morning of hard work that left us with a feeling of satisfaction. Spring cleaning was done and we were ready to fire up the grill and enjoy some outside living. Like it or not, our vacation had morphed into a staycation, and it was here at last.

I heard a ping and pulled my phone out of my sweater pocket only to see a pop-up notification that KLM flight 875 to Bangkok would be leaving in one hour. I rolled my eyes in disgust and regretted not removing that item from the calendar. Feeling annoyed, I shoved my phone back into my pocket and immediately heard a second notification. I sighed and wondered if I should even look. Chancing a glance, I saw that the universe was going to give me a little bit of balance.

> **Message to Barbara**: THE WINE STORE DELIVERS!! I saw it posted on FB this morning, so I called right away.
>
> **Barbara**: Does it come in keg size?
>
> **Me**: Now that I have home delivery, I don't have to worry about it. He's bringing us ten liters.
>
> **Barbara**: Are you sure that's enough?
>
> **Me**: For this weekend. LOL.

I was ready for a break. I put the brooms and cleaning supplies away, poured myself some water, and sat down at the freshly wiped table. A message appeared from Mom.

> **Mom**: So glad you got to talk with both of your boys. It makes it a little easier when you see they are okay. Barb and Brian were just here with tomatoes. The packing plant was selling a twenty-five-pound box

for five dollars. They had a glut since the restaurants closed and this allowed them to pay their employees and help the community. These are plum tomatoes, and some are still pink so they should last awhile. And make good pasta sauce! Everything is good here. Love you.

Ian was on his last day of quarantine in Pennsylvania, so he needed to have a plan for what came next. He understood he was not able to stay with his grandparents due to their age and his grandmother's health issues. My parents would've gladly taken him in if it were possible. But even if it had been an option, what would he do once he arrived there?

I wished he could make his way down to Will's apartment in Miami, since Will's roommate moved out and there was an empty bedroom. Without a car, that would pose a challenge, but I was sure we could get him down there one way or the other. Will, however, wasn't supposed to have visitors in his campus apartment so Miami wasn't a viable solution either. Obviously, heartbreakingly, frustratingly, he couldn't come home to Italy. What to do, what to do?

Message from Vickie: Time is so weird right now. I can't believe it's only been a week since our phone call. Some states are finally catching up with Italy and enforcing stay-at-home restrictions. Thankfully, Virginia is one until June 10th. How is Ian?

Me: Ian's on his last day of quarantine. I don't know what his immediate plan is. He does have a phone, so that's good. We're cleaning the porches and getting ready for staycation. The wine store is delivering—thank goodness—ten liters on the way this afternoon!

Vickie: Staycation? Is this the official start of your spring break? I hope that gives you a much-needed break from virtual teaching. Great news about the wine delivery!! Keep me posted on the Ian saga. It's a good update for me to use with the complainers.

Surveying the day's work, we felt productive and satisfied. We retreated back inside, got cleaned up, and made some snacks. We emerged with our plates and glasses and set up on the clean terrace for Navy Happy Hour. Tonight, we would enjoy the fresh air and sunset. Red sky at night, sailor's delight.

A few minutes later we heard the crunch of gravel in the driveway, announcing a visitor on the way. In the distance we saw a rise of dust appear, moving toward us like a mini tornado. Waiting and watching intently, I smiled when a little white utility van emerged from the dust cloud and stopped in front of the house. I wrapped a scarf around my face as a makeshift mask and headed out to the front gate with twenty euro in hand. The driver waved cheerily and jumped out with a mask, gloves, and two five-liter jugs of cabernet sauvignon. The wine delivery was right on time and this time Gene actually had a glass.

Sunday, April 5, 2020

We were able to have a video call with Barbara and Brian the next afternoon. They seemed in good spirits on their fifth day of lockdown.

"*Buongiorno*! You're looking well today."

"Indeed, indeed."

It was morning for them and they sipped their coffee while we chatted a bit about the challenges of being stuck at home. Barbara took the phone outside and showed me her kitchen garden.

"The good news is that I have a lot more time for this."

"Oh wow, look at your tomatoes!" I gasped with envy. Her vines were teeming with the plump red fruit.

I knew my own tomatoes would've been in the ground by now if I'd just been able to get the seedlings. After we hung up, I opened the refrigerator, checked the crisper, and found just what I was looking for. I grabbed a few soft cherry tomatoes and, out of desperation, squished them, and buried them in my kitchen garden. Giving them a sprinkle of water, I hoped I'd get lucky and they would sprout.

Teacher chat:

-- Hey, I just talked with an Italian neighbor, a judge who normally knows what's up, and he said that the proposed date for reducing the quarantine is around the 15th of May ... they're worried that if it's any earlier people might gather for picnics and parties on Liberation Day and Labor Day holidays. I asked him what he thought about schools reopening and he said they wouldn't because after 15 May, what would be the point? I said, "to have some closure?" but he didn't think they'd risk reopening for something like that. So, it does seem like we really might have nine more weeks of this. Anyway, *cin cin*, and happy spring break!

Things were getting pretty bleak on the meal menu. I hadn't been shopping in a while and my choices were dwindling. Looking for something that might work, I found frozen salmon fillets in the freezer. They had potential but I wasn't sure what to do with them. I put them in the fridge to defrost.

That evening, I did a quick scavenger hunt in the refrigerator and pulled out anything with possibility. The final creation turned out so tasty that now I make it every once in a while, when I'm in a cooking rut.

Whatever-You've-Got Salmon

Salmon fillets

Things from the back of the fridge like:
- jarred artichokes
- sun-dried tomatoes in oil
- garlic stuffed olives and capers
- red onion, sliced thin
- olive oil and lemon juice

1. Put everything on or around the salmon, sprinkle white and black pepper, splash with olive oil and lemon juice. Bake for 20-25 minutes at 350 degrees Fahrenheit.

2. Remove the salmon. Add hot cooked linguini or fettuccini (or whatever pasta is left in the pantry) to the baking pan to absorb the juices and mix it with the veggies. Stuffed pasta works well too. Put the salmon on top and serve from the baking pan.

Mmmmmm!

We tried it again later with chicken with the same success. For Whatever-You've-Got Chicken, follow the directions above and adjust cooking temp and time for chicken. Sprinkle with feta cheese before serving.

~

I was getting more and more concerned about Will being alone in his apartment. His demeanor was flat, his attitude defeated. This was not the confident young man we knew. At this point I didn't even care about his grades anymore, just his sanity. He was starting to remind me of Tom Hanks in his own private version of *Castaway*. I recalled the movie quote we sometimes referenced when times get tough:

"And I know what I have to do now. I gotta keep breathing."

Keep breathing, Will, keep breathing. You've got this.

Gene and I tried to talk to him about the importance of maintaining a routine, of exercising, and of making a point to stay connected with friends and family. I sent him a list of things he could do during his days alone—virtual field trips, audiobooks, crosswords, emailing the grandparents, etc.

"Shower and shave every day, don't go feral," I cautioned him.

I would have done anything to just go through the phone and be there with him, or better yet, for him to be here with us. We knew that couldn't happen so the best we could do was to keep breathing. We watched *Wallace and Gromit* together, another old claymation family favorite.

WEEK 7: INSIDE RECESS

Monday, April 6, 2020

Besides providing a much-needed and well-deserved hiatus from school, our spring break usually involved suitcases and a big adventure. Sometimes we stayed local and sometimes our vacations took us farther afield, but we always took advantage of the week to power down and recharge. Now that our planned trip to Thailand was obviously on hold, we decided to enjoy our week-long staycation by creating our own personal travel destination, an *agriturismo*.

In Italy, the countryside is dotted with *agriturismi*—rural lodgings or family-run working farms similar to bed-and-breakfast accommodations.

These unique travel opportunities allow travelers to venture out during the day and return in the evening to a welcoming country atmosphere. A comfortable room and delicious homemade meal make an *agriturismo* an advantageous choice for families. Ian and Will had played in the hay, captured fireflies, and harvested honey with beekeepers. We'd experienced impromptu cooking lessons, and left for home with jars of homemade jam, pesto, local wines, and cases of fresh vegetables.

We decided that come what may this week, we would have fun and enjoy a vacation in our own home. We dubbed it the *Agriturismo Bolzano Vicentino* and pretended we were somewhere far, far away. Despite the drafty windows, propensity for stinkbugs, and other peculiarities, we truly loved our little piece of paradise. I had chosen it for that quaint farmhouse feeling of comfort, coziness, and sense of space that living in the country gave us. And for its Italianness, for lack of a better word.

In the beginning, that wasn't quite so. When I transferred schools to Vicenza, Gene returned to Spain to finish out his time in the navy. I moved into a hotel with the boys so I could start work and they could start school. I scoured the area each afternoon after school and on weekends, searching for just the right house, looking at more than my fair share of possibilities. Finally, I found the perfect place, a farmhouse that came with a farmer, garden, and animals we weren't responsible for. After ten long weeks, we moved into the house of Gene's nightmares. The house itself needed a bit of work and the yard was a mud pit, but it had potential. We put in ceiling fans and air conditioning and made other minor repairs. We threw bags and bags of grass seed, planted flowers, and barked the beds. Finally, we had a place to call home and, more importantly, a place we wanted to come home to. This staycation would put that to the test.

We came up with a few staycation ground rules:
- Relax
- Do not do any schoolwork
- Do not be in a hurry about anything
- Do not go to the base, and most importantly,
- Do NOT grieve over our lost trip to see Ian

No need to pack, no early morning flights, no mounds of laundry upon return. There were some perks when I thought about it. We would make *limoncello* from *limoni*.

After lounging in bed an extra hour, we padded downstairs and poured coffee into our trenta-sized Starbucks mugs. I chose London and Gene chose Madrid. It made us feel like we were traveling, sort of. We settled in on the side terrace, lighting a small breakfast fire in the outside fireplace, sipping our coffee, and nibbling on jam and toast. We burned our expired travel documents.

We enjoyed the misty stillness of the morning, punctuated by the sounds of church bells, roosters, and ducks. Our colleagues had canceled plans as well and were on staycation in their own homes here in Italy, in Germany, in Spain, and in Japan. Gene sent out a message to our teacher friends far and near, inviting them to join us on the terrace.

ATTENTION: Virtual guests of the Agriturismo Bolzano Vicentino

Please join us fireside for cappuccino and a delicious continental breakfast followed by a virtual bird walk at ten o'clock. The ABV features mourning doves, ducks, chickens, guinea hens, and a stuffed snowy owl. Lunch will be served on the Mountain View Terrace at noon followed by the Mold and Fungi tour at one in the afternoon. There is still space available for the six o'clock *vini sfusi* tasting experience followed by dinner and a movie. Please contact the front desk to book your virtual activities now.

Kind regards,
Agriturismo Bolzano Vicentino

-- I'm in for the bird walk. What happened to the peacocks?
-- Could you please send some *café con leche* over to the Spanish Garden Room? With a side of friends?

It had been three weeks since I had shopped for groceries, and I often wondered what would be the thing that would force me to the commissary. I thought it might be coffee creamer, salad dressing, or peanut butter, but it turned out to be something else entirely.

"I made lumpia," my friend phoned to tell me. "Can you meet me in the commissary parking lot this afternoon for the drop?"

This was a great idea since I wasn't allowed to visit her home, but grocery shopping was completely permissible. A lover of Filipino food, I quickly agreed. So much for not going to base.

I knew I would need a face covering but supplies of masks and gloves in the local area had been depleted. I watched some DIY videos on YouTube to see if I could make my own mask, but I couldn't seem to get the hang of it. I couldn't even find a bandana, so I finally scrounged up a red neck gaiter from one of the boys' ski bags and pulled out the rubber gloves I kept in the cleaning bucket under the kitchen sink. They'd have to do because I was on a mission. I printed fresh travel documents, made sure my passport was in my purse, and headed to the commissary.

I circled the parking lot until I found my friend's car and we stealthily exchanged the lumpia for a bottle of *ripasso*. I placed my stash in a cold bag on the back seat and decided to press on inside to get some shopping done. The parking lot was filled with cars, an indicator of what was in store in the store.

My practical self thought, go in, you're here anyway.

My other self said, NO, go home, you don't need anything.

I listened to my practical self and decided to forge ahead. We could no longer use our own shopping bags, so I left them on the back seat by the lumpia. I put on the neck gaiter and gloves and puffed my way from the far end of the parking lot. Uniformed soldiers posted by portable sinks at the front door reminded shoppers to wash their hands before going inside. Do I wash with gloves or without gloves? I decided to wash my gloved hands. That was weird.

Checking items off my list, I raced down the aisles *Supermarket Sweep* style, attempting to get out of there as quickly as possible. My head was sweaty and itchy, my glasses fogged up. I touched my face a hundred times, trying to keep the neck gaiter in place over my mouth and nose. I didn't want to run into anyone I knew or stop and have a conversation. Not that I was being antisocial, I just wanted to go home and get this sweaty disaster of a mask off my face.

With Easter right around the corner, there were no eggs on the shelves. Cleaning supplies were scarce and what was left was being rationed. I stocked up on what I could, zoomed to the checkout line, and then waited. And waited. And waited.

"At least I'm not buying ice cream," the woman ahead of me turned and spoke.

While I was stuck in the ever-growing line, I thought maybe another loaf of bread, another coffee creamer, and another package of toilet paper would tide me over and maybe, just maybe, I could make it until the end of the month before coming back. Other shoppers obviously had the same idea and we took turns pushing and pulling the carts of those who ran back to get one more item.

Commissary baggers are usually efficient and helpful. When I finally reached the checkout, I discovered that new COVID-19 regulations prohibited baggers from working, so I had to pack everything myself. I was used to bagging my own groceries in the Italian store and at the self-checkout, with twenty items or less. I was not prepared for it here, however, with my cart filled to overflowing. By the time I'd emptied everything onto the conveyor belt, food was avalanching at the other end. Sweating and blinded by my steamed-up glasses, I hurried to get everything organized into the flimsy plastic commissary bags, which were impossible to open fast enough wearing those ridiculous gloves. People were waiting, the line was getting longer. To my chagrin, I ended up throwing everything willy-nilly back into the cart so I could make my escape. No doubt the bread was crushed somewhere down below but at least there were no eggs to worry about. I bagged everything in the parking lot. For the lumpia, it was worth it.

Arriving home, Gene met me on the back terrace. We unloaded the grocery bags outside, mindful to clean everything thoroughly with sanitizing wipes before bringing anything into the house. I carefully stripped off my clothes, washed them, and took a shower. What a hassle.

Still, for the lumpia, it was worth it.

I felt better after cleaning up. I found room for all the groceries then poured a glass of wine and went outside to enjoy the sunshine. The perfume of the wisteria wafted through the air.

Message to Mom: The wisteria is just starting to bloom.

Mom: Beautiful beginning. It will be fun to watch it open this week.

Me: I know. We're usually gone for spring break, so I don't really get to enjoy it that much. That's one of the good things about staying home.

From: Bill
To: Karin
Subject: Weekend

Karin,

I've been watching the WHO numbers for Spain, and I see they've finally overtaken Italy in the number of cases. It looks like the spread of the virus may have peaked in Italy, seems to be holding steady around five thousand new cases a day. How are you guys holding out? Is there still food on the shelves? Do you have access to the base? How are the boys doing, and where is Ian?

Things are the same here. We have had no personnel arrive on the island in over two weeks and no COVID cases. Nobody is quarantined, and only three people "sick in quarters" but they are all ruled out as COVID. We are still restricted to the ship as part of the global order.

The girls are doing fine. They are kind of stir-crazy being stuck in the house—kind of like being on a ship!

Be safe,
Bill

From: Karin
To: Bill
Subject: RE: Weekend

I just went out today for the first time in twenty days. Right now, we can still get on base, but we hear rumors that it might change. There is so much misinformation flying around right now it's hard to know what to think. I didn't get stopped by the *carabinieri* so that was good. And our wine store delivers so that's good, too. We're on spring break this week and making the best of it.

Ian is still in PA, his quarantine ended Saturday. He wants to get to

Virginia Beach to stay with a friend, or maybe go to DC where another friend has an apartment and then go to North Carolina with him. So many people we've known from Vicenza have offered to let Ian stay with them, but we don't know when this might happen or if he can even travel.

Will is still in his apartment in Miami and is getting a little stir-crazy being there alone. Kinda like being on a ship. We're watching *Seinfeld* with him every night, just to have some laughs and help him stay connected.

Mom and Dad love Walmart delivery. They're ordering every day. Thanks for checking in—glad you're safe and well. We are too.

Love,
Karin

Tuesday, April 7, 2020

ATTENTION: Virtual guests of the Agriturismo Bolzano Vicentino

Please join us for Spa Day at the ABV! After lunch don't miss the one o'clock *Riposo e Ripasso* in the pool. For those who prefer an evening dip, Soak Under the Stars happens tonight at nine o'clock. This event is adults-only and please remember no glass in the pool area; this especially applies to our guest from Okinawa, as you broke too many glasses on your last visit. Please contact the front desk to book your virtual experiences.

Kind regards,
Agriturismo Bolzano Vicentino

-- I'm so glad I signed up for the coffee and virtual bird walk. Are there still spaces available for tomorrow's 80s dance competition with the whistle and tequila shots?
-- Are swimsuits required?
-- No.

It was gloriously sunny, a perfect spa day at the *agriturismo*. Since we couldn't go to a real spa, we would fake it, enjoying the small hot tub we had ordered years ago from the navy exchange catalog and installed outside on the terrace.

Not wanting to be disturbed, we waited until *riposo*, the mid-day rest time, because we knew all of Italy would be taking an afternoon pause. Wrapped only in my sarong, I selected a bottle of *ripasso*, a delicious local red wine, and slipped outside.

Gene had already doffed his bathrobe and settled down into the warm water. Before I stepped in, I realized I'd need my sunglasses, so I slipped back into my flip-flops and headed to the house to fetch them. As I rounded the corner, my sarong flew out around me, and I was suddenly mortified to see a family on bicycles in front of our house. They were probably mortified to see me naked as well. Who were these people anyway and what were they doing in our private driveway? I was positive they were more than two hundred meters away from their house.

I wrapped myself up and ducked through the kitchen door, waiting a few moments before checking to make sure they were safely out of sight. I didn't know if they rode on into the corn fields or turned around and retreated back down the driveway. I retrieved my sunglasses, made sure the coast was clear, and ventured back out into the sunshine.

"Did you see the people on the bikes?" I asked Gene.

"Really? No, I didn't see anyone. Where'd they go?"

"I don't know. I think I scared them off when I accidentally flashed them." I giggled. "Oh, well, that's what they get for coming down here on private property."

I hung up my sarong and slipped into the steamy water, poured a glass of the deep red wine, and lazed. The sun splashed across the surface of the water, and I felt sublime as I sipped. I drifted in and out, dreaming of the day this craziness might be over. After a time, I thought I heard the rumble of tires on gravel; someone was coming down the driveway. Our private driveway. We certainly weren't expecting guests or a wine delivery. There was just one house, ours, and no one came down this dead-end driveway unless they were visiting us or Flavio. It was still *riposo*, so Flavio was asleep.

"Do you hear that?" I asked Gene.

"Hmmm?"

"Someone's coming down the driveway."

Feeling annoyed, I lifted myself up out of the water to get a better look and was horrified to see blue flashing lights. I quickly sank back down into the water.

"It's the *carabinieri!*" I hissed.

The vehicle wasn't the regular black and white squad car I was accustomed to seeing; it was a white SUV with *CARABINIERI* painted clearly in large letters on the side. It paused in front of the house, inched forward, then turned right and drove past the Batcave, stopping only a few meters away. Gene and I sank even lower into the water, hippo mode, eyes wide and hovering above the surface. The *carabinieri* paused there for a minute, two minutes, *ten years?*, blue lights still flashing. Then, ever so slowly, the SUV backed up, reversed course, and went back the way it came.

I slowly let out my breath and looked over at Gene. He gave me a sideways glance.

"More wine?" he asked, reaching for the bottle and pouring the last drops of *ripasso* into my party glass.

I didn't know if the *carabinieri* had come out to investigate a reported flasher or to look for a family that was roaming too far from home. Perhaps it was just a friendly visit to make sure we were safe and following the rules. They never came back and we'll never know. Just another COVID-19 mystery.

~

Later that night we had a video call with Will. I was glad to hear from him because I knew he'd been busy preparing for a big presentation.

"How'd it go?" I asked.

"It went really well but I'm glad it's over. This morning I just didn't feel like getting dressed so I did the whole thing in my shirt and underwear," he confided, laughing at the absurdity of the situation.

I laughed, too, finding it coincidental that both of us had a clothing malfunction kind of day.

Wednesday, April 8, 2020

ATTENTION: Virtual guests of the Agriturismo Bolzano Vicentino

Please join us this morning for mimosas in the Rose Garden followed by the Frogs and Lizards of the Terrace virtual tour at ten o'clock. This afternoon's 80s dance competition is now fully booked. Please contact the front desk to let us know how we can be of service.

Kind regards,
Agriturismo Bolzano Vicentino

My mother has suffered from lymphoma for many years. She was on a regularly scheduled regiment of treatments that had kept the disease at bay. This, combined with the other health complications of being almost eighty years old, kept her calendar full. I called in the evening, my time, to see what appointments were coming up. We could talk while I made dinner and she ate lunch. We would chat about food and recipes, books, and hometown gossip. I made it a point to check in at least once a week, and now a little more often, if possible, to make sure she and Dad were staying put.

"I'll need to check the calendar for the appointments, so I'll email that to you later today. We had a nice message from Will this morning," she continued. "It sounds like he's holding on for now."

"He is," I told her. "But I'm still worried about him. I have Gene here in the house with me and you have Dad there, but it's just Will and his plants. Even though Will can be a hermit sometimes, this situation isn't good for him."

"I know," she replied. "I hope this will go away soon and his roommate will be back."

"I hope so," I murmured as I tore lettuce for a salad. "The pandemic already nixed our trip to see Ian and it'd be highly annoying if it disrupted our trip home this summer. I can't imagine, really, it's two months away."

"I saw Ian's poetry in the Peace Corps magazine. I may try to email him. I just want him to know we enjoyed his writing and we're thinking of him."

"I think he'd like that. We aren't hearing from him as often as we'd like but he just has to work through this."

Later Mom emailed to update me on her approaching appointments.

From: Mom
To: Karin
Subject: Appointments

Almost all our doctors are setting up virtual appointments for patients who want them. I have rescheduled my dentist and my doctor. I don't see how she could listen to my chest via the computer, so I want to see her in person. I have to go to the Cancer Center tomorrow for Rituxan and that has been confirmed.

I sent Ian an email like I said I would. I hope it helps him to know we care about him.

Love,
Mom

From: Karin
To: Mom
Subject: Ian

I know Ian will appreciate the email. Thanks for reaching out to him. Also, thanks again for getting the ATM card sorted out. That was a nightmare and you were a huge help.

I'm glad you're getting your medication tomorrow. I'm sure the office will be clean and safe. And it's your first outing in about three or four weeks. It's not the best kind of outing but a necessary one. Don't go anywhere else!

Love,
Karin

Thursday, April 9, 2020

ATTENTION: Virtual guests of the Agriturismo Bolzano Vicentino

Come on down to the Lounge Lizard Café for Brunch and a Book. Join us at five this evening for the Flying Insects of Bolzano Vicentino virtual tour. We will go in search of the giant *calabrone*, the Godzilla of wasps. If we're lucky, we may catch a glimpse of *Mothra*, the endangered sphinx moth as well. Please contact the front desk to book your virtual experiences.

Kind regards,
Agriturismo Bolzano Vicentino

-- Any chance of seeing the stinkbug at this time of year?
-- Every day.

Despite Monday's commissary adventure, I was out of fresh fruit and veggies and the best place to get them was the Italian grocery store. My favorite place to shop, the Alì, was an easy stop on the way home from school, just one town over. It seemed ages ago since I'd been there, the day of the itchy throat coughing debacle that sent customers fleeing from the store. I hadn't returned and hoped that by the time I went back that incident would be long forgotten. I was disappointed that now I couldn't go, even if I wanted to, because we were only allowed to shop in our own *comune*. Being a creature of habit, I didn't want to go to a different grocery store, but I also didn't want to risk being the one fined for breaking the rules.

I stashed the neck gaiter and rubber gloves in my purse and headed to the Coop the market closest to our house. Once again, I was plagued by my sweaty neck, face, and hands. I enjoy browsing in the Italian grocery store because I never know what interesting items I may come across, but today I just needed to get in and get out. I flashed through the produce section and down the aisles at record speed, trying not to run over the other shoppers or ram their carts on account of my fogged-up glasses. As I approached the checkout, the cashier sensed my distress and generously gave me one of her own paper face masks.

"*Grazie, molto gentile*," I thanked her.

I love this country and I love these people and thank goodness I didn't cough in the checkout line.

~

I was relieved to finally hear something sensible happening on the news. The mayor of Miami, bless him, had ordered everyone to wear a mask in public. I wished this had been decreed for the entire state but hoped that perhaps other areas would follow suit and take this pandemic seriously. I just wanted everyone to play nice in the sandbox. Please.

Friday, April 10, 2020

ATTENTION: Virtual guests of the Agriturismo Bolzano Vicentino

Please join us fireside for a delicious continental breakfast followed by the From Farm to Table virtual tour at ten o'clock. This afternoon, you are invited on an excursion to the freshly planted cornfields and a sneak peek at the new duck pond currently under construction. Please contact the front desk to book your virtual experiences.

Kind regards,
Agriturismo Bolzano Vicentino

One reason Italian food is especially delicious is that Italians insist on seasonal local ingredients for their recipes. To get the freshest produce, most families have a small vegetable garden, an *orto*, in their yard. In the fourteen years we'd lived in our house there had always been a garden co-op in the backyard, four or five tidy little vegetable plots tended with care. I surmised that the gardeners were friends of Flavio, living in apartments without a yard or space for an *orto*. They rode their bicycles to and from the farm, even during the lockdown. Perhaps tending a garden was like grocery shopping and was considered an essential activity. Maybe the garden store was open for the same reason.

Gene and I walked down the bicycle path to the vegetable gardens. Lettuces, green and red, were already in full swing. Baby carrots and cabbages had been sown in the freshly raked beds, and onion sprouts were reaching for the sun. Pole beans, peas, and tomatoes had been staked in orderly rows. Little zucchini plants were in the ground, preparing for their summer of plenty. Oh, how I loved the zucchini and how I hated them, depending on the day and how many I found on my doorstep.

Walking through the *orto* with our virtual guests convinced me more than ever that I needed to find out if we could venture out to the garden store. We'd been waiting in anticipation for April 10 to hear the new government decree outlining the current restrictions, hoping that our situation would start to ease. When we finally got word, to our utter dismay, the new guidance was even tighter. We now had to wait until May 3 for the next decree in the hope we would gain a little freedom.

Saturday, April 11, 2020

Ian caught a ride with his coworker from Allentown to Philadelphia. With a hundred pounds of luggage in tow, he boarded a train bound for Norfolk, Virginia. The train was completely empty except for himself and one other masked passenger. He remained on board until Norfolk, where he and the other passenger both stepped out onto the platform and the train continued on its empty way.

One of Ian's friends from Vicenza High School had been attending college in Chicago. In March, due to the outbreak, he moved back in with his family in Virginia Beach. We knew them; the mom was Italian, from Vicenza, and the dad was retired army. I had taught the younger brother and sister when they were in kindergarten at VES. We were so relieved he was with a friend and a family we knew and trusted.

~

Gene and I made a cheese plate, set up the computer outside, and charged our glasses for Navy Happy Hour. It was comforting to connect with friends, even if it was just through the computer.

"Happy Saturday! *Cin cin!*"

Since we all had kids in school in the US, the first item of business was to report on their current locations and how they were surviving the chaos on their own. It was a continuing concern when dorms closed and students were sent home, because they certainly couldn't return to Italy. Some of them had gone to relatives or, like Ian, were searching out friends and couch surfing until they could get settled, whatever settled looked like at this point. We were so grateful to FIU for allowing Will to stay in his campus apartment. As isolating as that was, we knew he had a safe place to ride out this crisis without taking the chance of infecting other family members.

When happy hour was over, we bid our navy friends farewell and watched another episode of *Tiger King*.

Sunday, April 12, 2020

On Sunday, the last day of spring break, we greeted the day on the front porch with our morning coffee. I chose the Prague mug; Gene chose Paris. We were amazed at how lucky we had been with the weather all week. It had been sunny and mild and beautiful every day; the wisteria had started to unwrap and filled the air with a sweet perfume. Just that we could smell it made me smile.

I was working on a crossword puzzle, enjoying the quiet and trying not to think about work the next day. I looked up lazily, reaching for my coffee. From the corner of my eye, I caught sight of two large dogs running through the hayfield.

"It looks like someone's hunting dogs got loose," I said to Gene. "I don't see anybody out there with them."

He peered across the grass, watching the movement for a minute.

"I don't think they're dogs," he replied. "Look how they're almost hopping."

Shading my eyes, I squinted and noticed their little white tails. "I think they're deer."

Indeed, they were *capriole*, cavorting through the tall grass. Perhaps the lack of traffic, noise, and people had emboldened them to move freely about. It was a wonderful gift from Mother Nature to end our spring break staycation at the Agriturismo Bolzano Vicentino.

Message to Barbara: I hope you are having a Happy Easter and Happy Bubble Sunday. Happy birthday to Brian.

Barbara: Yes, yes, and yes.

In the spring of 1985, I was wrapping up my first teaching assignment on Guam. I recalled a song, "We Are the World," which was written to draw attention to and raise money for famine relief in Africa. I purchased the 45 and played it on my classroom record player for my first graders. It was a music lesson, geography lesson, and social studies lesson all rolled into one. More importantly, it was a lesson in compassion that I hoped my students would carry with them.

Musicians across genres and ages collaborated on the project, which led to the Live Aid Concert over the summer, raising millions of dollars to provide emergency relief. In January of the following year, it was performed on stage at the American Music Awards. Many of the original artists gathered for the rendition while others joined from around the globe via satellite, a truly spectacular pre-Zoom livestream event. The words of the song drifted through my mind now, calling for people of the world to work together in the face of this humanitarian crisis. I thought back to that time and to that appeal. How chillingly prophetic the lyrics seemed now and what an eerie feeling it gave me thirty-five years later.

Fast forward to the spring of 2020. Milan, in the heart of the outbreak, had been deserted for weeks. Photos on the internet revealed a hauntingly beautiful but desolate Piazza del Duomo, usually packed with hundreds of tourists. On Easter Sunday 2020, Andrea Bocelli, an Italian tenor, performed an emotional one-man show from the empty duomo. The concert, Music for Hope, was livestreamed across the globe and seen by more than twenty-eight million viewers.

The isolation being experienced by people worldwide was manifested in the heartfelt solo performance. Inside the cavernous sanctuary, four hymns were followed by an inspirational rendition of "Amazing Grace" from the front steps of the cathedral. Video of the silent streets of Paris, London, and New York accompanied the final piece in a visual echo of the lyrics of "We Are the World," calling for people around the globe to come together, for life, the greatest gift of all. This time, during a global pandemic.

WEEK 8: BACK TO THE IRONING BOARD

Monday, April 13, 2020

The bell rang. Recess was over.

"Noooooooo!"

I groaned and reached for the alarm clock. I rolled out of bed in slow motion and dragged myself to the shower. Then I shuffled downstairs, poured coffee, and checked in to school. It was back to business for us—not back to the classroom as I had hoped, but back to the computer.

I pulled the ironing board out from its hiding place behind the kitchen door and perched the easel on top. My kitchen was transformed into a classroom again. The Cat in the Hat, Thing One, and Thing Two went to hang out with Stella on top of the cabinets. They were replaced on the board with my stuffed Peter Rabbit, wearing his blue jacket with big brass buttons, radish in hand. I looked forward to seeing the kids this morning but was disappointed we were still meeting virtually instead of face-to-face. There was still so much left to do.

Kindergarten chat:

Good morning, friends, and welcome back! I hope everyone had a good break and enjoyed the beautiful weather. This week we will look at new spring plants. See you soon!

Our virtual morning meeting was joyful as we caught up on our spring break staycations. Each child was bursting, trying to wait to fill me in on the exciting details of the week.

"Mrs. Tramm! My fairy garden seeds are growing! There are little green leaves," one child exclaimed in delight.

"That's great!" I replied. "You can measure the plants every day."

Another voice blurted out. "We put up a pool in our backyard! I got to go swimming! But it was a little bit cold."

"I have a new basketball!"

"We have so much good news to share. Let's be respectful listeners

while others are talking," I reminded them, trying to rein them in
without bursting their bubbles. "Everybody will have a turn to talk. Just
remember to put an X in the chat box if you have something to say."

X

X

X

X

"I found some caterpillars on the plant on my balcony. They're black
and yellow and have prickles."

"We planted flowers, but the dog pulled them up."

"Look Mrs. Tramm! I lost a tooth!"

"You did! Now you have a window in your mouth," I replied with as
much enthusiasm as the kids. I was missing them so much.

Another chimed in with a lispy lilt, "And Mith Tramm, I have two
windows in my mouf and my new toof is growing in."

Monday mornings are hard but this one was definitely worth rolling
out of bed for. The delight we felt seeing each other again, the comfortable
familiar in the wake of this disruption, was joyful. *Andrà tutto bene.*

For story time I read *The Tale of Peter Rabbit*, one of my all-time
favorites. I thought this could be an interesting week if I could breathe
some life into our virtual classroom with some of Peter's misadventures.
I enjoyed weaving Beatrix Potter's animal characters throughout my
springtime curriculum, but this year I would have to be creative.

After the morning meeting, Gene and I had lunch outside on the
terrace, keeping that little piece of our agriturismo staycation routine in
place. During *riposo* I snuck Peter Rabbit out into the garden and took
a few pictures. Then I made a rabbit-sized scarecrow with his little blue
jacket and placed it in between some cabbages. I snapped a few more
shots. I posted the pictures for the kids to see.

Kindergarten chat:

Oh my! Look what I saw in my garden!

-- She caught Peter Rabbit!

-- Is it a scarecrow?

-- Is that his jacket?

-- It's Peter!!

-- What is growing in your garden?

-- My mom is growing some sunflowers.

I knew I could have some fun with this. Heart happy, I posted an answer to the kids:

-- There is lettuce, cabbage, and onions growing in my garden. And, yes, I think it is Peter's jacket! And his shoes! Do you think he will come back to get his jacket? Should I go get it for him? Will Mrs. Rabbit be mad? It's the second little jacket and pair of shoes he has lost in a fortnight.

Although Gene and I were feeling the frustration of confinement, Mother Nature was certainly not in quarantine. We paced up and down the driveway again for our afternoon walk and noticed the barely visible tips of the new cornstalks pricking up through the soil like little green spikes. We were heartily relieved that this year it was corn and not soybeans. The farmers liked to rotate between those two crops and, because soybeans seemed to be the favorite food of stinkbugs, soybean years were particularly dreadful.

It was hard to believe the corn was sprouting and harder to believe it would grow taller than Gene in just a few short weeks. As the days and weeks passed and we walked the same path over and over, the cornstalks became measures of time, not unlike the fading lines on a kitchen door jamb. Ankle-high, knee-high, waist-high, shoulder-high, taller than Mom, taller than Dad. Snap. In an instant.

From: Bill
To: Karin and Barbara
Subject: Anniversary

Barb & Karin,

All is well here, no changes in our status. We are still restricted to the ship and unable to go ashore, but Diego Garcia still doesn't have any COVID-19 cases. No new people have arrived here in about three weeks, so things are pretty safe.

Next Thursday (April 23rd) will be Mom and Dad's 60th anniversary. It's pretty sad that they will be stuck inside, but that is definitely what's best. I know they had a big trip to Italy planned … Do either of you have anything planned for them? This is really a terrible time to have an anniversary, let alone a big milestone like 60!

Hope you are all doing well and staying safe.

Love,
Bill

From: Karin
To: Barbara and Bill
Subject: RE: Anniversary

Barb and Bill,

We could get them a nice meal delivered and some flowers. They just got a wine shipment, so I think they have plenty of their favorite. I'm just anxious about too many people coming to the house, but they're getting deliveries from Walmart and UPS, and I think they have a system down. I'll check online to see if there are any restaurants that may deliver to them.

Love,
K

From: Bill
To: Karin and Barbara
Subject: RE: Anniversary

Karin,

A meal and flowers sound great. I think that's about as good as we can do at the time. I'll be happy to go in on whatever you think is best.

From: Barbara
To: Karin and Bill
Subject: RE: Anniversary

Funny that you mentioned the anniversary. I woke up thinking about that today. It's a terrible time for celebrations, (Brian's birthday was yesterday) … everyone needs to remain isolated.

I was wondering if we can figure out how to make a group video call work for us. Bill is that even a possibility for you? I'm sure Mom and Dad would feel very special if they were the center of a call from their kids all at the same time from around the world.

I found the attached article that lists the restaurants in Bradenton and Sarasota with their status. The big chains are also offering take-out dinners. I can pick up, wipe down and sanitize all the containers and run it over to their house. They would have to heat it up.

It does still scare me a little, having things delivered to their house. They feel obligated to interact with the deliverers and every item taken inside is another risk. Take a look at all the info and give me your thoughts. I'll wait to do anything until I hear from you.

Barb

Tuesday, April 14, 2020

The appearance of Peter Rabbit's blue jacket in my garden had created a surge of interest in what might happen next, and it proved to be a great lead-in to the rest of the story.

Kindergarten chat:

Good morning, friends! Today we will talk about that naughty rabbit, Peter. If you missed hearing about his adventures yesterday, please click on the link below to listen to his story. Pretend you are Peter. Would you go back to Mr. McGregor's garden to get your jacket? Today we will read *The Tale of Benjamin Bunny* to find out more. See you at our morning meeting!

There was good news. The two-hundred-meter limit had been lifted and people could exercise "within a reasonable distance" from their homes. Now we could stroll a little farther on our afternoon walks if we wanted to. Honestly, we had gotten used to our driveway loop, watching the corn come up, and trying to figure out what new project was underway at the duck pond.

It also meant that other people could wander a little farther out as well, potentially down our private driveway. We didn't like this new development because now there were unmasked runners and bike riders venturing our way, in our space, breathing our air. Hearing the ring, ring of a bicycle bell was startling and prompted us to jump into the hayfield as the rider passed. We felt anxious, still not wanting to get too close to people we didn't know.

From: Bill
To: Karin and Barbara
Subject: RE: Anniversary

First, wish Brian a happy (late) birthday! Did you give him a chocolate Easter Bunny? That's too bad having your birthday on Easter! As for the video call, we don't have the bandwidth to support that here, but I can call their home number when you both are on a video call. We just have to coordinate the time, so I know when to call.

Bill

From: Karin
To: Barbara and Bill
Subject: RE: Anniversary

I can set up a video conference; it just has to be after my school day is over. Bill, you can call in on Mom and Dad's home phone when we get that coordinated. What's your time difference?

I'll also order a flower arrangement sent to them. From Walmart, because maybe it will be the same delivery people and they know the house.

K

From: Bill
To: Karin and Barbara
Subject: RE: Anniversary

Karin and Barbara,

I like it. We are ten hours ahead of East Coast time. But plan on a time that is best for them. I can wake up in the middle of the night if I have to!

Bill

From: Karin
To: Barbara and Bill
Subject: RE: Anniversary

Okay, so you are four hours ahead of me. If we made the call around 10:30 in the morning their time it would be 4:30 in the afternoon here in Italy and 8:30 in the evening in Diego Garcia, so nobody has to get up in the middle of the night. That would work for me, but we need to make sure it's an okay time for Barb because she is working from home as well. I think we can do this!

Wednesday, April 15, 2020

I drove to school to put away my weather books and bring home some stories about plants. I planned to stay at school and hold my morning meetings from the classroom. It had been a month since I had been in the building, and it had a forlorn and eerie feel. The kindergarten wing was depressing to look at. The Welcome Back bulletin board seemed melancholy now and some of the Truffula trees in the hall were on the floor, as if the Once-ler had been busy chopping them down in our absence.

I didn't realize the extent of the impression it left on me until a year later when I read *The Lorax* to my students one morning in 2021. When I came to the part where the Once-ler began chopping down trees, out of nowhere my eyes started to well and I choked up.

"Are you crying, Mrs. Tramm?"

Nothing goes unnoticed.

"No, no, just something in my eye," I lied, voice cracking.

I glanced at the four Truffula trees I had rescued from the hall that day, now standing in a corner of my classroom, a reminder of that year-ago scenario. The emotion, which I had tucked in and tried to ignore, had been waiting, just waiting, for the right moment to come leaking out.

~

Looking around the classroom, I noticed something was different in the corner—my fish tank was missing. Some kind soul had been there and rescued our goldfish, or at least I hoped they had been rescued.

The straws we used to count the days of school were frozen in time at one hundred. One hundred straws, one hundred days. The tables were tidily set up, materials organized and ready, as if students were returning tomorrow. I wondered if I should put everything away but didn't have the heart to do it. Looking at the tables made me sad but seeing them cleaned off probably would have made me feel worse, so everything stayed the same. I remembered changing the calendar from February to March back when I thought we would only be out for a week or two. This time I didn't take the March calendar down to replace with April because I was afraid to imagine that we might be returning to school any time soon.

~

April is the Month of the Military Child. This year was a challenge as we had to come up with online activities and projects for the students to do at home. April 15 was Purple Up Day at Vicenza Elementary School, purple being a color that symbolizes the combined colors of all military branches. I had put on my Purple Up shirt in the morning with a special sense of pride.

Kindergarten chat:

Good morning, friends! Happy Purple Up day! I hope you are wearing your purple today! Many of you have a mom or a dad (or both!) in the army or work to help the army. What an important job they have to keep our country safe and free. Purple Up Day is a day for YOU! It is a special day to remember the big job you do being part of your family.

During the morning meeting I could tell the kids could see the classroom, our classroom, and wondered why I could be there and they couldn't.

"Mrs. Tramm, are you at school?"

"Yes, I'm at school but we can't come back to class right now. I'm here to get some new stories to read and to make sure our class is clean and safe for when we're ready to come back."

We read *Bumblebee, Bumblebee, Do You Know Me?* a story about different kinds of flowers. I asked the children to go out and look for dandelions in their yards.

"Don't forget to make a wish!" I reminded them.

Hardy dandelions are the official flower of the military child, representing their ability to survive, take root, and bloom where they're planted. This year that idea took on an additional dimension. Just as the children were blossoming in our classroom, they were abruptly uprooted. And just as children will do when transplanted, they took root and continued to survive and thrive under their new circumstances. Resilient, strong, and yet yielding at the same time, remarkable.

During our discussion one of my students said, "Mrs. Tramm, my dad cut the lawn yesterday and now all the dandelions are gone."

I smiled and assured him, "Don't worry my friend, they'll be back tomorrow."

Oh, how I wished my little dandelions would be back in the classroom tomorrow.

~

Dandelions are considered a spring delicacy in the Veneto. Their sunshine-yellow faces line the roadsides, squeeze up between the cracks in the sidewalks, and dot the grassy fields. Every April Flavio would bring over a load of dandelions, pulled straight from the hayfield out front. I'd find them laid out carefully atop old newspaper, waiting for me on the doorstep when I arrived home from work. After removing the dirt, roots, and flowers, tender leaves awaited. Although they are tasty in a salad, my favorite dandelion dish is delicious *dente di leone* risotto.

Dandelion Risotto

Risotto is easy! I use a large wok pan, but any large pan will do. Gather olive oil, a shallot or onion, a package of cubed *pancetta* or smoked bacon, 2 cups, give or take, of arborio rice, two quarts or more of hot broth, butter, grated cheese, salt and pepper, and last but not least, the clean dandelion greens!

Heat the broth while sautéing an onion in olive oil then add the cubed *pancetta* to the onions and stir a minute or two. Throw in handfuls of greens, adding to the pan until they are wilted, add pepper, then remove them to a bowl.

Drizzle and heat a little more olive oil in the pan, adding the uncooked arborio rice, allowing it to toast for a few minutes until light golden. Pour in two or three ladles of hot broth, stirring gently and adding greens from time to time, stirring, stirring, stirring, until the broth is absorbed. Continue adding broth and greens, stirring, and repeating until the rice is tender and a little al dente. It usually takes about twenty minutes and demands steady attention and stirring. If I run out of broth, I use a little hot water. Taste for texture and salt and if there are any greens left, serve them on top. To finish, turn off the heat, add butter and cheese, and garnish with a dandelion flower. Pour a glass of prosecco. *Buon appetito!*

I left my classroom and smiled as I noticed the dandelions scattered across the school lawn. I made my way to the parking lot and left for home, stopping for groceries on the way. The commissary wasn't jam-packed this afternoon and wasn't nearly as overwhelming as the last time. There was no hazelnut coffee creamer, still no sanitizing wipes, and now cheese was being rationed too. But none of that even mattered when I spotted four tomato seedlings in the produce section—I felt like I'd won the lottery!

This time I was able to go through the self-checkout. I scanned and bagged my own items, paid, and sped home. As soon as I had wiped everything down and put the groceries away, I hurried out to the kitchen garden to plant the tomatoes. I couldn't believe my eyes when I saw some tiny green seed leaves poking up through the soil. They were from the squished cherry tomatoes I pushed into the dirt ten days earlier. I felt triumphant, like the little boy in *The Carrot Seed*, who grew his carrot against all odds. This year I would have a bumper crop of tomatoes, even in a pandemic!

~

We called Will and chatted for a bit, asked about classes, and we watched an episode of *Seinfeld* together. I hoped he had been staying busy and his feelings of isolation were beginning to ease. When the program was over, he shared that he'd been writing a new song to stay busy.

"Will you play it for us?" I asked.

When Will was still living at home he would practice his guitar every night before going to bed. Most nights I was already turned in and could hear his music drifting into my room as I fell asleep. It was a comfort to know he was home and safe and content. I wished for that more than anything now.

Hearing his music through the phone was the next best thing. He picked up his guitar and played his latest song for us.

Too Fast/Too Slow
by Will Tramm

Waiting for the posters to fall
Come and go as the plants grow tall
My mind goes where I am unable
Silence at the empty table.
Wake up to a calendar dance
Seems nice from a window glance
Long arm moving too fast, too free, for me
A stranger is all I can see
Right now. Too slow. Right here. Oh no.
Time doesn't care about your long, long hair.
Right then. Too fast. How long will it last?

~

From: Barbara
To: Karin
Subject: RE: Anniversary

OMG ... living through an abrupt, huge restructuring and downsizing at work. Coronavirus is affecting businesses in a BIG, long-lasting way. We've been spinning, trying to re-group and keep things going; at the end of the last two days, I've been beat and haven't engaged with my personal email at all. Sorry about that.

10:30 in the morning sounds like a plan for the call. I should be available working from home unless they schedule some kind of conference call, and then I should know in advance.

Let me know further your thoughts on the food.

Barb

Thursday, April 16, 2020

Spring is my favorite part of the school year—it's the crescendo of kindergarten. By now the class is like an orchestra, everyone playing their own part but working together as a team. They've hit their stride; they know what to do and they do it. We're comfortable with each other; we have inside jokes. It's the glorious payoff of months of collaboration.

When children start kindergarten, they come from a variety of backgrounds and have had an array of experiences. Some have been to preschool, either at the Child Development Center on post or in the Italian *asilo*. Some have been in home daycare or Sure Start, a version of Head Start. Some have never been to preschool. They all come in on a different page, and they leave on a different page. I assure parents that as long as the children are turning pages, they're right where they need to be; they'll bloom and grow, like dandelions in the field. They always do.

Most of my students were capable and confident beginning readers. There's nothing more rewarding for a teacher than witnessing that first spark of realization when something clicks and they have just read a book by themselves. The wide eyes, the excited fluttering of hands.

"I can read it, Mrs. Tramm! I can read!"

These words are music to any teacher's ears. I've put hundreds of children on the path to reading and it never gets old. This is why kindergarten teachers love their jobs. This is why I keep coming back.

I was missing that teacher vitamin this spring. Virtual learning was vastly different, impersonal in many ways. While we were using our online reading program, I was unable to see children's faces as they read, the screen only featuring the selected text. I felt a little cheated, missing their expressions, their smiles, their joy at the printed word. Something had been stolen from us and I didn't want our year to end this way.

~

We had a video chat with Ian while on our driveway walk. He seemed much better than the last time we talked. He was happy to see his high school friend again. We were relieved and grateful to the family for taking Ian in. He was regaining his footing and reprioritizing his next steps.

Ian missed his bicycle as he had to leave it behind with his host family in Thailand. He had spent the last fifteen months bicycling the twenty to twenty-five kilometers each day to and from his job in various schools. Not having transportation now was challenging for him.

Message to Vickie: I hope all is well with you in Virginia Beach. You'll never believe it, but Ian has landed in VB for a few weeks. He is staying with a friend and just said to us he wished he had a bike to ride. So, I was wondering if you have an extra bike he could borrow for a couple of weeks, maybe an old one of the boys' bikes lying around. Let me know.

Vickie: There are a lot of old bike parts but am not sure if there is a whole bike out there. I'll check and get back to you.

Me: Thanks, *amica*!

Risotto was on the menu, always an easy and delicious choice. Stirring, stirring, stirring, is time-consuming but I could read, talk on the phone, or message family. And have a glass of vino. I checked in with my sister.

Message to Barbara: How was your day? Surreal right now?

Barbara: Surreal is right. More communication on the lay of the land today. Looks like I have a new boss, a pay cut, fewer people, some new staff, and will up my advertising responsibilities from seventy stores to ALL five hundred stores. I need wine.

Me: I'm pouring some for you right now. In a big glass.

Barbara: Good, have two. I'll join you later ... I keep getting pulled into these phone calls now and I probably shouldn't start slurring yet.

Me: I shouldn't have two, but tomorrow IS Friday.

Barbara: Why stop? It's Friday, Jr.

Me: LOL! You're right!

Message to Ian: I'm sorry, Vickie said they don't have a working bike, only a bunch of bike parts. She said she would let me know if she found a whole one.

Ian: Okay cool! Thanks! Also, what was the address of our Virginia Beach house again and what elementary school did I go to?

Me: Cooke Elementary. Remember when your bus driver would stop at our house after school and pick up Will and drive him around the block over the big bump?

Ian: I do!

Friday, April 17, 2020

I delighted in sharing Beatrix Potter's stories about naughty Peter Rabbit and his friends. They were childhood favorites that I'd read to my sons and to my students throughout the years. It was fitting that on the last day of this author study, a bright green tree frog joined Gene and me for lunch on the terrace. He was resting on the back of a chair at the table, motionless and wide-eyed. When we finished lunch, we picked up our trays and went inside. He was still there, eyes now closed, basking in the sun. I went back out and snapped his photo, along with a lizard on a flowerpot, and posted it in our virtual classroom.

Kindergarten chat:

Look who came to my house for lunch—a tree frog and a lizard! They reminded me of another favorite story by Beatrix Potter—*The Tale of Jeremy Fisher*. You can click on the link in the classroom library tab to hear it. Listen to find out what Jeremy Fisher had for lunch.

During our afternoon meeting I asked, "Who listened to the story about Jeremy Fisher? What did he pack in his picnic basket?"

"Jeremy Fisher ate a butterfly sandwich for lunch!" someone unmuted and shouted.

"Gross!"

"I would eat a butterfly sandwich."

"My dad ate a worm," the conversation started to swerve.

"Yuck!"

"Oh my! Thanks for sharing." I responded, trying to get us back on track.

"We've got lots of lizards at my house," someone else chimed in.

"Did you know their tails come off?"

Oh, how I missed our spontaneous spiraling class discussions.

From: Mrs. Tramm
To: VES Kindergarten 2019-2020
Subject: Kindergarten in the Kitchen News, Friday, April 17, 2020

Dear Kindergarten Families,

Thanks again for your patience and understanding as we continue to navigate digital learning. We appreciate your hard work with the kids as we all learn together. I'm making a section in our virtual classroom for our daily story time and the morning messages, so your child won't miss out even if they are unable to attend the morning meeting.

Mrs. Dee has created a new digital scrapbook of the photos that were submitted to us this week. We loved the dandelion pictures, the flower art, and someone made lumpia—YUM!! Thanks all for sharing your ideas and comments with us. Have a great weekend!

Karin Tramm
VES Kindergarten

I folded up the ironing board and parked it behind the kitchen door. This week was over, and *voila!* my classroom was turned back into a kitchen. The kindergarten team had a virtual happy hour. I made a spritz and we toasted the fact we had survived yet another week of remote teaching, then lamented about missing out on this glorious time of year with our students.

Saturday, April 18, 2020

After Ian's message, I had been thinking about our Virginia Beach house. In 1999, after leaving Iceland, Gene was stationed on board the USS Theodore Roosevelt, an aircraft carrier homeported in Norfolk. We had found a nice house within our budget and within walking distance of the beach and the Virginia Aquarium and Marine Science Center. We could enjoy the sun and surf we had sorely missed at our last duty station.

Ian managed to locate the house and took some photos to share with us. The house, no longer seashell pink, had been repainted bright yellow but still had the wide driveway where the boys used to ride their Big Wheels. There was the front porch, where Will, wearing his Pokémon pajamas, would wave goodbye as his big brother climbed aboard the school bus each morning. Then flooding my memory, Ian's face, eyes wide with excitement, as I put him on the bus for his first day of kindergarten; I was jealous his teacher would get to know him in a way I never would.

I remembered serving the boys waffles for breakfast and dancing to the *Shrek* soundtrack while getting Ian ready for school. Ian said he remembered waiting by the mailbox for the bus to arrive each morning. And I recalled his bus driver who was so kind and had a son in Ian's kindergarten class. Some days after school, instead of dropping Ian off, she'd stop and pick up Will, let him ride around the block on the bus, then drop them both back off.

It brought to mind how she cried with me when she dropped Ian off on September 11, 2001.

"Y'all okay?" she asked, wide-eyed, as Ian climbed down from the bus.

"Yeah, okay, I think. His daddy's already gone. They called everybody to the ship. They're leaving this afternoon. Now. Yeah, we're okay."

My mind skittered. My voice trailed off, and my eyes pooled as I nodded, not really sure if we were okay or not, but knowing that somehow, we had to be. I glanced up and saw tears running down her cheeks as the doors closed and the bus pulled away from our mailbox.

It was a horrible day in so many ways. Gene didn't get to say goodbye to Ian, who was at school, in first grade at the time. Later I watched on TV as the enormous aircraft carrier steamed out of Norfolk toward the Persian Gulf, blasting "New York, New York" over the ship's PA system. I had the difficult task of trying to explain why Daddy wasn't coming home for dinner that night, or for a while, in a way that was appropriate and made sense to a five-year-old and a six-year-old.

I did my best to keep the TV news off and to shield the boys from the horror that was our world at that moment. Despite all of that, they overheard things and asked tough questions. Returning home from the commissary one afternoon with groceries and a bonus bag of doughnuts, I heard Ian's small six-year-old voice from the back seat.

"Mommy, if this Daddy dies, can we get another one just like him?"

I had to pull the van over as waves of nausea washed over my soul.

Fortunately, Gene returned safely from deployment, back to the seashell pink house in Virginia Beach. The boys only have happy memories of their time there. Big wheels, buses, and big beach waves.

Ian: It was super familiar, the drive up to the house. And the main street, too.

Me: You used to ride your Big Wheels across that busy street, in the crosswalk, of course, to the marine science museum.

Ian: Hahahaha. Fearless.

Me: Then and now.

Navy chat:

-- Let's meet early for Navy Happy Hour tonight because the Air Force Academy graduation is at 6:45 and we want to watch. Can we meet at 5?

-- OK for us. I'm going to invite Misty and Andy. Even though they are army folks, they are riding this out down in Sigonella on a navy base. I think they can be honorary navy.

We welcomed our southern friends to Navy Happy Hour; we sorely missed them since they had left Vicenza for Sicily last summer. First things first, we caught up on our displaced kids. They shared the story of their daughter, a freshman in college, who was dealing with a car wreck, a closed dorm, and trying to find a place to stay during her latest life reshuffle. Over spring break, she had been on her way to a friend's house when she was nicked by a semi on the interstate. She swerved, overcorrected, and bounced back into the truck. She was okay but the car was totaled. Her parents got the nightmarish call at one thirty in the morning.

Luckily there was a family nearby, friends from Vicenza, who generously offered to let her stay with them for as long as she needed. This sense of community, embraced by our military families, even by families who had relocated back to the States, was gratifying and humbling. Trying to straighten out challenging situations from overseas was something most of us were all too familiar with, but trying to deal with a crisis during a pandemic added a whole new layer to this horror story.

After we all signed off it was still hard to let go. My phone pinged with a new message in the Navy chat.

-- What a fun happy hour! Thanks Misty and Andy for showing up; it was great to see you smiling back on the screen and to get the latest update from the States. *Mamma mia!*

-- Thanks for letting us hang with the navy. It was awesome to see you! I miss you guys!

-- Soon.

Sunday, April 19, 2020

Message to Barbara: I hope you've been able to step back from work a bit this weekend. I just got off the phone with Mom and Dad. They said they bought steaks to grill for their anniversary on Thursday! *UGH*—We were going to order a meal for them. Let's brainstorm about what to do.

Barbara: Are you able to do a video call or are you going somewhere—LOL

Me: Haha, very funny. Yes, call me.

After talking with Barbara, Gene and I put on our walking shoes and headed down the driveway for our daily stroll. The sun wedged through the afternoon clouds striking tender young corn leaves, creating the illusion of hundreds of neon green flames flickering skyward. We looped back to the duck pond where we noticed stealthy upgrades in progress.

Corn was the main crop on the farm, but sometimes something different would pop up in the fields. One summer the doorbell rang and the landlord asked me to go for a walk with him for a *sorpresa*, a surprise. At the end of the dirt driveway was a shimmering sunflower field, a glorious secret garden. Long after the blooms were dried, harvested, and plowed under, volunteer sunflowers still lined that stretch of the driveway and the edges of the field. Then came the duck pond.

There had always been a small pond out by the chicken coop for the ducks and geese that lived on the farm. However, now a new and improved much larger pond evolved from the sunflower field. And it wasn't for the farm ducks; it was to attract the wild ducks that our landlord and his *amici* hunted every duck season. The field, now surrounded by sunflowers, was dug out and flooded. A ramshackle lean-to and hunting blinds had been constructed and it looked as if islands of corn were being planted in the middle of the pond. An old camper appeared painted camouflage colors, sunken into the ditch on the far edge of the water, the windows eye level with the ground. I could imagine the gleeful comrades, gathered inside waiting for the ducks, telling lies and drinking *grappa*.

Flavio was always careful to alert us as to the first day of hunting season so we wouldn't be shocked at the crack of dawn by shotgun blasts in the yard, dogs barking, and strangers clad in bright orange hunting vests striding around on the property. Some mornings, shot scattered into the yard while we were enjoying our coffee on the porch. We tried blasting classical music to alert the hunters to our presence, or to keep the birds away, thus keeping the hunters at bay. This year there was a perfected piece of hunting heaven, but at least it was away from the house.

We passed the new duck pond and headed back. I didn't even want to imagine what this hunting season held in store for us.

WEEK 9: AN ANNIVERSARY

Monday, April 20, 2020

The ironing board squealed in protest when I retrieved it from behind the kitchen door and put it back in service. I shared the sentiment on yet another virtual Monday. I made breakfast, signed in, and prepared for the day. During our morning meeting, one of my kids unmuted, but instead of reading out loud he asked in a small voice, "When are we going back to school, Mrs. Tramm? I miss it."

I was so unprepared for this question and suddenly all eyes and ears were on me. My voice caught in my throat when I answered.

"I don't know, but soon, I hope."

I attempted to be cheerful but felt heartbroken. The kids were trying to be brave, but this was so very hard for them. A crack in the façade had appeared.

~

Barbara, Bill, and I continued to play time zone tag trying to plan a surprise for Mom and Dad's anniversary.

Message to Barbara: Vase or no vase? Is vase easiest for you?

Barbara: Vase is easiest. Hopefully it will be smooth; that's easier to wipe down.

Me: Okay, one dozen rainbow roses, vase included. It looks smooth. I asked for delivery on Thursday the 23rd but when I checked the receipt it said Wednesday the 22nd. I guess you get to enjoy them for a day.

Barbara: Either is fine. Thanks for doing that. I'll cover the food.

Me: We'll help with the food, too. You're doing all the legwork. I hope work is going okay for you today. Hang in there. You're getting paid and your commute is to the coffee pot. And the bathroom. And you can wear the clothes you slept in. And no bra.

Barbara: I did get asked to go into the office for a meeting today. I know it'll be fine. Just a little crazy now. Tomorrow I'll wear PJs all day.

Tuesday, April 21, 2020

And the sun rose on another day of COVID-19 exile. I logged on to our virtual classroom to greet my kids.

Kindergarten chat:

Good morning, friends, and Happy Tuesday! What kind of trees are growing in your yard? Do they have leaves or flowers? Will they have fruit? Today when you go outside and look at the trees, think about these things: Is the bark rough or smooth? Can you see the roots? Why does a tree have roots? Today we will read about trees and talk about the job each part of the tree does. See you soon!

Later, during our morning meeting, the kids had much to tell me about the trees in their yards.

"I have orange, apple, pear, cherry, olive, kiwi, and grape vines," one student listed off.

"Wow! You have a lot of fruit trees," I said. "I bet the flowers are beautiful right now."

"I have strawberries."

Hmmm. Not really a tree, I thought, but okay.

"We have an olive tree and a pomegranate tree."

"I don't like olives!" someone else blurted out.

"In my yard we don't really know what kind of tree it is, but it had white flowers."

"Ahh, you have a mystery tree," I said. "You'll have fun watching to see what kind of fruit grows."

~

Barbara: I had to step away from the computer for a minute because I couldn't stand it any longer. I went outside and noticed my new form of gardening—just cut down the plants and let them grow back—it's working. I have new eggplant!

Me: Yum! You should grill it!

Barbara: Are your tomatoes coming up?

Me: Yes! I can't believe it, but some volunteers are coming up from the squished tomatoes I planted last month, and I found four starter plants in the commissary last time I went. Your tomatoes look great—I'm jealous! I can't wait for mine to be ripe.

Wednesday, April 22, 2020

I attempted to scan through my email each morning before I got started with school. Between my teacher email, my student email, my joint email with Gene, and my personal email, I worked hard to keep the electronic flow in check. These days email traffic was heavy and laden with parent questions, admin tasks, and family communications. In addition, my parents' Walmart grocery emails piled up in my inbox. I didn't mind those emails and frankly was relieved that my parents were finally grocery shopping safely online. However, the number of communications associated with one order was considerable, so it was my habit to forward those immediately and then delete them.

Scrolling through my inbox I saw another email from Walmart and immediately sent it on to Mom and Dad. Finger hovering above the trash can icon, my eyes flew open when I noticed the words in the subject line: "Rainbow roses delivery delayed." In my haste to clean out the inbox I had accidentally forwarded what I thought was a grocery receipt but was really a notification about the upcoming flower delivery, the surprise flower delivery. Argh. What was I thinking?

I was sure they would still be asleep due to our time difference. No problem, I thought, I'll just recall this message like I did with my school email program. Only I didn't see any options for that on the toolbar. I searched online and found that yes, I could've recalled it, if I'd done so within thirty seconds of sending. Well, that wasn't happening now. I sent Mom and Dad another email and told them to disregard the last email from Walmart, as it wasn't meant for them. I'm sure that prompted them to open it right away and read it, after all, that's what I would've done.

Let it go … let it go … let it go, I told myself. I rolled my eyes, heaved a sigh, and started my virtual school day.

Kindergarten chat:

Good morning, friends! Happy Earth Day! How can you help take care of our earth?

-- You can water plants.

-- You can throw away all the trash people put on the ground.

-- I made some Earth Day cookies!

-- I planted some collard greens today.

-- You can plant trees.

-- You can recycle.

-- I only recycle toys I don't like. And bottles.

I loved the kindergarten chat. Sometimes it made me giggle and sometimes it made me burst out laughing. I recycled lots of bottles, too, especially during COVID-19 lockdown.

I was not laughing, however, about missing all of our usual Earth Day activities this year. We wouldn't be able to walk out to the dumpsters to sort our recyclables, a fun and favorite field trip. We wouldn't be able to make paper. We wouldn't have a tree-planting ceremony in front of the school. We wouldn't make Earth Day seed bombs. The best I could do was read *Curious George Plants a Tree* to my computer, and we would live vicariously through our little monkey friend.

~

I called Barbara later in the evening to touch base about the next day's plan. I also needed to try to explain that not only had I spoiled the flower surprise, but that now the flowers were going to be delayed as well.

"Do you want me to find some flowers here?" she asked. She had to do everything—I felt awful.

"No, since the email just says delayed, maybe they'll come tomorrow," I replied hopefully. "If I don't get an update by tomorrow then that'll be Plan B, I mean Plan C. Sorry."

"Yes, Plan C."

Dad always told us, never start with Plan A, always just jump straight to Plan B. And of course, he was right.

Thursday, April 23, 2020

My parents were married on the 23rd of April, 1960, at the nondenominational church in Sarasota, Florida. For their fiftieth wedding anniversary we'd celebrated with them in Italy. Barbara and I toasted them with prosecco, followed by a glorious lunch in a Palladian villa. The chef came out to congratulate them on *cinquant'anni*, fifty years of marriage. We enjoyed an afternoon stroll through the rose gardens before ending our day with *gelato*. Ten years later, having a family celebration was proving to be a bit more complicated. We rose to the occasion as best we could, but this time with a very different plan.

Message to Barbara: It looks like the flowers are on the way. I don't know what time, but I guess you'll be home. Does 10:30 this morning still sound okay for the group call?

Barbara: Yes, that works, my next conference call is at 11:00 a.m. I'm looking at our email trail and I wrote in Bill's email 4:30 our time, but that's your time…do you think Bill knows? I hope I didn't mess that up!

A few minutes passed.

Barbara: Okay, I just sent him an email to clarify. My brain is fried right now. If he's not available this morning, can we give it a try again later?

Me: Okay, I'm confused. I thought it was 4:30 my time, 8:30 his time. If we need to do 4:30 your time it will be 10:30 my time, 2:30 in the morning his time. *Mamma mia*, I can't even think straight!

Barbara: I'm good for this morning; I don't want Bill to have to get up in the wee hours. I just wrote the wrong thing to both of you in the last email. I'm an idiot and no one even questioned it. Let's call them at 10:30 this morning my time, 4:30 p.m. your time, and see if Bill calls in at 8:30 p.m. his time because that's what we originally discussed. If he doesn't call, we will try again later. OMG.

Who's on first?

10:30 a.m. Florida, 4:30 p.m. Italy, 8:30 p.m. Diego Garcia:
Message to Barbara: Now, of course, I'm having technical difficulties ... hold on.

Barbara: Holding on, lol, not going anywhere.

Starting with Plan B, Barbara and I finally managed to connect. I added Mom and Dad to the group video call.

"Happy Anniversary!" Barbara and I chimed in together.

They were thrilled to see us both on their screen. We chatted for a long time waiting for Bill to call in on the landline. Five minutes ticked away, then ten minutes. Apparently, he didn't get the memo. We said our goodbyes and went to Plan C.

Barbara: Okay to call back at 10:30 your time?

Me: Yes, I'll do that. I'll initiate again. Did you hear from Bill?

Barbara: No, he's probably sleeping so he can get up at 2:30 a.m.

Me: I've got the tech issue figured out, so I'll call back at 10:30 my time, 4:30 your time.

Barbara: Perfect. Have a few glasses of wine first.

Me: I shall.

Four hours later I called my sister.

"Did the flowers come?" I asked, "I got an email saying that they were delivered. I was careful not to forward this one to Mom and Dad. I can't believe I did that!"

"Yes, they're here," she confirmed, "I haven't taken them out of the box yet. Right now, I'm putting out a fire at work."

"Okay, wait, did they really come in a box? Seriously? I thought they were supposed to be in a vase!" I was exasperated.

"Yes, they came in a box, zip-tied. But also with a vase. And it's smooth."

"Okay, can I see them?" I asked.

"Hang on a sec."

She propped up the phone while she lifted them out of the box, clipped the zip, and held them out for me to see. Then she busied herself with fitting them in the vase.

"They're really pretty," she said. "I need to trim the stems and reposition them a bit. We lost a few petals but overall, they're good. Mom will love them."

"Thanks for taking care of this. Again. Sorry you're stuck with delivery service."

"It's fine—you set it all up. We're just all doing what we can. Hey! Look!" Barbara held a small piece of paper out. "I just found this cute anniversary card in the box that I was getting ready to throw away."

"Good save on the card," I laughed. "Okay, I'll talk to you later; let's try again in two hours."

Two hours later. Ping!

Barbara: Should we try to connect now before Bill calls in and they're all flustered?

Me: Yes, I'm on it now. *Momento*.

Barbara: I just got an email from Bill. He's up and ready. It's 2:30 a.m. his time. Oops!

We were successful this time around. Technical troubles solved, Barbara and I called on the cell and Bill called in on their landline at 4:30 p.m. their time, 10:30 p.m. my time, and 2:30 a.m. his time. Sorry, Bill! We talked and laughed and enjoyed being together as a family, even for just a few minutes.

I was up way past my bedtime, but Friday would be forgiving. At least it wasn't 2:30 in the morning. My first meeting wasn't until 8:30.

Years ago, my dad made a triple clock that still hangs by their telephone, the kind you might see behind the desk at a hotel indicating the time in different cities across the continents. Each clock face is labeled with a name, Karin, Barbara, and Bill. It was a stroke of genius to keep track of their globetrotting children in multiple time zones. Back then I thought it was a cute idea, but now I understand the necessity.

From: Bill
To: Karin and Barbara
Subject: RE: Anniversary

Barb / Karin,

Thank you so much for calling in to Mom and Dad today. I think that was really special for them to be able to talk to all three of us. I was able to hear both of them well but had difficulty hearing both of you. I could hear you speaking but couldn't understand most of it. Toward the end, I heard the tell-tale crackling of my phone line which usually happens in bad weather just before we lose the satellite and the connection. Please let me know what the dinner and flowers cost and I'll pitch in for my part. Thanks again.

Bill

Friday, April 24, 2020

I was thankful Fridays were set aside for make-up sessions and lesson planning for next week. It made for a little bit more flexibility this morning after my late evening on the phone. Combing down my bedhead, I made it downstairs in time for my first make-up meeting, followed by coffee, planning, and another online reading lesson.

I read *The Great Kapok Tree* to the kids at our morning meeting and then heated up leftovers for the mid-day meal. Gene and I juggled our trays through the kitchen door and outside onto the terrace.

"Well, well, look who's here," Gene said with a nod at the table.

I looked and saw our tree frog friend, Jeremy Fisher, lounging on the chair back. He opened one eye and shut it, seeming to wink at us as he joined us for lunch again.

From: Mrs. Tramm
To: VES Kindergarten 2019-2020
Subject: Kindergarten in the Kitchen News, Friday, April 24, 2020

Dear Kindergarten Families,

It was a wonderful week celebrating Earth Day and learning how we can all take care of our planet. We had some great conversations about trees and why they are important. I saw lots of colorful bark rubbings; nice job! We learned about recycling, and I hope that all of the children can participate in that at home. It's an age-appropriate chore that allows your child to contribute to the care of your home and the earth.

Next week we will learn about shapes. On Monday, we will begin with a short review of flat shapes—some of our students still confuse triangle and rectangle (because they sound similar) and may need a review of hexagon as well. Next comes Tangram Tuesday. There will be lots of fun and games with tangram puzzles. On Wednesday, our lesson will be about spheres and Thursday's lesson will be about cubes.

Finally, thanks again for the teamwork. Have a great weekend!

Karin Tramm
VES Kindergarten

Saturday, April 25, 2020

Since 1946, *Anniversario della Liberazione d'Italia*, has been celebrated on April 25 to commemorate the end of fascism and the Nazi occupation. Usually a festive day of parades and picnics, Liberation Day 2020 was a quiet tribute to a different kind of resilience. Although no one was liberated from quarantine on this day—Italians did their duty, buckled down, and followed the rules. They stayed home, and when they had to go out, they wore their masks. The very hardest part, a miracle in my opinion, was that everyone practiced social distancing. I hoped liberation for Italy would come soon.

We had been granted a modicum of liberty when the two-hundred-meter exercise limit was modified. An Italian friend biked over with a load of lettuce from her *orto*.

"*Ciao! Come va?*" How are you?

She dropped the bursting bag on the front porch, backed her bicycle away, and parked at a safe distance. I retrieved the bag and also found red and green radicchio inside.

"*Grazie!*" I called, excited about the fresh produce. I could taste more springtime salads already.

She stood by her bike for the next hour and proceeded to fill me in on all the gossip of the neighborhood I had been missing, and apparently I had missed a lot. I found out who wore their masks while exercising and who did not and who had been taken away in an ambulance in the middle of the night. She spoke no English and my Italian was only so-so, but in that moment it didn't matter. We were having a real conversation.

From: Barbara
To: Karin and Bill
Subject: Anniversary call

Bill,

Thanks for the follow-up email. Sorry again about the confusion on timing; I hate that you had to get up at that hour to join. It was fun to all be in one place together, even if it was virtual —that seems to be all the rage these days.

The flowers arrived in the afternoon, and I sanitized the vase and food containers before we took everything over. Dad had set extra chairs out in the front yard so they could come out to the porch and we could have social distancing happy hour. They seemed really happy about all the attention. I also ordered them a layered chocolate dessert to share and stuck candles in the top of the Styrofoam container—very classy! I think overall the day was a great success!

Love,
B

From: Karin
To: Barbara and Bill
Subject: RE: Anniversary call

   Thanks Barb. You did all the heavy lifting for this. I'm glad you got the chocolate cake—I looked at getting a dessert when I was ordering the flowers, but all their cakes were in-store pickup. It's good that you were able to get one somewhere else. I hope you're having a restful weekend and can stay away from work.

   K

Ian was the lucky recipient of a stimulus check. As a Peace Corps volunteer, he lived on a small stipend and did not have the opportunity to sock away any substantial savings. This came as a boon to him and he was thankful for every penny. As much as he would've liked to work, at the moment he had no car, jobs were scarce, and he needed to be ready to pack up and go back to Thailand as soon as the Peace Corps gave him the green light. The highly anticipated funds arrived in my parents' mailbox in Florida and Mom called with the good news.

   "Ian's check is here. I know he's anxious to get it, so I'll send it on to him today."

   "Thanks. That's great news. We're relieved he's got some funds to tide him over until he goes back, hopefully soon."

   "Also, I put in a grocery order yesterday with delivery tomorrow," she continued. "Then we tried to add to it, but I'm not sure it worked. If you don't get an email confirming it, we'll just set it up as a second order, which I had to do once before, so I know what to do. If I add to that order, you may get another email for the second order; sorry."

   "Okay, no worries. I saw the grocery order from yesterday and forwarded the email, but I haven't seen anything else since then. If I see it, I'll send it on. Barb said she and Brian came over for an open-air anniversary happy hour with you."

   "Yes, we had a good time. It was just nice to have some real human interaction, even if it was from several feet away."

   What a bizarre turn our lives had taken.

Navy chat:

-- Hey everybody! Another week, another meet. 6:00 p.m. with drink in hand. I just got a new ration card!

Gene and I set up outside and we joined our navy friends at six o'clock. We caught up on the kids and shared rumors, news, and gossip. Someone said the garden store was delivering and would accept online orders. Maybe I could put some geraniums in soon; a garden project was just what was needed.

Sunday, April 26, 2020

I woke up to the sound of a cuckoo bird right outside my window. When we first moved into the house, I heard the cuckoo and thought one of the boys was playing a joke on me, but no, we had a resident cuckoo somewhere nearby. Mother Nature's alarm clock continued trilling as I went downstairs to open up the house and make coffee.

When I pushed the heavy wooden front doors aside, bright light streamed into the foyer. I blinked and saw to my surprise, an entire flat of lettuce on the front steps. Someone had been up early working in the *orto* and was kind enough to share the bounty with us. One of the many benefits of farm living was the constant flow of eggs, fruit, and vegetables from the garden. I appreciated getting the fresh produce, especially when I was trying to limit my trips to the grocery store.

Of course, fresh from the garden also meant roots and all, snails, slugs, and mud. I carried the flat to the side of the house and gave the lettuce a preliminary squirt with the hose. I paused. I needed coffee first.

I returned to the kitchen and poured two steaming cups. Gene and I sat outside and enjoyed the quiet while drinking our coffee. When we were ready, we rolled up our sleeves and got to work cleaning. He pulled off the sandy roots and I rinsed with the hose. After determining that we had relieved the lettuce of its critters, we brought two large dishpans of clean lettuce leaves into the house. I soaked them in the sink, spun them, and laid them out on towels to dry. Then I took a picture of our lettuce haul and sent it to Barbara.

Message to Barbara: OMG, would you look at all this lettuce? I think we'll be having salad for dinner. Forever. I wish I had your tomatoes.

Barbara: Wow! Did you grow that lettuce? I wish I had your lettuce.

Me: No, I didn't. It was left on the doorstep this morning. An entire flat of it—roots, snails, and all. Another friend stopped in yesterday and gave me two big heads of lettuce but each a different kind so that was good. And some radicchio. I've been cleaning lettuce for a couple of hours now. I'm not much in the mood for a salad.

Barbara: It will be delicious later.

Of course, she was right. Salad season had arrived and it was exquisite. There was Caesar salad, chef salad, taco salad, Spanish salad, seafood salad, caprese salad, and just-plain-salad salad. Lucky for us we like salad.

~

Each year in April, the Valpolicella region hosts the ultimate event: *Magnalonga*. The wine walk covers roughly eight kilometers, meandering through villages, vineyards, and villas, each stop serving a local wine and food pairing. Participants are provided a wineglass, a wineglass holder to wear around the neck, and a punch card for each stop.

At the end of the day, wine lovers have enjoyed a spectacular hike, an eight-course meal, delicious wine, live music, and dancing. A group of us had made this progressive dinner a tradition for the last four years and were sorely disappointed when this year's *Magnalonga* was canceled due to the pandemic. Gene and I decided to host our own virtual *Magnalonga* at Agriturismo Bolzano Vicentino. Gene created a Team Vino chat group, and we planned our day.

ATTENTION: WINE LOVERS!

Please join us for the first ever (and hopefully the last) Virtual Wine Walk. This year's *Magnalonga* will stroll along garden paths and historical landmarks on the beautiful grounds of the ABV. Be ready at three o'clock this afternoon to uncork and unwind from the convenience of your own home.

Kind regards,
Agriturismo Bolzano Vicentino

Our afternoon driveway trek had increased to three laps now, and although not nearly as scenic as Valpolicella, we would make it a grand wine walk just the same. We changed into our Team Vino t-shirts and walking shoes. We dug out the wine glass holders from last year, found the matching glasses, and hung them around our necks.

Outside at the wisteria arch we popped the cork on a small bottle of prosecco and filled our glasses. We opened a package of *grissini*, breadsticks, and munched our way down the driveway. We stashed a bottle of *vino sfuso* in the shade so when we passed the gate we could refill and proceed. We ambled along to the cornfield, where the young stalks were now ankle-high, and enjoyed our vino with some potato chips. We toured the chicken coop, the *orto*, and the fishpond, stopping here and there for refills and to make some videos for our virtual wine walking trail buddies.

Since the two-hundred-meter rule had been lifted we were seeing more and more walkers, runners, and bikers intruding on our personal space. Sure enough, heading toward us as we wobbled along the third and final loop, we encountered a dad and two kids on bicycles.

"Oh lord!" I cringed and turned to Gene. "Please don't let it be the same family that rode down here on our spa day."

As the Italians are the most social of all human beings on the planet, the family stopped to talk, even though we didn't know each other, or at least I hoped we didn't know each other. We attempted to maintain our social distance by moving off the driveway and into the hayfield. They must have wondered about these strange Americans wearing Team Vino t-shirts, making videos, and carrying wineglasses around their necks.

The father pointed out one of the new houses being built nearby and told us that he and his family planned to move in over the summer when construction was finally completed. We put two and two together and figured out that he must be the son of Farmer Cow, the owner of the dairy farm and the hayfield to the right of our driveway. Farmer Goat, the brother of Farmer Cow, raised goats on the left side. The kids pedaled away but Papa kept talking and we kept our distance in the hayfield. Finally, he announced he would invite us to a BBQ when his house was finished this summer.

"*Arrivederci!*" he called. He waved, mounted his bike and was once again on his way.

"*Ciao!*"

We finished the last loop, returned to the house, and opened a bottle of amarone. The final stop on our wine walk was dinner on the terrace.

Team Vino chat:

-- We missed you friends but hope you'll put your reservations in early for next year's event!

-- I hope next year we'll be walking in Valpolicella again.

-- Agreed.

-- Haha! This wins the Vino-Quarantino Award!

-- I had to pace back and forth on my balcony! I don't think I got my miles in, but I did drink the vino! Thanks for not letting me drink by myself—LOL!

-- *Cin cin!* Let's do it again! Thanks, ABV!

-- My favorite stop was the *sfuso* and Doritos pairing.

-- Mine was the Shrine to Our Lady of Stinkbugs.

WEEK 10: L IS FOR LETTUCE

Monday, April 27, 2020

By now the students, parents, and I had adjusted to the online learning schedule. Although it wasn't the best situation, we made it work and I felt like I was still providing my kids with valuable instruction and the predictability and routine they needed. It was a new routine, but a routine nonetheless. I needed the routine as much as they did.

The kids had gotten most proficient at muting their microphones and pinning the speaker to the screen. Most of them showed up on time and ready to learn, although for some, every day was pajama day. In addition, there was still the conundrum with one of the parents, Mrs. Double D. I was struggling to figure out how I could politely caution her about leaning over to adjust the computer while wearing her workout shirt. We were getting an eyeful every day. Should I say something?

Kindergarten chat:

Good morning, friends, and Happy Monday! This week we will be learning about plants. What do plants need to grow?

-- They need water and a pot and some dirt.

-- We planted flowers over the weekend!

-- Can you please show me your flowers? I love flowers.

-- Here is a picture, they have a lot of colors. I like the pink ones best.

-- I like your flowers. We are going to plant a butterfly garden with a lot of different colors so the butterflies will come.

-- That's so cool!

-- We planted some lettuce.

During this time, I wasn't the only one trying to figure out stateside complications; many of my colleagues were dealing with their frontline duties in Italy while trying to juggle precarious situations back home. I was anxious for my friend down the hall who shared that her father had been diagnosed with COVID-19 last week and was in the hospital. I understood the fear and helplessness she was experiencing being far across the ocean. Traveling was nearly impossible and there was nothing she could do from over here but say a prayer and hope for the best.

My concerns about Will continued to escalate as I felt like his continued isolation was leading to despondency. I could tell he felt like a prisoner in his apartment and suspected that he'd given up on his schoolwork. Exam week had just finished and I was sure that hadn't ended well. I encouraged him to reach out to the campus counseling service. We still communicated with him every day, but I didn't know what else to do. I was consumed with fear and self-doubt. Should I call someone to look in on him? Was that overstepping? I couldn't decide if I was being neglectful or paranoid.

~

It was scary to watch the pandemic fallout, not just on the health of citizens, but on the health of the economy; so many people were being laid off. My sister had navigated a precarious situation at work but managed to keep her job when she emerged from the tumult.

Message to Barbara: I hope work is a little calmer for you this week.

Barbara: Thanks. I've been called in today to clean out the offices of the people who were let go. Ian sent us an email and I told him we are always here to help if there's anything that he needs. You know that's true. And for Will, too.

Me: Thanks. They know. It's a relief for me to know you're there for both of them. I hope it doesn't come to that.

Captain Kangaroo and *Mister Rogers' Neighborhood* were the first programs I was allowed to watch on TV. Gene and I both have old black-and-white photos of our preschool selves riding our Wonder Horses, eyes locked on the screen in fascination. Then along came *Sesame Street* and although I was older, I still watched with my younger siblings, Barbara and Bill. Big Bird, Bert and Ernie, and Cookie Monster were my BFFs. When I was a beginning teacher, I purchased a few *Sesame Street* LPs. The singalong songs tickling me with cherished memories. My first graders in Guam sang *Sesame Street* number songs and learned "Rainbow Connection" in sign language with Kermit the Frog and Miss Piggy.

As we grew and changed, *Sesame Street* grew and changed as well, adapting across the generations. Who would have guessed that thirty years later my own sons would be riding the very same resurrected Wonder Horses watching *Elmo Saves Christmas* and singing "C is for Cookie"? *Sesame Street* never disappointed and truly encouraged a lifetime love of learning.

Over the years my students have become less familiar with the friendly neighbors who live on Sesame Street. But, I still like to call on my old Muppet friends from time to time.

I came across an excellent town hall meeting for children put together by *Sesame Street* and *CNN*. My eyes swam as I watched the familiar characters talk with Dr. Gupta about COVID-19, wearing masks, handwashing, coping with loss, dealing with feelings, and staying healthy. Who could have fathomed that fifty years later this would be happening? *Sesame Street* imparted such a powerful message delivered in a positive, hopeful, and age-appropriate manner. I passed the link to parents, hoping that Elmo and Big Bird could reassure the kids in a way that we adults hadn't been able to. And who knew, perhaps the kids just might make some new BFFs.

~

Friends continued to bring us smiles and buoy our spirits. I received a message from a neighbor we had met in Iceland when the boys were just toddlers. We made fast friends with many of the stairwell neighbors in Keflavík family housing, the big blue house, as the boys called it. We hunkered down together during the cold, dark Icelandic winters, the closest thing to a lockdown I'd experienced until the pandemic. We crossed paths here and there, as most military families do, but it'd been a long time since we'd caught up.

June: Funny your Facebook post about the wine walk showed up this morning. I've been thinking about you and hope you're all well. My cousin is turning seventy and this afternoon the family will have a surprise Zoom party for him. Jimmy Buffett is the theme. We spent yesterday making FIN hats to wear. I always remember that concert we went to. I need to go to another one and take my sixteen-year-old granddaughter who has no appreciation for Jimmy.

Me: I remember that concert and how we were so lost in the parking lot afterward! That would be a good song title, wouldn't it? "Lost in the Parking Lot." I think I'll suggest it to Jimmy—LOL. Here's a picture of Ian and my niece at their first Buffett concert two summers ago. He's a little bit bigger than last time you saw him. We made them wear banana suits. They had way too much fun and probably got lost in the parking lot, too.

Tuesday, April 28, 2020
Surely all teachers suffer stress dreams on a regular basis, especially when deluged with out-of-control workloads at the beginning and the

end of the school year. I read that stress dreams were actually beneficial because they processed anxiety at night, allowing more mindful focus during the day. Stress dreams were our friends, the article said. Good thing I had so many friends.

My stress dreams almost always involved snakes, and last night's dreams were no exception. Snakes, as usual, were the opening scene. The bad dream continued to unfold, moving on to a sunny vacation at an unknown destination. I was on the beach chatting with friends, very excited to be getting a break. Panic ensued when I realized I'd forgotten to put in a leave request and I hadn't written any lesson plans for my substitute. The conclusion of the nightmare had me back at home in front of the computer screen, holding a virtual class meeting. I fell out of my chair and stood up only to realize I wasn't wearing any pants, in full view of my students and their parents. Perhaps I'd been too judgmental about Mrs. Double D in her workout clothes. A therapist would've had a field day with all that material. I didn't know what it all meant but I hoped that at least that nightmare would make the next day a little less stressful.

~

In the morning I gave up trying to figure out the puzzle of my stress dreams and focused on another kind of puzzle, the tangram, a kindergarten favorite. A tangram puzzle is comprised of seven flat shapes that fit neatly together into a square. They can be used to compose hundreds of images and patterns. Originating in China, the tangram puzzle spread overseas to Europe and the Americas. They are great tools for teaching shapes and construction.

Kindergarten chat:

Good morning, friends, and Happy Tangram Tuesday! What is a tangram? Check out your math assignment to find out and have fun making shapes from shapes! We will read *Grandfather Tang's Story* later today. What tangram animal is your favorite?

In the afternoon we talked about the tangram puzzles the children made earlier in the day.

"How many shapes are in a tangram puzzle?" I asked.

"Seven!" came back the reply.

"And what shapes did we use?" I continued.

"A square, a lot of triangles, and one of those funny ones, I can't remember," replied one of the kids.

"That's a hard one to remember. It's a rhombus," I explained.

"Mrs. Tramm," someone excitedly broke in, "The tangrams were really fun. I liked making the spaceship the best."

"I don't remember a spaceship in the story but I'm glad you made up some of your own pictures."

"I made a dog and a fish."

"And I made the turtle!"

"My sister made a cat and my cat is named Callie and my cat is white and brown."

~

After our initial wine delivery, I figured out that the *enoteca* was indeed considered an essential service, and therefore was open for business. Barbara got it right; this was Italy. After the virtual *Magnalonga*, we'd depleted our ten liters and were ready for a refill. I rinsed the wine jugs, remembering to save the water to use for my flowers. I printed new travel papers indicating I was going to the *enoteca*, laughing and thinking perhaps instead of burning these I'd keep them as a remembrance. I collected my passport, keys, mask, and wallet before heading to the car. It was only a three-minute drive to the wine gas station, but I felt like I was taking a grand tour.

The large window in front was propped open so I could pull in, walk up, and get a refill without even going inside the store. This was brilliant, quick, and easy—a wine walk-up window. I reclaimed my freshly filled wine jugs, paid twenty euro, and was on my way home. I hoped this would alleviate some stress as well. Returning to the ABV, I found a head of lettuce, waiting to be cleaned, on the front porch.

Wednesday, April 29, 2020

The spring nights were cool and crisp followed by rosy dawns. Not being in a hurry on these slowed-down days allowed for a new awareness of the changing of the seasons. Peering out the window, I blinked and took a double-take when I spotted a fresh powdering of snow shimmering on the mountains. This was a late-spring surprise, a gift, and much better than waking up from a stress dream. A new day was dawning and by noon there was more lettuce on the front porch. My refrigerator overflowed.

~

Another friend reached out on Facebook Messenger. She and her family had recently moved back to the States—was it last summer or the summer before? I truly felt like I was in a time warp as one day melted into another. I had met her ten years ago when her youngest daughter was in my kindergarten class. She was also a teacher and we'd worked together at the elementary school. Her son and older daughters had been in Gene's physics class at the high school.

Missy: Hi Karin, I hope you're doing well. I just went on a rare trip to Facebook and my daughter was standing right behind me. She instantly spotted Gene's video of the wine walk and said, "Please play that; I want to hear his voice." Sweet, huh? Don't tell Gene—it will go to his head. Miss you two!

Me: Aww. We're doing fine—virtual teaching has been a challenge but we're making it work. The hardest part is being over here away from our family and worrying about them from afar. I hope you and the family are safe and well. We miss you, too!

Missy: This new way of life is working about the same for us. I'm teaching second grade this year. I'm absolutely loving it but prefer to be in the classroom with the kiddos. I'm working this morning and just sent a meeting request to the entire school instead of just my class! Why do they let people like me have access to technology?

I'm happy to see you and Gene are still doing your wine walks—so funny! Our wine stock is getting low, it's about time to return to Italy. XO

Me: Thank goodness the wine store is still open—he delivers, too! I'm probably funding his kid's college education. *Ciao* for now my friend!

Miraculously, there was encouraging news from my kindergarten colleague. Her father was on the road to recovery and would be sent home from the hospital later this week. It was joyful news for her and her family. Sometimes we may feel helpless, but never hopeless.

Message from Will: I woke up with a dry throat this morning. I don't think it's coronavirus because I've been isolating but I can't be sure. Just wanted to let you know.

Me: Have you been drinking water? Do you have a thermometer? Do you feel like you have a fever?

Will: No fever, drinking water, and staying in bed.

Me: Maybe you're just run down and tired from exam week. Can you smell?

Will: Yes, and I can taste.

Me: OK, that's a very good sign.

With this news my stomach roiled. Now it was my turn to feel sick.

Thursday, April 30, 2020

In the morning my head was spinning and my ears were ringing. Maybe it was allergies, maybe it was just stress. Maybe life in kindergarten is always so loud that I just hadn't noticed that my ears were ringing all the time. Not feeling up to speed was okay for now; I didn't have to write sub plans and I was thankful for that. I would make it through this day.

This morning there was red lettuce on the doorstep. We would have salad for lunch. Again. For this I was thankful as well

Kindergarten chat:

Good morning, friends! Today we will read *Eating the Alphabet.* Please bring a fruit or veggie snack to eat. We will also play fruit and vegetable bingo while we read. You can make your own homemade bingo card by dividing a piece of paper into eight equal rectangles and writing one letter in each space. The letters should be random and no duplicates. Have a crayon or marker ready to X out the letters as we play. I hope to see you today for a story and a garden snack!

Story time bingo was an overwhelming success and we decided we needed to play bingo more often. We enjoyed apples, carrots, grapes, and more as we munched our way through the alphabet. And yes, L was for lettuce. Lots and lots of lettuce.

Message from Will: Checking in! I've been resting, made some soup, and I feel OK, still tired. No fever or cough. My throat is still sore.

Me: I'm glad you are feeling okay and are resting. If you have an appetite, that's a good sign. Try some hot tea with honey and lemon if you have any. Do you feel like watching *Seinfeld*?

Friday, May 1, 2020

I flipped my Wine Time calendar to the May page. It read, "Does running out of wine count as cardio?" Haha! I snapped a picture of that and sent it to Barbara. She shot back, "The answer is NO! It counts as an emergency. But not for you because you have home delivery."

Neither cardio nor an emergency, teachers were being required to participate in yet another day of professional development, virtually. Just the thought of it gave me a hot flash. Teachers are constantly made to feel that somehow, we're not doing things right and frankly, it gets tiresome. I sent out my favorite PD Day meme to the kindergarten team: "When I die, I hope it's at a faculty meeting or a teacher in-service because the transition from life to death would be so subtle."

This PD focused on our new language arts curriculum and the topic was interpreting "visual graphic displays." Can't we just say pictures or, if we want to use a big word, illustrations? Educational jargon is the worst! For the kindergarten team this was decidedly frustrating because that's exactly what we do all day, help students make meaning from pictures.

Even more annoying, the materials used were from the fourth-grade curriculum. Sigh. How we longed to have meaningful training that was actually written for and beneficial to kindergarten teachers and students. Long ago I had grown tired of this genre of PD and now, with everything else going on, I couldn't believe we still had to suffer through it.

Although the PD was virtual, the kindergarten team decided to work together in person at school so we could collaborate and commiserate, in our own classroom space, with masks in place … and plenty of brownies.

We finished the modules, polished off the brownies, and got ready to go home. I packed up books and files for the upcoming unit. I added puppets and math visuals to my school bag. Before packing up my computer, I quickly scanned my email and wrote my parent newsletter. As my finger was hovering over SEND, my inbox pinged and I saw a new email notification slide across the bottom of my screen. It was from the district superintendent's office and confirmed what I already knew in my heart: the kids wouldn't be coming back to school this year.

I sighed and put my head in my hands. My heart was heavy and tears of frustration ran down my face. Even though this news came as no surprise, it hit home when I saw it in writing. It was official. I walked across the room and ripped down the calendar. When I felt a bit more composed, I quickly rewrote the newsletter and sent it. Separation anxiety took on a whole new meaning as my teary-eyed gaze swept the classroom a final time and I locked the door.

From: Mrs. Tramm
To: VES Kindergarten 2019-2020
Subject: Kindergarten in the Kitchen News, Friday, May 1, 2020

Dear Kindergarten Families,

As you probably heard, it was announced today that we will finish out the remainder of this school year with virtual learning. I'm not sure how we will close out the classroom and get all your child's work and belongings back, but as soon as I know I will update you.

I came across an excellent town hall meeting for children put together by *Sesame Street* and *CNN*. Even if your child doesn't watch *Sesame Street*, this is a very well put together piece about COVID-19, wearing masks, feelings, staying healthy, and other things that are age-appropriate topics regarding our current situation. It's long, so it's broken down into six separate segments, maybe fifteen minutes each. I highly recommend that you sit down with your child and watch one session at a time and talk about it. You can find the link on our virtual classroom.

Thank you again for the enormous effort you are putting forth to team teach with us. We are so grateful for your feedback, your patience, and your dedication in this situation. Have a great weekend!

Karin Tramm
VES Kindergarten

From: Mrs. Grant
To: Mrs. Tramm
Subject: RE: Kindergarten in the Kitchen News, Friday, May 1, 2020
    Hi! I knew this news was coming but it's so very hard to digest. You've been SO fantastic this year and I'm sad that our kids didn't get to spend the whole year in the classroom with you and Mrs. Dee! You both are amazing teachers and people, and I thank my lucky stars that we had the time we did. Big hugs to both of you!

Mrs. Grant

From: Mrs. Tramm
To: Mrs. Grant
Subject: RE: Kindergarten in the Kitchen News, Friday, May 1, 2020
    Thank you. I was actually in my classroom when we got the word and you're right, even though we knew it was coming, it was devastating to read the official memo. My classroom is still set up to go, with the centers all prepared. In my heart I was hoping maybe one Monday we'd get back to business and there you'd be at the art center like all the other Mondays. I guess now I really need to wrap my head around it and figure out what to do next and how to approach it with the kids. We still have six more weeks of fun and learning and we'll get through it together! You are an INCREDIBLE parent and I'm so grateful for your support.

Big hugs to you!
Mrs. Tramm

Good news from Will brought a little balance back to my life after the disheartening news from school.

Will: I just woke up and my throat feels a little less sore today! Not 100%, but I'm getting there.

Me: Awesome! Maybe you can get out and take a walk. Fresh air and exercise would be good for you.

As for me, my ears were still ringing even louder than before. Everything sounded far away, the same feeling I'd get after scuba diving or right before my ears would pop on an airplane. The left ear was especially clogged and was becoming problematic. It was already hard enough to understand kids with missing teeth and poor internet connections but losing my hearing in one ear made it so much worse. I told them I was having trouble with my ear, but sometimes it was so bad I needed Mrs. Dee to interpret for me and write it in the chat box.

I tried the old jumping up and down on one foot trick. This worked when we were kids and had water in our ears from the beach, but this time to no avail. I wondered if the ringing was due to wearing my earbuds while listening to audiobooks, something I was indulging in more and more while at home. I didn't want to go to the clinic, so my last resort was Doctor Google. After doing a bit of research, I found a few ideas I could try at home.

Saturday, May 2, 2020

I was feeling melancholy, thinking of Ian on his birthday. Where had the time gone? One minute he was bouncing through the Monterey Bay Aquarium in a baby backpack, and the next minute he was off to work for the Peace Corps. We knew he was still bothered about his evacuation and hoped that he'd be able to return to Thailand soon, even though it seemed incredibly far away. Selfishly, I wished I'd be able to set eyes on him before he went back.

When I was off to Guam after graduating from college, my parents must've been beside themselves. No cell phones, no email, and my house phone wasn't even capable of calling the States back then. Instead, I had to drive downtown to the RCA store to place a long-distance call. My mother was quick to bring that to my attention on the day I told her Ian was going to Thailand. Such a happy/sad day.

It'd been a while since Ian had been home for his birthday. I thought back on some of his birthday cakes. There was the dinosaur cake, the train cake, the Chuck E. Cheese cake, and the many cakes with Lego figures on top. When he was sixteen, he wanted to blow up his birthday cake with firecrackers. We did that out in the driveway. Thank goodness we didn't have any neighbors, except for Farmer Cow and Farmer Goat across the fields.

When he turned eighteen, his cake was emblazoned with the Florida State University seal. Earlier this year Ian sent me a picture of a birthday cake made of Italian sausage links and frosted with mashed potatoes. He said he wanted that sausage cake for every birthday from now on. I wished I could make it for him this year and hoped someone would do something special for him on his special day.

Peering through the front door I noticed a present on the front porch. Not for Ian, but for me.

Message to Barbara: Unbelievable! Peter Rabbit's been here again. Another flat of lettuce is on the front step.

Barbara: That looks like a good problem to have.

Me: It is. I shouldn't complain. It's helping me not have to go to the store so often. I wish I had a refrigerator just for lettuce.

Navy chat:

-- Loved the Tramm wine walk last weekend—hilarious!

-- Charge your glasses and we will see everyone tonight at 6!

We gathered our wine and our thoughts and moved outside. We joined our navy friends and caught up on all the kids. I laughed and shared with them how twenty years ago on this day Ian was celebrating his fifth birthday in Virginia Beach, and now a quirk of fate had put him there again. I chuckled remembering how we had to politely ask Chuck E. Cheese not to sing "Happy Birthday" when he brought the cake out because Ian hated for people to look at him. Isn't it funny how life's path sometimes loops and twists and leads around to an old yet new place?

Message from Vickie: I think you're busy with virtual happy hour now. I hope so!! Anyway, happy birthday to Ian. We're supposed to have sunny days again finally and if he's still in Virginia Beach this next week maybe he can come sit on our outside deck—it's huge, you can see it on Google Earth, so plenty of room for social distancing. We could drink a birthday spritz and discuss Thailand and Italy and other favorite places.

Me: I gave Ian your phone number, and yes, he's still in Virginia Beach. If there is a spritz involved, he will probably be there.

Vickie: I am happy to be a spritz ambassador!! I know he needs transportation so we can figure something out when he calls.

Sunday, May 3, 2020

We heard a buzz that the Italians would go back to school in mid-September. The rumor (there were so many) was that the students would go part-time face-to-face in the classroom and part-time virtual school. We didn't know what that would mean for the local American schools, but they did try to follow the Italian schools. It seemed like a long time away to make these kinds of decisions because anything could happen between now and then. I just wanted it to be safe for the kids and the teachers.

In the meantime, a new decree came from the Italian government late in the evening. New word came loosening the leash just a little bit more. There was a ray of hope on the horizon.

From: Bill
To: Karin, Barbara, Mom & Dad
Subject: Going home

To Everyone,

I just found out yesterday morning that there will be a chartered flight to bring personnel to Diego Garcia. My relief is flying to Norfolk on Tuesday to start a fourteen-day quarantine at a hotel with all other crew members coming to DG. They will fly from Norfolk straight through to DG, with only one stop for fuel. Once the aircraft arrives and the air crew gets their mandatory rest, the off-signing crew will board the plane and fly straight back to Norfolk, with one stop for fuel. I assume we will fly home on commercial flights from there. I don't think we will be quarantined going home. If all goes perfectly, I should be home around May 25th. I'll end up with around 180 days aboard the ship, which is the longest trip I have ever had. It will certainly be good to get home.

Love
Bill

From: Karin
To: Bill
Subject: RE: Going home

Bill,

This is excellent news! I know the family will be so happy to have you back home. We're still status quo here. Some of the restrictions will be loosened on Monday—for example, now I can shop at my favorite grocery store in the next town over and I can go to a cemetery or a funeral if I want—with a mask, of course. The very best thing, however, is that now restaurants are open (for take-out only). At last, we can have pizza on Friday night again, after two months!

It was finally announced on Friday that we would be doing virtual school for the rest of the year. We pretty much knew that would happen but now it's official. I have mixed feelings about it. Gene and I certainly have settled into a new routine, but I do wish we could have some kind of closure with the kids. It's heartbreaking when the kids keep asking when they can come back to school. This will be hard on all of us. Of course, I do love that I can mute some of the naughty ones or eject them from a meeting. So, there's that.

So happy to hear you have light at the end of your tunnel!

Love,
K

PART 3

THE END OF THE BEGINNING

"Toad, Toad, wake up. It is May now."

Frog and Toad Are Friends, Arnold Lobel

WEEK 11: THE BIRTHDAY SEASON

Monday, May 4, 2020

When the month of May rolls around, our family enters the birthday season. Ian's birthday kicks things off on the 2nd, followed by mine on the 4th, then Gene's on the 11th, my uncle's on the 17th, my niece's on the 25th, then my sister's and my cousin's, both on the 31st. My parents follow in June and July. Weave in Mother's Day, Father's Day, and graduations, and we always have a lot of celebrating to do. We like that.

Kindergarten chat:

-- Good morning Mrs. Tramm! A little birdie told us it's your birthday. Happy birthday, Mrs. Tramm!

-- Good morning, friends! Thank you for the birthday wishes. Did you know that today is also Goldilocks's birthday? We will read *Dear Peter Rabbit* to find out who she will invite to her party. There are many characters from the story in the illustration below. I can see Peter Rabbit, Goldilocks, the three pigs, the three bears, Red Riding Hood, Mr. McGregor, and Mrs. McGregor. I especially love their party hats. You can zoom in and see many details from the story. What are they eating? How many party hats can you find?

After the read-aloud we talked about all the characters from different stories that came together in the book.

"This is a great book! I love the pig's plate hat!" remarked the speech teacher who was collaborating on the lesson.

"I see Mama Bear and Papa Bear out in the woods."

"And in this story, Mr. McGregor is Goldilocks's dad!" I was so happy they were noticing details in the illustrations and nuances of the text.

"My birthday is next week!" came an excited voice.

"Today is my dog's birthday!"

The kids sang "Happy Birthday" to me. It was heartfelt and touching and made me miss them so much. Gene picked flowers from the yard and placed them on my school desk in the kitchen.

From: Bill
To: Karin
Subject: Happy Birthday

Karin,

HAPPY BIRTHDAY!! I know it must not be much fun being stuck inside for your birthday, like Mom and Dad during their anniversary. At least your wine store is open! And other things are starting to open up there as well. I've noticed that the new cases each day seem to be staying below 2,000 in Italy, so that's a big improvement. I hope they open things up slowly and not too fast like what is happening in the States.

I got a laugh out of your comment about being able to mute some of the kids during the class discussion. I sure wish I could do that sometimes here on the ship. When you get a chance, update me on how your boys are doing (all three of them).

Happy B-Day—
Bill

From: Karin
To: Bill
Subject: RE: Happy Birthday

Thanks for the birthday wishes. I can't remember where I left off with tales from the trail of Ian. He's still in Virginia Beach with his friend that he's known since sixth grade. We're grateful he is with someone familiar. He's doing so much better now that he has a phone plan, ATM card, and Italian food in his belly. He'll be there a couple more weeks. God bless that family!

Will starts summer session next week. He's doing okay but is feeling isolated and alone in his apartment. He misses his friends and especially his music. We talk to him every night and watch an episode of *Seinfeld* together.

Gene's fine. He's feeling much better but is still anxious about the virus, not knowing for sure whether he actually had it or not. He feels vulnerable, I think turning sixty next week is on his mind.

Ciao for now!
Karin

Message from Barbara: HAPPY BIRTHDAY!! Hope you can sneak in an extra walk down the driveway!

Me: My treat today is to go grocery shopping at the Alì.

Barbara: Is that the one where I saw baby food made from horse meat? And rabbit?

Me: Yes, and it's the same store where I had the coughing incident—I haven't been there since.

Barbara: That IS a treat. I hope Gene made you coffee in bed this morning.

Me: And he mowed the lawn and picked flowers from the yard.

Barbara: He remembered and was creative. So sweet! He definitely gets points for that!!

Me: He's even ordering Mother's Day flowers for his own mother right now. We're going to order some for Mom and have them delivered to you. Or not. Be honest. They'll be from all of us.

Barbara: Yes, that's fine, whatever you want to do. She also mentioned some things she can't get delivered, her favorite jam and butter, so I'll pick some up and take them with the flowers.

Me: I'll take care of the flower order. What delivery day is best?

Barbara: Saturday delivery.

Me: To your house?

Barbara: Yep.

Me: OK. Thanks for delivery duty. Again. I'll be careful not to accidentally forward the order confirmation to her. Again.

The revised travel restrictions allowed me to go back to the Alì in the next town over. I gathered my shopping bags, mask, and gloves, and drove to the supermarket, trying not to speed in my excitement. There was no line outside. It's amazing the things we used to take for granted.

Wearing my mask and stylish latex gloves, I cruised the aisles and stocked my cart with fresh fruits and vegetables, cheese, salami, breadsticks, biscotti, fresh pasta, prosecco, and Aperol—all the things I had been missing. I didn't even cough at the checkout. What a great birthday!

Message from Ian: Happy Birthday Mom! What are you guys up to tonight?

Me: We're getting ready to eat spaghetti and octopus. One of my friends at school prepared the octopus and shared some with me. It's been in the freezer waiting for today.

Ian: Oooh! Yum! I'm jealous!

Me: I know you've been eating well too.

Ian: Indeed I have. The other night for my birthday we did linguini with clams and shucked oysters and ate them out of the shell. So good.

Me: Yum! I'm glad you had a good birthday meal and some local food.

Ian: Me too! It was so good. And my friend got me a poetry book that I'm super excited to read.

Message from Will: Happy Birthday Mom!!

Me: Thanks. I'm so happy, I got to go shopping at the Alì! I was thinking of you when I passed the *frutti di bosco* yogurt.

Will: Yum! That would be pretty good today. I'm feeling much better. I think whatever I had is gone for good.

Me: Awesome! That's the best birthday present!

~

The state of Florida also loosened some restrictions, entering phase one of reopening. Beaches, parks, stores, and restaurants resumed business with limitations, but were open nonetheless. To me this seemed surprisingly soon and I felt growing concern for my family. I continued to annoy my parents and Will, continually reminding them to stay home. This pandemic seemed far from over.

Tuesday, May 5, 2020

I was awakened at 4:47, not by the cuckoo bird, but by a loud rushing noise. I stared at the red numbers on the clock, time counting on like an odometer in a speeding car. I wondered if I was hearing a train, but the sound was continuous; it didn't fade away as a train might. I had flashbacks to the series of earthquakes we experienced a few years back. Was this another temblor coming? Was I hearing it before I felt the jolt?

But no, earthquakes rumble and this was more of an unceasing roar, a tremendous roar so it seemed to me.

I got out of bed and peeked out the bedroom window, almost afraid of what I might see. I wondered if it was an explosion or a fire. What else could make a noise like that—something dreadful was happening and it sounded intense. I could see nothing. *Niente.* Maybe, I thought, it was just this weird thing going on with my ears. I went back to bed and listened to the sound ebb and flow, but never stop. I managed to fall back asleep for a brief time and when I awoke the rolling racket was still there. Daylight streamed through the window, but nothing seemed out of the ordinary except for the noise, like typhoon winds rushing toward me from the distance.

Then it dawned on me—it was the highway, a kilometer or so beyond the hayfield and through the trees. It was the sound of cars and trucks heading for the *autostrada.* Over the years we'd become so accustomed to hearing the traffic that we ceased to notice it, especially in summer and winter when the windows were closed. When we were outside or when the windows were open, we joked that it was the sound of the ocean calling. Only now I realized I hadn't registered, nor appreciated, the complete silence of the past two months. It was in sharp contrast to the sound of so many cars and trucks hitting the highway on this day, the second day of a little bit more freedom.

~

Usually, Mrs. Dee and I would meet individually with six or seven students each day. We'd chat with our little friends, read a story together, and do a short math lesson. At the end of each meeting, I touched base with the parents to see if they had any questions I could answer or any concerns that needed to be addressed. It was an important time to reinforce the home-school connection and keep the lines of communication open. I had a very tight-knit group this year and I missed working with my parent volunteers as much as I missed the kids.

As we neared the end of my first meeting, I asked my student, "Is your mom close by? I just want to talk to her to see if she has any questions for me."

"No, she's at work, but my dad's here," she answered.

She picked up her tablet and took off to go get her dad. Her virtual run through the house made me a little seasick but the screen soon steadied, and I was horrified to realize she was in her parents' bedroom.

"Dad! Dad! Wake up!" she called, "Mrs. Tramm wants to talk to you!"

"NO, NO! Don't worry about it, never mind," I tried to tell her, "Don't wake him up!" But it was too late.

"Hello?" Dad's groggy face appeared on my computer screen as I apologized profusely.

"I'm so sorry! I didn't know you were asleep! I was just checking in to see if you had any questions. I'm so sorry, really, I am. Please just go back to sleep. We can talk next week."

Note to self: from now on make sure to have a visual on the parent before asking.

~

Message from Misty: Hey! Happy late birthday—hope it was good.

Me: Another backward birthday. I'm getting younger every year, ya know.

Misty: I'm stealing Tangram Tuesday.

Me: Good, glad you like that, we had fun with it. Read *Grandfather Tang's Story* with it.

Misty: Also, I need to reschedule our meeting on Friday.

Me: Friday morning is a mess, lots of make-up meetings already. Let's try at 1:00 after lunch, if it works for you. And then maybe a follow-up at 3:00, after my group meeting. For a quarantini. Miss you!

Villa Sceriman, Vo'Euganeo:

We are open! We are happy to welcome back all of our customers from the Veneto region! It is not possible to consume our wine here yet, but we will be ready to host you as soon as we are able. We will continue with our cantina sales and deliveries during the month of May. You can't see it, but we are smiling under our masks!

As was the rest of Italy, Vo' was returning to life.

Wednesday, May 6, 2020

Kindergarten chat:

-- Here is a picture of a bird nest in my front yard. I can't believe how fast the birds are growing. Last week they didn't have feathers and this week they do. The mother and the father bird work together to bring food to the chicks. Today we will read a story about a baby bird searching for his mother. It's called *Are You My Mother?* See you then!

Stories about birds are always a kindergarten favorite. At this time of year, they are especially relatable as the children are seeing real live birds returning home, building nests, and searching for food. The kids were fascinated by the pictures posted in our chat.

"Aww, they're so cute."

"How long will they be in the nest?" someone asked.

"I don't know; we'll have to wait and watch," I answered.

"I have a bird's nest by my front porch," another added.

"Awesome! You'll get to see the chicks grow up, too!" I said.

"What kind of food do they eat?"

"I think these birds eat worms and insects," I replied. "The mother bird searches for food and brings it back to the nest. Because they're just babies, they can't chew it themselves, so she chews it up for them and spits it in their mouth. It's bird baby food."

"EEEWWWWWW!!!!!" the collective cry came forth.

~

The corn was knee-high now and the hayfield was getting tall as well. As we were finishing our afternoon driveway stroll, Farmer Cow fired up his tractor and commenced the first cut of the season. Dust and grass flew in every direction as we hurried through the gate and back up to the house. We were always at the mercy of the wind when this happened. If the breeze blew south, all would be well. If it blew north, we'd have to clean the entire front porch again. Either way, tomorrow beautiful rolls of hay would polka dot the freshly cut field. The cut grass smelled so good, and it was so good that we could both smell it.

~

Message from Vickie: Was thinking of you yesterday wondering what kind of birthday you were having in quarantine? It's one for the memory books. I know it's your first quarantine birthday and hopefully the last!

Me: I celebrated by going to the next town for grocery shopping. We hadn't been allowed to leave our towns until Monday, so I was ready with a long list. Ian said he was going to take you up on your offer of spritz so stand by.

Vickie: I saw on the news that they relaxed a few restrictions on your birthday. What a great gift!

Thursday, May 7, 2020

My father's sister, Lillian, was affectionately known to us as Aunt Babe. She was ninety-five years old and a spitfire. A boat enthusiast, like my father, she had also raced in her younger years, as had her daughters. Much to her chagrin, she'd been residing in an assisted living facility for the past year. It was a beautiful place, a tableau of fountains and tiled courtyards, but she missed her home, her view of the water, and her freedom. The facility, like others in Florida, had restricted visitors two months ago due to COVID-19. The isolation had proven difficult for her.

Aunt Babe was tenacious, sometimes irreverent, and maybe just a little bit ditzy. I always made a point to visit her when I was home in Florida during the summer. Last time I was there I gathered her up for a morning outing to the grocery store where we stocked up on coffee and snacks. We went to lunch at her favorite seafood restaurant and in the afternoon treated ourselves to a manicure. We had a fabulous day and I was sorry to bid her goodbye until next summer.

Mom texted me and asked me to get back to her when I could. I called her while I was making dinner so we could enjoy our own "Cook and Chat Show" that had become our routine.

"I just wanted to let you know that Aunt Babe is in Sarasota Memorial," she began. "She went in because she fell at the nursing home, multiple times. They had to have her checked out."

"Okay," I said slowly. "How is she?"

"She was also having trouble with a cough and breathing. They can't get her oxygen levels up and they're afraid it'll affect her kidneys." Mom paused and then added, "Her systems are shutting down. Hospice is going to be called in. And she'll be tested again for COVID-19."

Suddenly I lost my appetite. I turned the flame off and tried to focus on the conversation.

"This is terrible news and it's even worse because I know you and Dad aren't allowed to go to the hospital. How's Dad doing with all this?" I asked.

"Really very well," Mom answered. "He's sad but realizes it's just her time. They talked on the phone yesterday and she thought she was at a big party."

I smiled to myself. That was so Aunt Babe.

"A nurse has to hold the phone for her." Mom went on. "She doesn't know who Dad is. I left a message with Barbara to call me when she can so I can tell her. Then I have to email Bill."

"This is hard for me to frame right now, both the bad and the good of it. Thanks for letting me know."

We talked a bit about what else was going on in Florida—what was open, what was still closed. We talked about books and TV, and what we were making for dinner, but my mind kept wandering to Sarasota.

"Okay, Mom, I gotta go now; my dinner's almost ready. Keep me updated on Aunt Babe."

"Will do. Love you!"

"Love you, too!"

I ended the video call and drained the pasta, feeling a bit emotionally drained myself.

Friday, May 8, 2020

The first week of May is traditionally Teacher Appreciation Week. This year it should have been called Teacher and Parent Appreciation Week as parents were real heroes holding down the fort at home since February. One of my parents stealthily contacted the others and had the students each make a short video. She compiled them, set the entire thing to music, and presented the slide show at our morning meeting. Mrs. Dee and I were speechless.

One of my students appeared on the video, jumping on his trampoline. "Hi Mrs. Tramm and Mrs. Dee. Thanks for teaching us."

Another student appeared, dressed in his Sunday best, including a tie. "You're the best teachers ever!"

I wasn't sure if I could watch this in front of my kids. The screen flooded with photos of our classroom, students, and parents, all working together. Then a shift, a photo followed of my kitchen classroom, taken from the other side of the Google Meet. Then pictures of the kids at home, eating green eggs and ham, holding up *Andrà tutto bene* rainbows, the fairy garden, and then more video clips.

"Thank you, Mrs. Tramm and Mrs. Dee."

"I miss you."

"You are the awesomest teachers ever!"

The video finished with one of the girls performing a cartwheel and blowing a kiss at the camera.

"Thank you for being our teachers!" she exclaimed, grinning ear to ear.

It was one of the nicest things a parent has ever done for me and it could not have been more meaningful this year. I cried in front of the class. I'll never be able to watch that video without crying. I sent the link to Mom and Dad, thinking they might need a warm fuzzy, too.

From: Mrs. Tramm
To: VES Kindergarten 2019-2020
Subject: Kindergarten in the Kitchen News, Friday, May 8, 2020

Dear Kindergarten Families,

Thank you all for the beautiful video today. Mrs. Dee and I were surprised and beyond words. I'm touched and honored to be the teacher of your children. I'm so proud of them, and of you, parents, for stepping up and doing the job that had to be done this year. It has been a monumental team effort.

We also have a new slide show, "Our Little Dandelions," on the virtual classroom. If we don't have your child's photo there, please email it to us and we can still include it. I will also put a link to today's video there so the children can watch it again if they like. I know I will watch it at least a hundred more times.

Next week we will be learning about birds, where they live, and what they eat. Please help your child notice birds around your home. Feel free to post pictures of your feathered friends in the chat.

Also, next week on Thursday morning we will have a special guest reader from the post library to tell us about the summer reading program. Please know that attendance is optional, but we hope your child will be able to be there to enjoy the story and hear all about the summer reading fun offered by the library.

Happy Mother's Day to all of our awesome moms who do sooooo much more than we even know. Thank you! Have a great weekend!

Karin Tramm
VES Kindergarten

Mom: Your dad and I just saw the video you sent. What a nice thing they did. It made me cry. We are so proud of how you have made this work. I know it's been hard for you and Gene. We love you!

Me: The video made me cry too. It was a surprise and they showed it during my morning meeting. It was so sweet. I'm glad you liked it.

Saturday, May 9, 2020

The Mother's Day flowers arrived at Barbara's house a day early. Once again, she was tasked to wipe everything down and deliver to Mom. She made a basket of goodies to accompany them.

Mom: Thank you! How pretty and what a beautiful way to start the day. Bill called just a minute ago. That was also a wonderful surprise. Happy Mother's Day to you and I hope you get to go out.

Thank you also for the food items Barbara delivered. And best of all, thank you for the iPad for our early birthday present! Barb and Brian stayed quite a while and helped your dad set it up. She said she would let Bill know about it, so I won't thank him just yet.

Me: You're welcome. We thought you should have it early in the birthday season this year. Now you can use it for video calls, too, instead of your phone.

Mom: Also, just so you know, I had a message that Aunt Babe's oxygen was turned off. She was comfortable last night and stable. Love you and thank you so much.

Sunday, May 10, 2020

The new decree allowed even more freedom. Now we could have a fifteen-kilometer radius to exercise in. This meant longer walks and bike rides, new scenery, and the opportunity to drive somewhere to exercise. The update was welcome news for many of our friends who were single and had been stuck in their apartments alone.

After a long bike ride, two friends dropped by with a bottle of prosecco for Gene's upcoming birthday. We sat on the back terrace and enjoyed the sun and a spritz. We chatted awhile, feeling almost normal, before they were on their way again. I gave both of them a big bag of lettuce.

-- Thanks for the lettuce. I had a most delicious salad. It was really nice to see you guys in real life, although I think it makes going back to being alone a little bit harder.

-- It was so good to see you, too. Come anytime. We'll always have prosecco. And lettuce.

Gene and I realized how lucky we were to be managing this lockdown together. Being together alone was a challenge for some but we were getting along. We were exercising. We were enjoying meals together. We were fortunate to have each other and we knew it. Every day.

The missing plates at the table belonged to Ian and Will. It was hard to keep them out of my thoughts, especially on Mother's Day when the void seemed even more apparent. When the boys first left, Gene and I slowly adjusted to our empty nest status. We filled our days with new restaurants, art shows, and adventures. Now, in this pandemic, days like this made family separation more acute, the gap ever widening between when I saw them last and when I might see them again. I thought back to their birth days and wrote letters to both of my boys.

Dear Ian,

Thank you for rocking my world. You changed me. You taught me. You gave me a new perspective. Just when I thought I knew everything, you helped me understand that, in truth, I knew nothing.

You were born after twenty-three hours of labor. Grandma and Grandpa were there. Dad was there. We were all waiting for you, but you were quite comfortable and weren't convinced you were ready to meet the world yet. When you finally arrived, you were blue. You wouldn't breathe. You wouldn't eat. And so it went with you, my stubborn, willful, beautiful baby boy. As an infant it was scary. As a five-year-old, it was exasperating. As an adult, you have dogged determinism, grit, and persistence. These are clearly the qualities that have given you the fortitude to navigate your current situation. You are absolutely resilient.

I love you.

Mom

Dear Will,

The doctors didn't know why you were coming so early. An air ambulance lifted me away from Monterey to San Francisco. I said goodbye to Dad, and he drove as fast as he could to the University of California San Francisco hospital, three hours away.

We waited two long days for you to be born. There were fourteen people—doctors, nurses, and medical students—in the delivery room when you arrived. They whisked you away and took good care of you while one of the doctors showed me the knot in your umbilical cord. He said you were a swimmer in your early days and made a loop and swam through it. Maybe it's true that you really came from the fish world like Dad always says.

The doctor told me that usually a knot in the cord causes a miscarriage early on, or if the pregnancy proceeds full term, a stillbirth. It was a miracle that you were born nine weeks early, the magic moment of survival. The doctor told me that the knot hadn't caused your premature birth, but I know in my heart that you were born early for a reason. You are here for a purpose.

I love you.

Mom

Message from Ian: Happy Mother's Day! Love you!

Me: How do you do that? I was just thinking about you and picked up my phone when your message popped up. Don't forget about Dad's birthday tomorrow. The BIG 6-0!

Ian: Because I'm extremely intelligent. And I know it! What a geezer!

Me: Birthday party at 5. Our time.

Message from Will: Happy Mother's Day!!

Me: Thanks, Will. Don't forget tomorrow is Dad's birthday. The BIG 6-0!!

Will: I know!!

Me: Don't forget to send him a picture of his favorite dog card.

Will: Again?

Me: Yes, he wants the same card every year.

WEEK 12: TRANSITIONS

Monday, May 11, 2020

Gene was turning sixty years old. Although he kept telling me he didn't want a party or a fuss, sixty years was something to celebrate, even if we were still in the midst of a partial lockdown. Now that I knew how to set up a video conference, I mustered a menagerie of friends from near and far and planned a virtual surprise party.

Dear Friends and Family,

Gene Tramm will be turning sixty years young today. Drop in to visit and share a toast tonight between five and seven (Italy time). Don't forget to wear your party hats!

When the school day was over and we'd walked three driveway laps, I made a plate of snacks and poured two glasses of prosecco. On the stroke of five, I moved the ironing board out of the way and pulled up two kitchen chairs as my computer screen came alive. One by one, friends from all over the world popped in for the virtual birthday party to wish Gene well.

"Happy birthday!"

"*Tanti auguri!*"

"*Buon compleanno!*"

"*Feliz cumpleaños!*"

It was a loud, chaotic gathering, almost like real life. Everyone wore party hats, and we splashed our wine and clinked our glasses. We laughed, told stories, and for a short time forgot about the chaos that surrounded us. Ian even made a short appearance from Virginia Beach—in his banana suit, of course.

Tuesday, May 12, 2020

As we all became more comfortable with the virtual classroom platform, many of the students and parents made their own videos to share with the class. It was fun to watch the kids and see how everyone was growing and changing, to see their homes and families, and to see what was new and exciting in their lives. We had videos of art projects, science experiments, cooking, and Lego creations. One of my students made a video about a delicious plant she found growing in her yard.

"Hello everybody. This is mint. I found it growing in my yard. Maybe I'm going to eat some now."

She bravely munched on a leaf and eyed the camera as if waiting for a response.

"Mmmmmm," she continued, beaming. "Thank you for watching my video about mint."

Naturally, we had to have a discussion about mint during our afternoon meeting.

"We have mint growing in our yard, too, but I don't like it!" one student shared. "It's too spicy."

"You got so tall!" exclaimed another.

For three long months, we hadn't seen each other in person, only in our boxes on screen. It was noticeable how much taller she had grown when we watched the video and saw her walking in her yard.

"Did you like the mint?" someone asked.

"Yeah, I liked it," she answered. "It tickled my nose."

"Hey! Now you can make mint ice cream!"

~

Now that I was sure we wouldn't be returning to the classroom, I needed to come up with a way to pack up my students' belongings. Besides their school supplies, journals, artwork, and rest time towels (yes, we still had rest time, the best time), there were bags of spare clothing and other personal items to return. The school had supplied each classroom teacher with small plastic commissary bags for each child, but they weren't nearly big enough to hold everything kindergarten.

One of the parents saved the day. She had some large reusable shopping bags from a local grocery store and they were the perfect size.

"How many do you have?" I asked.

"Probably twenty-five or so. More than enough," she assured me.

"How'd you get so many?"

She laughed, "My husband always forgets to take the bags into the store, so he just buys a new one every time. I've gotta get some of them out of my house; I don't have any more room!"

"Thanks, that's a huge help. When can I get them?"

"Today, please! I'll put them in his car."

After my last meeting, I logged off my computer and drove to post to pick up the bags. I laughed when I saw them, no wonder she wanted to get rid of them. Win-win!

"Thanks!" I called as I loaded them.

The entire back seat of my little car was full of bags. School was only five minutes away, so I drove over to drop them off. I passed the playground and noticed the tricycles were still scattered willy-nilly along the fence. I'd have to do something about that sooner or later.

As I entered the room, I inhaled the stale smell of abandonment. A musty, silent twilight zone. Afternoon sun angled through the windows, highlighting the dust motes dancing on their empty stage. I opened the bags wide and put them in a large circle on the floor, waiting to be filled. I swapped out my books and supplies once again and went back to the car.

Pulling out of my parking space I saw a large shiny puddle where the car had been parked. I pulled back into the adjacent space and checked the liquid. It wasn't oil and it wasn't water. As I drove home, I was relieved that no indicator lights came on, but I knew this shouldn't wait and I had to get it checked out. I hoped the garage would be considered an essential service and would be open for business.

~

In the evening I called Mom and found out that Aunt Babe had tested negative for COVID-19. This allowed her to move to hospice care and to have next of kin, her daughter, at her side. Her vitals were good, but we all understood what came next.

Wednesday May 13, 2020

One of my students posted a picture of some baby birds she'd found in distress in her backyard. The kids were very interested, and it sparked a lively discussion during our morning meeting.

"*Buongiorno amici.* Happy Wednesday!" I began. "One of our friends helped rescue some baby birds in her backyard. Did you see the pictures she shared?"

"Aww that's sweet!"

"What a good helper," someone added.

"Those birds look the same as the ones by my front door."

"What kind of birds are they?"

"Where is their nest?"

"Why did they get out?" the questions continued.

"Where are the mom and dad?" Someone was worried. "Will they come back and feed them?"

A quiet settled on the screen, eyes on me.

I appreciated how our students were making real-life connections. I wished I could be in our classroom sharing my collection of bird feathers, eggs, and nests. The kids had still grasped ideas and made meaning in their own world, even if their world, at the moment, was no further than their own backyards.

~

My great-grandfather, Verdi Burtch, was an amateur ornithologist, and I've always had an affection for our feathered friends. The bird clock in my kitchen belonged to his son, Kirk. After Grandpa Kirk passed away, no one else in the family wanted the clock; the bird calls that chimed every hour were loud. Since I already had a house full of noisy boys at the time, I became the proud new owner of the bird clock. Shortly after, Ian and Will built a bird feeder that we hung on the fence outside the kitchen window. While we sat down to breakfast, we would watch the birds enjoying their morning meal at the bird feeder—many of the real birds singing songs we recognized from the clock.

We spotted male and female cardinals in the winter, noting their contrasting plumage. We saw the robins arrive in the spring, joined by wrens, finches, and cowbirds. We watched the blue jays bully the other birds and the squirrels trying to commandeer the feeder. We kept the *National Audubon Society Field Guide to North American Birds* on the kitchen table to learn more about our newfound feathered friends.

One spring we noticed the cardinals arrive at the feeder with their babies and one mismatched chick. Doing some research, we learned that cowbirds lay their eggs in the nests of other birds and leave them for the adoptive parents to raise. The cardinals regularly appeared with their own two chicks and their foster cowbird chick as well, until one day the chicks were gone, flying away to start their own lives.

Whenever I heard the bird clock it reminded me of my grandpa and my boys, and now, I was so lucky to be able to share it with my class. It was right above my computer and every hour on the hour, a different bird call would sound. At eight o'clock the black-capped chickadee sounded for my first meeting of the day. The northern cardinal and the white-throated sparrow also kept us on schedule. At eleven o'clock our large group meeting would commence with the call of the white-breasted nuthatch. When the kids heard the bird call through my computer, they knew it was the signal to sing the "Hello Song" and then mute their microphones. My grandmother was a teacher too, and somehow, I knew she would be smiling down from heaven when the bird clock sang.

~

We called to see if the auto mechanic was considered an essential service and to our relief he was. After my last afternoon meeting, I drove the car to his shop to get the leak checked. Gene followed and we rode home together. How strange it felt to both be in the same car at the same time, like we were on a first date. For the past three months, all our outings had been solo because only one family member at a time was allowed to shop, per the regulations. From the passenger seat I could witness the world go by. The roadside, brilliant with color, reminded me of the Italian flag with clusters of bright red poppies cropping up in the green grass, and white calla lilies crowding the ditches. I wasn't too happy about the car needing work, but the drive home was a glorious treat I would have missed otherwise.

"No surprises," I murmured as we turned down the driveway toward the ABV.

"No surprises."

~

In the evening Mom messaged me to call her. Sadly, I knew what that meant.

"Hey, Mom, what's up?" I asked, but my heart already knew.

"I just wanted to let you know that Aunt Babe passed away a few minutes ago."

"I'm so sad and sorry. How's Dad doing?"

"As well as can be expected. He has to take care of a lot of paperwork."

"Well, I hope everything is straightforward and he can limit face-to-face meetings."

"So far, yes, he hasn't had to leave the house, but he will down the road. Also," she continued, "someone posted it on Facebook already, so please let your boys know as soon as you can before they see it."

We reluctantly said our goodbyes and hung up. I took a big breath and sighed. There would be no funeral service, no closure. Her daughter was with her when she passed and that was a comfort to both of them. We would all miss her spunk, but her spirit would remain alive in all of us who knew and loved her. She was ninety-five years old and had led a very full life.

Message to Ian: Aunt Babe passed away earlier today. I thought you'd want to know.

Ian: Yeah, I saw it on Facebook. Have you talked to Grandpa? How's he doing?

Me: Dad's okay. He talked to her on Sunday, but she didn't know who he was. He knew it was coming and that it was her time, but I know he's disappointed he couldn't be there with her at the end.

Message to Will: I hope you had a great day of class. I'm sorry to tell you Aunt Babe passed away today. There's nothing you need to do but I wanted you to know.

Will: Ian told me. She was ready.

Me: I know. You're doing okay? Staying in your apartment?

Will: Don't worry, Mom. I'm staying home.

Thursday, May 14, 2020

Kindergarten chat:

-- My birds are gone! They are not in the nest anymore!

-- Don't worry, my friend. They must be out learning to fly. That's what all little birds do.

~

The post library had been closed almost as long as the school had. However, the lovely ladies of the library continued to reach out to the kids in the community. Ms. Amy had been doing a virtual story time each week for the past year, and she started reading nightly as soon as school had gone virtual in February. Families could join Ms. Amy every night on Facebook, where she streamed in her PJs, bathrobe, and towel-wrapped hair, reading to her Frenchie dog, Normandy, and to the children. She soon became a virtual community celebrity.

The librarians were old friends, both of them having had children in my kindergarten class. Ms. Amy had been one of my supermoms then, even volunteering in my classroom after her daughter went to first grade. I called to see if she would be willing to be a guest reader during our morning meeting so she could talk to my students about the library summer reading program. Even though it would be virtual, I wanted to encourage my students to get involved with the library and keep reading over the summer.

Ms. Amy, wearing her striped cat eyeglasses, appeared on the screen. I heard the kids' delight.

"Look, it's Ms. Amy!"

"I know her!"

"There's Normandy!" one of the kids pointed at the Frenchie on the bed beside her.

Ms. Amy had a similar reaction. She later told me it had been so long since she had seen the kindergartners, she gasped and reached out for the screen when she saw their faces. I completely understood this and that is why I love her.

She shared the cover of the book, *Miss Bindergarten Celebrates the Last Day of Kindergarten* and began to read. Right away I saw crumpled faces and the questioning looks of my kids. I realized I had made a huge blunder in not preparing them for this particular story. I failed to tell the class that today was NOT the last day of kindergarten. After the story I tried to smooth things over and made sure the kids understood there would be kindergarten tomorrow and next week. I assured them we were just getting ready for the last day of kindergarten, but I could see the looks of anxiety and betrayal on their faces.

~

I called Mom and Dad to see how everyone was holding up, health-wise and otherwise. They seemed to be doing well, considering all that was going on in their lives: lockdown, death in the family, etc. Then Mom had some exciting news to share.

"I finally got out of the house today," she told me. "I had a little outing."

"What?! Why?! Where'd you go?"

She went on to tell me that she had driven herself over to the hospital to attend a friend's retirement party. Mom had retired from Manatee Memorial Hospital several years earlier, having worked in the surgery unit for many years. She was feeling the frustration of being confined to the house for the last three months and was anxious to get out and have some social interaction. I got that, but I still didn't like it.

"Mom, it's dangerous for you to be around other people right now, especially at the hospital. You should only go there if it's an emergency. You could get exposed to all kinds of stuff," I reminded her cautiously.

"Don't worry, it was outside in the parking lot. We all wore our masks and stood far apart."

Sigh.

Friday, May 15, 2020

I dreamed I went to the grocery store. I was inside before it dawned on me that I had forgotten my mask and gloves in the car. I left my shopping cart and headed back outside in a panic when I noticed no one else was wearing a mask or gloves either. Then, in my dream, I realized that the pandemic had really all been a bad dream and things were just as they had been before. What does that mean when you have a dream that you had a dream?

At least in this dream there were no snakes. And I was wearing pants.

~

Kindergarten chat:

-- Happy Friday, friends! Can you name a bird that can swim but cannot fly? Do you know the smallest bird? Can you name a bird that runs very fast? Get your bingo cards ready because this afternoon we will play bird bingo and learn more fun facts about birds! See you soon!

We talked a lot about birds. We talked about why baby birds leave the nest. We talked about why kindergartners go to first grade.

Much like the hundredth day of school, the last day of school is looked forward to as a day of celebration. Sometimes. Kindergartners don't really know what to expect for summer break. After all, they've never had a summer break before. They're comfortable in their predictable routine, and the change in their everyday normal can prove difficult for some of our young friends. This was especially true this time, this year having been anything but normal. When I promised them that the hundredth day of school wouldn't be the last day of school, I was very wrong. Very,

very, wrong. Perhaps the hundredth day wasn't technically the last day of school, but it was the end of our kindergarten world as we knew it. Now we faced another difficult transition, one even I was not sure how to navigate.

For military kids and others attending overseas schools, the last day of school is bittersweet. Summer is moving season for a large number of military families. On average, military schools experience a 30 percent turnover each summer. For students, the last day of school means freedom from teachers and freedom from classes, but it also means saying goodbye to friends, sometimes forever. For teachers, it means freedom from lesson plans and admin demands, but also saying goodbye to students and colleagues, sometimes forever. We cry and wave hankies as the buses depart, joking that the tears are really tears of joy. Some of those tears are, but not all.

Get ready to fly little birds ... be strong ... you can do it.

From: Mrs. Tramm
To: VES Kindergarten 2019-2020
Subject: Kindergarten in the Kitchen News, Friday, May 15, 2020

Dear Kindergarten Families,

We had a sweet week learning about birds. We know that birds are covered with feathers, that most birds fly but some can swim as well. We learned that a bird's feet are especially designed for its habitat, and a bird's beak is especially designed for its food. We know that birds lay eggs in nests and nests can be found in many places, even by your front door! And most mama birds chew the food for their chicks—*EEEWWWW!* We also know that in time baby birds grow up and fly away. Next week we will learn about insects. Dig out your magnifying glasses!

One of my favorite end-of-the-year activities is to have students present an animal project to the class. The children can choose any animal and do a little bit of research on it. Next week during our individual meetings I will talk to the children about their topics, what they are learning, and where they are doing their research. The following week, instead of individual meetings, we will have optional small group meetings so the children can present their work if they choose. They will also have the opportunity to have questions and answers with their classmates.

Again, thanks for everything, every day. We couldn't do this without you! Have a great weekend and see you on Monday!

Karin Tramm
VES Kindergarten

~

It was Friday night and Gene and I were very content to slide back into our comfortable pizza and wine routine. I had sunk deep into the sofa when I heard my phone. Where was that thing? Digging it out from under a pillow, my heart missed a beat when I saw that it was my sister. I knew it was two o'clock in the afternoon, her time; she should be at work. Now that she was back at the office, she would never call at this time of day. I answered in a panic.

"Hey, Barbara, what's going on?" I asked, my mind racing

"Everything's okay, but Mom had an accident. She drove herself to the allergy clinic to get her shot. When she was leaving, she pulled out of the parking lot onto Manatee Avenue and was struck broadside by a truck coming in the far lane."

"Driver's side or passenger side?"

"Passenger side," she replied.

"Well, thank God for that."

Barbara was calm. She went on to reassure me that Mom was okay. She refused to be taken to the hospital because she was concerned about the possibility of being exposed to COVID-19.

"That's totally my fault!" I lamented. "I scolded her yesterday for going to a retirement party at the hospital."

"She's okay. She was checked by the paramedics and they released her. She's at home. Resting. The car's another story. It's totaled."

Big breath. Exhale.

Saturday, May 16, 2020

Packing up my students' personal items was a daunting job and something I was not looking forward to. I knew I couldn't avoid it any longer, so I drove to school to get started. Being a Saturday, I knew I could work uninterrupted, and if I needed to stop and stare at the walls, I could do that, too. No one else would be there and I wouldn't have to wear a mask. It looked to be a productive day.

I put on my earphones and listened to an audiobook while I worked, trying to keep my mind off the disheartening task at hand. The shopping bags were a godsend, adorned with cheery arrangements of fruits and vegetables made to look like hearts and flowers. Very Arcimboldo-esque, I thought. The art teacher would approve.

I spread the bags out around the room and labeled them. I retrieved the rest time towels, rolled them, and tried to remember who the unlabeled ones belonged to. It seemed so long ago we had last used them. I snapped some pictures and put them in the kindergarten chat, hoping to clear up a few mysteries.

I made piles of papers on the reading table and organized their work into folders. There were science journals, writing journals, and portfolios. There was artwork from the hundredth day of school, still on display in the hall. Then there was the jumble of miscellaneous personal items I'd harvested from the classroom: spare clothes, books, games brought in to share, confiscated toys, a pair of mittens.

Mrs. Dee had been in and taken down the Welcome Back bulletin board and made a pile of those pictures. One long bulletin board beside the door served as our travel wall and was covered with postcards from their adventures so far this year. Venice, Rome, Florence, London, Paris, and more. Did these kids have any idea how lucky they were? It was an impressive collection, and I was thankful they'd been able to get out and see so many places before their lives had folded inward.

I worked for a couple of hours and then called it a day; the rest could wait and there was plenty of time. Or was there? I felt like I was in a time warp, Dali's limp melted clock in the foreground of my thoughts. Time flying and time standing still, in motion and interrupted, synchronized and shattered in the fluid dance of circumstance.

~

Message to Barbara: Thanks for the call last night. I called Mom and Dad after I talked to you. Mom was okay, they seemed in good spirits and were self-medicating with a bottle of Montepulciano d'Abruzzo.

Barbara: Good to know. I was, too. I talked to Mom a little bit ago and she was very chipper and said she felt better today than yesterday.

~

Gene brought my laptop outside, and we settled on the terrace; I brought the snacks and Gene poured two glasses of wine. We clicked on our private Navy Happy Hour link and waited. The chat pinged.

-- Be there in a minute.

-- Our internet keeps going out!

-- Are you coming back?

-- Trying.

-- You're frozen.

-- Aghhhh! This internet is horrible lately!

-- Oh no, our battery just died!

-- Are you coming back?

-- Trying.

-- We're moving inside—it's starting to rain.

-- Karin, are you coming back?

Sunday, May 17, 2020

On Sunday mornings in spring, we liked to have our breakfast on the front porch. We wanted to enjoy this time of year before the heat and the bugs drove us back inside. I picked up a magazine and some biscotti and headed outside with my coffee. The roses were just beginning to bloom in the adjacent flower bed. The sun was just right, and the quiet was consolatory. Gene came out to join me. We breathed.

After the deer sighting last month, we were keen to keep our eyes open to see if our spritely friends might return. We spotted movement in the hayfield but not quite the same as the deer. It was a group of wild hares, *lepri*, frolicking in the tall grass. Their huge ears could be seen bouncing this way and that, as if they were playing a game of tag. The hares continued to entertain us for more than an hour. It was as if the real Peter Rabbit had come to visit.

WEEK 13: THE BIRDS AND THE BEES

Monday, May 18, 2020

Insect Week is oh so sweet in kindergarten. Most kids are outwardly grossed out but inwardly fascinated by their six-legged friends. The first year I taught on Guam I asked my students to bring in an insect for homework. Every last one of them brought in a cockroach. I shouldn't have been surprised because our classroom was rife with them. In the beginning, I couldn't figure out what was chewing up the paper, especially the gluey papers. The little rainbow-colored sprinkles I found on every desk in the morning were a mystery as well.

I came to school one fall evening for Open House and flipped on the classroom lights. I was stunned to see an entire army of cockroaches, giant ones, skittering across the desks and floor to their hideaways in the wall, the scratching clatter of their retreat making my skin crawl. Then it became clear to me that the sprinkles were, in fact, cockroach poop, rainbow-colored from their diet of crayons. I don't know if I was grossed out or fascinated, but I could never look at rainbow sprinkles on a cupcake in the same way.

During today's morning meeting we had a conversation about bugs.

"Mrs. Tramm, I saw some ants in my kitchen."

"Sometimes I have some ants in my kitchen too." I replied. "They're always searching for something to eat."

"There's some cockroaches in my kitchen," someone blurted out. I saw his mother widen her eyes and cringe in mortification, as if her son were disclosing family secrets.

"I saw a lot of flies and bees outside. And some big ants, too."

"I found a beetle and a ladybug in my yard."

"Did you see my picture of the giant butterflies? We saw them this weekend at the lake," one friend asked, describing the photo his mom had helped him post earlier that morning.

"Yes, I did! Wow!" I replied. "Thanks for sharing. They were so beautiful and have perfect colors to help them hide. You were so lucky to see them."

"They were bigger than my hand!" he continued.

"You know, I have a lot of insects around my house, too, especially stinkbugs," I confessed to the children. "Have you ever seen a stinkbug? Have you ever smelled one? P-U!!"

"Yuck!" came the reply in unison and then an explosion of stories about stinkbugs, or what I appropriately term now the "Italian cockroach".

~

Each week we reclaimed a little more space and place. Businesses continued to reopen, and I hoped we could get to the garden store. We were allowed to travel together in the car, but the rule still stood that only one person at a time could go into a store. We continued to be restricted to the region, but the Veneto was diverse and far-reaching. It stretched from Venice and the Adriatic beaches in the east, west to Verona, and north to Asiago and the Dolomite Mountains.

One of the most welcome differences was that passports and travel papers were no longer required to leave the house. This was a huge relief because I lived in constant fear of being stopped by the *carabinieri* and by chance having the wrong travel documents. I cut the old docs into quarters, stapled them, and made scratch paper pads.

The most exciting change by far was that now people could visit with their families and friends again, as long as the group was no larger than eight people. This was the true breath of fresh air we'd been waiting for, and, like little bugs, we all began to scuttle out of our hideaways.

Tuesday, May 19, 2020

Kindergarten chat:

-- Good morning, friends, and Happy Tuesday! Look at this picture of soil. It's crawling with worms, ants, and millipedes. These are nature's recyclers. They chomp through the things that fall onto the ground, like leaves and sticks. These critters chew the dead things into smaller and smaller bits until they become part of the soil again. How many insects can you spy? You may need to use a magnifying glass.

Today we will read about many different kinds of insects in *The Very Quiet Cricket.* See you soon!

~

The mystery fluid under the car turned out to be the result of a radiator leak and—good news—it had been repaired and the car was ready for pick up. Gene and I drove together and immediately noticed the increased traffic, much heavier than when we dropped the car off only a few days ago. As each new decree eased restrictions, more and more cars eased out of their garages and back onto the roads. They filled the streets and clogged the traffic circles, zipping, beeping, barely creeping. Even traffic that had been annoying in the past took on a joyous resonance.

I stopped for groceries on the way home. The commissary was busy and still out of bleach and wipes, but the hazelnut coffee creamer was restocked. I picked up two. I continued on to the Alì and found fresh strawberries and white asparagus, a local specialty. With a chicken in the slow cooker, this would make a perfect meal. Indeed, life was ever so slowly resuming its natural cadence.

Wednesday, May 20, 2020

Kindergarten chat:

-- Good morning, friends, and Happy Wednesday! Today's insect habitat is a flower garden. We like flowers because they are pretty, but to insects they are food. Did you know that honeybees have to visit more than 20,000 flowers to collect enough nectar to make just one spoonful of honey? That's a lot of flowers!

After the morning meeting everyone had something to say about insects.

"Mrs. Tramm, in that picture I saw eighteen insects."

"I think there are one hundred."

"I think there are one thousand."

"Did you know that my grandma has honeybees and sends me honey?" one of the boys asked excitedly.

"Can I tell you something? Butterflies like flowers, too."

"Yes, they do," I replied. "Butterflies are pollinators, and they drink nectar from flowers. Today we're going to read about butterflies. Our story this afternoon is called *Waiting for Wings*. See you at two o'clock. Goodbye, little butterflies!"

~

While living in Spain we saw some amazing flower-filled patios, even in the humblest of homes. We were inspired to make our outside living space an essential and elegant part of our Italian home as well. When we first moved in, the terrace was covered with crumbling red brick tiles, plants pushing up through the cracks. We did our best to spruce up the space, pulling weeds, trimming the kiwis and grapevines that covered the pergola overhead, and filling the planters with brightly-colored flowers. We purchased two loungers and a tile table to complete our outside dining room.

We lined the low walls with flower boxes, but snails tortured our efforts and peacocks ate the tender young plants. Attempts at growing bougainvillea were snuffed out by freezing temperatures, the beautifully painted Spanish pots I had brought from Rota cracked and broken beyond repair. Despite all that, we continued to experiment with what worked best in our space.

One summer we returned from the States to find the disintegrating tiles replaced with new paving stones. The transformation was beyond measure. We spent many a Saturday morning at the garden store choosing new plants that might work—pansies in winter, geraniums in spring, petunias in summer, and mums in fall. We put a small waterfall in one corner. Finally, we had created a little oasis where we could enjoy family meals and entertain guests. We had a renewed sense of pride in the patio, although, I have to admit that now and again I miss the volunteer snap dragons that used to erupt through the cracks every spring.

We'd been biding our time and finally, finally, the garden store was open for business. We followed the one-person-at-a-time rule and Gene was the lucky one who got to go. He texted pictures of the flowers to me so we could choose together. Arriving home, he unloaded a rainbow of color from the back of the car. There were purple petunias, red geraniums, orange begonias, yellow margaritas, and pink impatiens. He also picked up basil, parsley, and arugula for my kitchen garden. *Andrà tutto bene!*

The patio came together beautifully. If only the boys were here to enjoy it with us, I couldn't help thinking. This was the time of year when in the past they'd both arrive home from college long-haired and tired, with stinky laundry and sometimes friends in tow. The patio took on new life as they filled it with music, friends, and stories I might not want to hear. I missed those nights, the long dinners, the laughter.

~

Message to Barbara: I broached the subject of not driving anymore to Mom. She said she'd love to stop driving but at the time she was taking an online driver's course so she wouldn't lose any points on her license. I didn't know what to say. We need to gently reinforce this idea.

Barbara: Good, because when I brought it up the day after the wreck she was offended. LOL

Me: Let's keep on it and then we can task Bill with following up.

Thursday, May 21, 2020

Kindergarten chat:

-- Good morning, friends, and Happy Thursday! We have a big surprise for you at our morning meeting. See you then!

Mrs. Dee was going to have a baby. We'd known before school closed in February, but the kids and parents were not yet aware, as the computer had hidden her baby bump from view. She had the brilliant idea to have a baby reveal for them using our morning message. We had eighteen of our twenty-one students present. At the sound of the bird clock, they sang the "Hello Song" and dutifully muted their microphones.

I put the whiteboard easel in camera view and asked the parents, the students' home-teachers, not to say anything aloud when they figured out the mystery word in the message.

"Okay, boys and girls, we're ready to read. Put an X in the chat if you see a word you know. Remember, if someone reads your word, it's okay for you to read it again. We'll figure out all the words together before we work on the mystery word."

The message written on the whiteboard easel read:

Mrs. Dee has some good news to share with you today.
She is going to have a b _ _ _!

Immediately we saw the parents' faces light up as they silently typed direct messages of congratulations into the chat. It was hard for me to keep a straight face throughout the lesson. The students took turns reading a word and telling me their strategy for figuring it out. It went quickly, as most of the students were fairly competent readers by this time. We identified all the words and then began to talk about the mystery word.

"What letter does it start with?" I asked.

"B!" came back the reply.

"Good, and how many letters are in this word? Let's count the spaces."

"One, two, three, four," we counted together.

"What would make sense?" I finally asked.

"Birthday!" came the first guess. Of course, someone would say birthday because what could be more exciting to a kindergartner than having a birthday? I wrote "birthday" on the whiteboard below the message.

"Let's look at this word. Does birthday start with B?" I asked. I saw the kids nodding their heads up and down and talking to their parents.

"Yes, it does," I confirmed.

"Does birthday make sense? Talk to your home teacher about this." I watched the individual conversations taking place with their parents in the Hollywood Squares.

"Does it fit—does birthday have four letters?" There was a pause, some conversation. "Hmmmm, why can't the mystery word be birthday?"

X in the chat. "Because it has too many letters."

"Ohhh, yes," I replied, "Too many letters. Any other ideas? What else starts with a B and makes sense?"

Unmute. "Baby?"

"Maybe so, let's check it out. Does baby have four letters?"

"Yes!"

"Does baby start with B?"

"Yes!"

"Does baby make sense?" I watched their faces focus into understanding and happiness.

"Yes!"

"All right my friends, what's the last thing we need to do?"

"Read to make sense!" they chorused.

"Let's read it one more time together."

The sweet sound of kindergarten voices came together:

Mrs. Dee has some good news to share with you today. She is going to have a <u>baby</u>!"

"Does Mrs. Dee have a baby in her belly?"

"When can we see it?"

"My mom had a baby in her belly, too."

I closed the meeting by asking the kids to think of a good name for Mrs. Dee's baby. Parents typed the kids' ideas into the chat: Kayla, Layla, Eva, David, Henry, Robert, Rocky, Parker, Rosa, Daisy, Lily, Violet, Diamond, Peppermint, and Little Egg. We would just have to wait and see.

Friday, May 22, 2020

I tossed and turned through another night of stress dreams. This time I dreamt I kept missing virtual meetings with my kids. My computer wouldn't work, the power went out, someone was knocking on the door, my phone was ringing, my ears were ringing, everyone was talking to me. All at the same time. Thankfully, it was just a dream, just a nightmare.

Once awake, I was relieved to remember it was Friday and I had some planning time to start my day. The computer worked, the power did not go out, no one called or knocked on the door. No one brought lettuce.

~

When Ian was still in Thailand, he sent me a short video of himself sampling something that looked rather disgusting. He loved trying to shock me with his antics. Smacking his lips, he tossed the mystery snack in the air and caught it in his mouth.

"Mmmmmm, crunchy!" He smirked and munched and crunched.

I decided to find that video and post it for my students. I wanted them to guess what he was eating.

Kindergarten chat:

-- Good morning, friends, and Happy Friday! Check out the video and tell me what you think Ian could be eating. And don't forget today is Friday and that means bingo! We will read *The Icky Bug Alphabet Book* while we play. Have your bingo cards and snacks ready! Mmmmmm, crunchy!

For our afternoon meeting everyone came prepared with their bingo cards and their snacks. Before we started, I asked them about the video.

"I think those are raisins and rice," came the first guess.

"Well, you're right about the rice," I said.

"I think they're cockroaches," suggested my little friend whose father ate a worm.

"Is it chocolate candy?" asked another with a less adventurous palate.

"Are those crickets?" someone guessed.

"Is that your son?"

"Good guess! Yes, they're crickets! And yes, that's my son, Ian."

"Ewwww!" Everyone was either grossed out or fascinated.

"Ready for bingo? The first letter is C. C is for cricket."

~

From: Mrs. Tramm
To: VES Kindergarten 2019-2020
Subject: Kindergarten in the Kitchen News, Friday, May 22, 2020

Dear Kindergarten Families,

Congratulations to Mrs. Dee! She will be having a baby in October. Thanks for all of the name suggestions. I know it will be hard for her to choose the right one.

This week we learned all about insects. They have six legs and three body parts. They have an exoskeleton that they shed when their body grows. They are egg layers. You can even eat some insects!

Next week we will learn about animals that live in lakes and ponds.

Mrs. Dee has done an amazing job with the digital yearbook signing pages. Please help your child sign the pages of his or her classmates. There is a short tutorial to watch before you start. You can email Mrs. Dee with any questions.

Don't forget that Monday is Memorial Day so there will be no school. June second is the designated pick-up day for kindergarten materials and supplies. If you have more than one child in the school, you can come on either day. Thanks to Mrs. Taylor for donating the bags.

Thanks again for your teamwork and support! Have a great weekend and see you on Tuesday!

Karin Tramm
VES Kindergarten

~

FIU sent news that for now, faculty and students would continue with online instruction through the end of the summer session. In the fall, they planned to gradually reopen the campus when the time was right and be decidedly careful. They also shared that physical distancing, face coverings, and other mitigation measures would be part of their reopening plan.

I was glad Will's university had a plan in place. I hoped Florida would follow the example of Italy and other countries that were flattening the curve. It was disconcerting to me that some people were refusing to wear masks and ignoring social distancing—or worse, spreading the rumor that COVID-19 wasn't real.

Saturday, May 23, 2020

The latest decree by the Italian government announced we would be allowed to socialize in small groups again. We decided our next Navy Happy Hour would be in person, with appropriate social distancing. We chose to meet at our friends' home to take advantage of their rooftop terrace. It would allow for fresh air and spreading out.

It was still an odd feeling to be riding in the car with Gene, as if we were breaking a rule and might get in trouble. We parked the car, put on our masks, and rang the bell on the gate. I wondered who else had touched the bell and the gate. I thought the same thing about the elevator buttons and wondered who had been in there ahead of us. Should I hold my breath? There were so many considerations in my head that never would have crossed my mind four months ago. I was so glad I carried hand sanitizer in my bag and gave Gene a squirt on the way up.

If I thought being in the car felt strange, the real awkwardness was being around people again, even friends I knew well. Cheek kissing was definitely out, as was hand shaking, but was elbow bumping still okay? Wasn't that getting a little too close?

We sat outside, ate, and enjoyed the evening breeze. It was exhilarating to be out and have a normal human conversation yet exhausting to be mindful of the circumstances.

For this Navy Happy Hour, we were missing Misty and Andy, our Sigonella friends from down south.

-- Y'all enjoy your dinner! We're envious but happy it has gotten to the point you get to see each other! We are missing friends, food, and fun in Vicenza.

-- If you're ever missing anything from this area, I can send you a box!!

-- Can y'all fit yourselves into the boxes?

Sunday, May 24, 2020

I had yet another round of stress dreams. In this nightmare it was announced that school would resume in person the next day. I drove to work on a rain-spattered road only to discover that the school had been moved to a new location and I didn't know where it was. When I finally found the building, I couldn't find my key and was locked outside. When I finally got inside, I couldn't find my new classroom.

Then I was in my car again, this time Ian was with me in the passenger seat. I looked over at him, he smiled, opened the car door, and jumped from the moving vehicle.

I woke up gasping and in a cold sweat. It was Sunday so I didn't have to get up right away, but I couldn't get back to sleep.

WEEK 14: DISMISSAL

Monday, May 25, 2020

Memorial Day dawned crisply but we didn't get out of bed. A federal holiday meant no school for students or teachers. We lamented that our long weekend would go to waste, but waking up at the Agriturismo Bolzano Vicentino wasn't too bad. We slept in, lingered, and drank coffee in bed. We puttered around and then took our afternoon walk, strolling past waist-high corn and ripe cherries.

Cherry trees lined the hill back behind the chicken coop. The cherries were free for the picking, but the last thing Gene and I wanted to do was pick fruit. When Ian and Will were here, they didn't mind that the trees were buggy and choked with undergrowth. They and their friends picked bucket loads every year, probably eating more than ever made it back to the house. It had been quite some time since we enjoyed fresh cherries.

On one of our daily rambles, we noticed piles of brush along the ditch edging the hill where the cherry trees grew. By the looks of it, someone had been clearing the area. Gene eyed the brush piles with suspicion, always wary of what a new project on the property might mean. The next time we passed the house he went inside and returned with a plastic bag.

"I'm going up there," he announced, turning off the driveway and stepping into the cornfield.

I had no inclination to trample through the mud, so I let Gene do the investigating. Trekking past the toolshed and through the chicken coop, he determined that Flavio had been pruning trees and creating some open space to better access the cherries. Our lucky day! Gene returned to the house, not too dirty, with a bag of the dark red fruit. There were some stinkbugs, too, but we picked them out and washed the cherries well. We ate a bowlful right then, out on the terrace, spitting the pits into the yard. I covered the rest with cold water and stored them in the fridge. Right now, life was not a bowl of cherries, but this treat came mighty close. Even with the stinkbugs.

Tuesday, May 26, 2020

When we moved from the navy base in Spain to the army post in Italy, Will brought his two pet turtles, Speedy and Bebe, with him. We packed them in their traveling terrarium and loaded them in the car for the weeklong trip. We hauled them into hotels and even smuggled them on board the overnight car ferry from Barcelona to Genoa.

Animals weren't allowed in the cabins, but Will was distraught at leaving them in the car. We threw a towel on top of the box and proceeded up the stairs.

"*Che cos'è?*" the porter asked. "What is that?"

"*Tortarugas,*" Gene replied in bastardized Spanish/Italian.

The porter looked confused, shook his head, and waved us on.

Arriving in Vicenza, we were hotel bound for an indefinite period. I searched out the local thrift store and found a spacious hamster cage. We refurbished it with a small turtle-sized pool, and Speedy and Bebe went to live at school as the adopted classroom pets. My students were enthralled with them, so even after we moved into our house, I left the turtles in my classroom. One day, months later, the assistant principal noticed them and decided it wasn't safe to have turtles at school. Speedy and Bebe had to leave.

The turtles came home to live with us in Bolzano Vicentino. We dug a small pond in the front yard as a home for them and added some goldfish as friends. Lily pads and water irises provided resting places for frogs and dragonflies. Two other turtles, from another classroom, came to join them. Soon we had our own little wetlands project. With an expanded living space, the turtles continued to grow bigger, until one year they managed to escape over the rocky wall. Farmer Cow reported seeing them in the hayfield on the way to their new home in the irrigation ditch.

The turtles were now long gone, but the pond was usually full of tadpoles this time of year. Will used to catch a few for me so I could take them to school. The kids were always thrilled to watch them pop out one leg and then another, tails shortening, mouths widening, until little froglets crawled up onto the rocks at the edge of the tank. Then I would bring them home one by one for Will to dutifully release back into the pond. Doing it virtually this year just wasn't the same.

Kindergarten chat:

-- Good morning, friends, and Happy Tuesday! Have you ever been to a lake or a pond? What plants and animals live together there? Watch this video about a pond to find out. Today we will read a story called *The Teeny Weeny Tadpole*. See you soon!

When we met for our morning meeting the kids were beside themselves to tell me about their big pond adventures.

"Mrs. Tramm! We went to the lake yesterday and saw baby swans!"

"Baby swans are called cygnets," I told them. "You're so lucky to get to see them. Were they fuzzy and grey?"

"Yes, and they didn't look like the big ones."

"You're so lucky to get to go to a lake," one of the kids cut in.

"We went for a walk around the lake and saw lots of tadpoles. I wanted to bring some home, but my dad said no. And then we saw some turtles swimming. And some bugs."

It sounded like a joyful field trip.

~

Message to Will: Turtle benefits?

Turtle benefits had become part of the Tramm family lexicon years ago when Ian and Will were in middle school and finally cajoled us into getting them each a cell phone. Checking in with them, I'd text *tutto bene?* Everything good? They'd reply, *si, si, tutto bene.*

Unfortunately, English autocorrect and Italian words don't always play nicely together and hence, the Italian phrase "*tutto bene*" morphed into "turtle benefits." I didn't always catch it. One night it came up in conversation at the dinner table and ever since then it was our inside joke. After a while we didn't even bother to correct it and lapsed into further linguistic laziness by just using the turtle emoji.

I texted Will again, "Turtle benefits?" Later a turtle emoji appeared on my screen. If a smartphone was really smart, it would be able to tell me if this was the truth. Was he really *bene?* I needed to know.

~

After school Gene made a trip to the hardware store. He hadn't done any recent shopping except for groceries and plants, so this was a big adventure. He came back with everything on his list and a safety update.

"There was definitely a limit to how many people were allowed in the store at one time because there was a line outside, a short line, but still a line. There were tape marks on the sidewalk for social distancing. There was even an employee out front to make sure everyone was wearing a mask and using the hand sanitizer from their dispenser. Inside there was another employee at the entrance to take your temperature."

Italy was still very serious and for this we were grateful.

~

Message from Mom: Bill's home. He's going to call tomorrow. FYI.

Me: Great news! He must be exhausted!

Mom: Yes, he is. He said he had a 23-hour flight and needs to decompress.

Wednesday, May 27, 2020

Our morning meeting began.

"Good morning, friends, and Happy Wednesday! Today I have a special book, one of my favorite books. It's about a fish and a frog who are friends. It's called *Fish is Fish* by Leo Lionni.

"We love *Fish is Fish*!" one of my parents exclaimed.

"Me, too! I'm so glad. Leo Lionni is one of my favorite authors," I said.

"In the book, the cows and the birds and the people all look like fish," her son told me. "They're pretty funny!"

"Ya know what? I have two goldfish," someone added. Then a pause, "Wait, who's feeding our fish at school?"

"They're living at Mia's house and she's taking care of them. Thank you, Mia!" Mia's mom waved from her Hollywood Square and smiled. She was a science teacher at the middle school and had been helping us in the kindergarten science lab all year. She'd been our mystery fish rescue hero.

"We'll post a picture," she promised.

~

From: Karin
To: Bill
Subject: Welcome Home

Bill,

I hope you're over your jet lag and are now hard at work on that honey-do list. Glad to hear of your safe arrival—I know everyone's so happy to have you back. Mom said you had some big adventures and four-star accommodations with a cardboard bed on a cement floor. I bet your own bed felt mighty good after all that!

Gene and I are both well and heading into our last two weeks of school. Will's slugging away at CALC 2 in summer session. Ian's in Chicago helping his friend move back to Virginia. The plan is for him to still make his way to Florida at some point. If and when it's safe.

In one week, Italy is reopening its borders but only to the EU. We'll see how the summer plays out but sadly, I don't think we will be able to travel back to Florida this year. We'll see. All for now.

Love,
Karin

From: Bill
To: Karin
Subject: RE: Welcome Home

Karin,

Yes, it is wonderful to finally be back home. I'm working hard on the honey-do list. I talked to Mom and Dad yesterday and they bought a new (used) car to replace the crashed one. Good to hear that Italy is opening up again, even if it's only to the EU. Looking at the graphs for Italy, Spain, Germany, etc., it looks like the peak numbers were very short-lived. The US peak has lasted for over a month now. People here refuse to be told what to do and I think that's most of the problem.

So, that's it from here.

Be safe,
Bill

Thursday, May 28, 2020

Parents were scheduled to begin picking up their children's personal items soon, so I needed to finish the terrible task I had started the week before. For health and safety reasons, the school building was only allowed to be 30 percent occupied at one time. Teachers were required to sign up for a specific day to work in the classroom so the numbers did not exceed the limit.

I drove to work early and found the school in the same location, my key worked, my desk was just as I had left it. It was not the same nightmare I had Sunday, but it felt like a nightmare just the same. My classroom was discombobulated. Someone had come in and rolled up the carpets. I wondered if carpets would even be allowed next year. Furniture had been pulled out from the walls, I imagined in preparation for some kind of deep cleaning. Mrs. Dee had been in and taken down the postcards and other items, sorted them, and had started to put some things away in the bags. Sadness.

The yearbooks had been delivered, placed on my desk in a stack beside a loose pile of artwork. I picked one up and flipped through it to the kindergarten section. A lump formed in my throat when I saw our class picture, my shirt proudly proclaiming: Get your CRAY-ON! It's the 100th Day of School!

There we all were, smiling and saying cheese, totally unaware that it was the last day we would be together. I closed the book and dropped a copy in each child's bag.

I turned on my computer, put on my happy face, and paused to hold the morning meeting with my kids.

"Good morning, friends! Happy Thursday! I'm going to post a video that you can watch to see a frog egg grow into a tadpole and then into a frog. You can watch it after our morning meeting."

"We have lots of toads that live in our yard. They only come out at night," one friend commented. "I posted a picture so everyone can see."

"Interesting, "I said, "They're nocturnal. And I love their camouflage colors. I wonder where they lay their eggs."

"I think they lay them in the wet dirt," she replied.

"Mrs. Tramm, why are you at school?" Nothing escaped their notice. "Why can't we be there, too?"

"I've got some cleaning up to do today but I didn't want to miss reading this story to you."

We talked more about frogs and toads and other animals that live in a pond. We read *Turtle Splash!*

After the meeting, I looked around at what else I might do while I was there. Teachers had been asked to sign up for an additional workday next week to come back to clean and organize their classrooms once the students' belongings had been disbursed. I thought I'd get a head start because not only did I have to deal with the classroom itself, but the kitchen, bathroom, and kindergarten playground also had to be cleaned and organized.

I cleared the materials from the tables and put away the art project for the one-hundred-first day of school, the day that never happened. I stored it in a folder for next year, whatever next year might look like. I took down posters and cleared the tops of the cabinets. I organized and shelved books. I wondered if the kids would even be allowed to touch books next year. I finally packed my schoolbag and headed home. It felt like an entire week's worth of work had been accomplished in just one day, another bizarre time slip.

When I got home, I was welcomed by the *profumo del paese*, the perfume of the country—cow poo. On any other day I would be highly annoyed when the honey wagon (that's what my grandpa used to call it) rolled up and sprayed its reeking load in the hayfield. The noxious smell permeated the house, even with the windows closed. This time, however, I didn't mind. I was comforted by the fact I could still smell, even if it was cow poo.

~

I hadn't heard from Vickie in a while, so I was happy to see an update from her on my Facebook Messenger.

Vickie: Well, it got a little crazy with virtual graduations. And not to sound like an old person, which I am, but the weather has been so crappy and rainy here. It was a very disappointing Memorial Day weekend being locked down.

Has Ian moved south yet? I feel like it's *Where's Waldo—Where's Ian*? It could be a new series. I'll try to catch you later this week for a phone call. I've got a funny update on Miami you'll appreciate.

Me: Sunday is the best day for a call. We're actually going to a restaurant to eat lunch on Saturday. First time since forever!

Vickie: That will be an exciting day—lunch at a restaurant!! It's looking more European here in Virginia Beach. Restaurants have to serve outside so now there are tables in parking lots. Just like Naples!!

Friday, May 29, 2020

Kindergarten chat:

-- Good morning, friends! Happy Bingo Friday. Did you know there is a lizard that squirts blood from its eyeballs when it gets mad? Did you know a chameleon's tongue is three times longer than its body? We will learn more fun facts about reptiles this afternoon when we play Yucky Reptile Alphabet Bingo. Have your bingo cards ready!

In my opinion, maintaining a positive relationship with students is one of the most important and challenging goals of virtual learning, at least for kindergartners. I tried to facilitate that bond by carving out some one-on-one time at the end of each individual meeting. I cherished the time to just chat, and trust me, they always had a lot to say. One of my students was so excited about getting some new smelly markers in the mail from her grandmother. At the end of our meeting, she held them up proudly for me to look at. One by one she called out the colors as she popped the lids off and took a big sniff.

"Purple is grape. Blue is blueberry. Green is watermelon. Yellow is banana. Orange is orange." She laughed at that one, then she pulled the lid off the red marker and held it up to the computer screen.

"Red is my favorite," she confided. "It smells like a strawberry. Here,

Mrs. Tramm, you smell it. Do you like it?"

Oh, how I wished I could just go through the computer and smell that marker. And give her a hug.

~

The birthday season continued for Mrs. Dee and for my friend Misty.

Message to Misty: Happy Birthday! I have my evaluation meeting at 9:30 and a group meet at 11:00. How is your morning looking?

Misty: I have meetings all morning until 11:30.

Me: OK, let's do our collaboration meeting after lunch and then let's do virtual happy hour for your birthday.

~

From: Mrs. Tramm
To: VES Kindergarten 2019-2020
Subject: Kindergarten in the Kitchen News, Friday, May 29, 2020

Dear Kindergarten Families,

The kids did an awesome job this week with their animal research projects. They were great presenters and respectful listeners. They used a lot of resources to find information and asked thoughtful questions. They had beautiful illustrations. I learned a lot from them!

This week's individual meetings will include a self-selected shared read and some addition and subtraction activities.

Thanks for helping your child sign the digital yearbooks. This will make a nice keepsake for your child, and Mrs. Dee personalized all of them to make sure each was unique. You will be able to print your child's pages now that they are all complete. The yearbooks have arrived, and they are with your child's school supplies that you will pick up next week.

A few reminders:

Registration for next school year is happening now. You can find the links and the registration information on our virtual classroom page. Our staffing is based on the number of students registered so it's really important that all returning students re-register now. Please spread the word to friends who have upcoming kindergartners! They need to register as well and the sooner the better.

Tuesday, June 2nd is Kindergarten Pick Up Day and the next Tuesday, June 9th, is the Kindergarten Online Farewell.

Have a great weekend!

Karin Tramm
VES Kindergarten

~

Message from Will: Are you up for an episode of *Seinfeld* tonight?
Me: Yes, give us some time to get the pizzas. We need to fetch some vino, too. How about in an hour or so?
Will: *Perfetto*.

It was pizza night and we were grateful Gioia was open. We picked up two pies and refilled our empty wine bottles at the wine station across the street. We settled in front of the TV and watched an episode of *Seinfeld* with Will. When the show was over, we chatted for a while about school and life. Will played a few songs on his guitar. The music was soothing and brought back fond memories of him practicing in his room every night after homework, and me listening to the notes as I fell asleep.

"Do you want to hear a new song?" he asked. "I'm still working on it, but I think you'll like it."

"Of course," Gene answered. "What's it called?"

"We Will Live."

Yes, we will, Will, I thought. Yes, we will.

With pizza night back in place, a little wine, and a little song, I was content for this moment and my heart was happy.

"More wine?" Gene offered.

"Why yes, thank you. More of everything."

Saturday, May 30, 2020

Our bicycling friends called last week and asked if we wanted to join them for lunch at a favorite restaurant.

"Are you ready to venture out?"

Hmmm. It was one thing to go to someone's house to eat, but another thing entirely to sit in a restaurant filled with strangers. Honestly, Gene and I both felt a little nervous. After a conversation about living a life, but not living in fear, we said YES! She made the reservation for four people.

It felt like it had been ages since I'd gotten dressed to go out. I wondered if I could get away with wearing yoga pants to the restaurant. I'd gotten far too comfortable during our lockdown, but I knew stretchy pants really wouldn't do. Italian women dress to the nines just to take out the garbage. I was certain I could manage something more presentable.

I put on makeup and fixed my hair with much more care than I usually did for a class meeting. I was in desperate need of a haircut. Oh well, after the lockdown everyone else probably had pandemic hair too, I thought. Some jewelry would spiff me up; nice earrings and a bracelet sounded about right. Maybe I would actually put my contacts in instead of wearing my glasses. My fingernails needed attention as well.

Picking up my keys, I glanced around the entryway as I was leaving the house. Instead of jackets on the coatrack, now there were masks hanging on the hooks. A bottle of hand sanitizer was on the barrel table by the door, ready for us to use as soon as we got home. I thought maybe I should get a decorative soap dispenser for that; it was probably going to be there for a while.

"Do you have my wallet?" Gene started the car and made his same old joke. "Do you have any money?"

Ah, the more things change the more they stay the same, I thought. As we drove away, I could see the corn reaching for the sky. Soon the house would be blocked from view. Summer was on the way.

Being together in the car still had that strange feeling, new and not new at the same time. Driving down the road I noticed rainbow-splashed *Andrà tutto bene* banners hanging from houses and fences. Yes, we were going to be fine! Red, white, and green Italian flags fluttered from homes and businesses. Stores were open and Italians, all wearing masks and dutifully socially distanced, stood in line waiting outside for their turn to enter. The orderliness and rule-following were unprecedented for Italy. We sped down the road, a little too fast we found out later, when a traffic ticket arrived in our mailbox. We were in wonder at the reawakening of the Veneto.

We met our friends at a favorite restaurant in Valdobbiadene, Villa Sandi. Wearing masks, we entered and were seated in the glass-enclosed terrace. The tables were spread far apart, the windows thrown open to allow fresh air and light to stream through. Masks were required if we left the table but could be taken off while eating. *Prosecco, prosciutto, tagliatelle, salsicca, tiramisu.* Forget the yoga pants; pass the pasta. We caught up, laughed, and told stories of school, lockdown, and family.

Sated with food and friendship, we gathered our things and went to the bar to pay the bill.

"*Bentornato!* Welcome back!" the bartender beamed at us.

The wine was on the house. I LOVE this country!

Sunday, May 31, 2020

One of the beautiful things about Italy is the plethora of art museums and temporary exhibits that are available to the public. One such exhibit in the nearby town of Treviso featured still-life paintings, *natura morte,* from the sixteenth century to the present. It concluded with a comparative display of contemporary still-life photography. A wannabe photographer myself, this exhibit piqued my interest and had been on my list to do.

I was terribly disappointed I wasn't able to go before the show closed months ago amid pandemic restrictions. May 31 would have been the final day of the exhibit. I checked the website to find out where it would be on display next, hoping I could catch it at another venue in the future. I was excited to discover that it would stay and reopen in Treviso, extended until September. This would be on my summer to-do list for sure.

I thought about the photographs on my own phone. I'd been scrolling through them earlier and was startled by the divided history of the images. The pre-pandemic pictures featured my students sitting side by side at the art center, playing dress up, and working on puzzles together. There were travel photos of festivals, parades, Christmas markets, and dinners. Everyone was close together, touching, laughing, and talking.

Abruptly the photos shifted. There were photos taken from the windows of my house, my kitchen classroom, the stinkbug on my toothbrush, Stella the shelf elf on the kitchen cabinets above the sink, and the beautiful double rainbow. There were plenty of memes, a screenshot of Ian and Will when we had our group video call, and virtual happy hours. There was Peter Rabbit in the garden and Jeremy Fisher joining us for lunch. The most recent photos were from the day before at Villa Sandi, selfies with masks and smiling eyes.

Someday down the road those photos would make an interesting exhibit.

~

Message to Will: Good to talk to you last night. I love your new song and I'm so happy about your calculus grade. I just saw on the news that Miami has an 8 p.m. curfew. Thank you for staying home.

Will: Making pasta. Staying home. Turtle benefits.

I hadn't heard from Ian in a bit. I knew he had taken a trip to help his friend clean out his college apartment and get things moved back to Virginia Beach.

Me: Where are you?

Ian: I'm back in Virginia now. We went to Chicago with his dad, a good trip. We rented a U-Haul, cleaned out everything, and drove it back. I'll call you in a few days to tell you all about it.

Me: Glad you could help out with the move. Probably fun to take a boys' trip, too, although maybe not these days.

Ian: How are things over there? Can't be crazier than over here right now I'd imagine.

Me: Our biggest crazy right now is the last week of school coming up. We're slowly coming out of lockdown. I'm going to send a case of wine and some groceries from the Italian grocery store to Virginia Beach. See if you can find out some of the foods they might be missing.

Ian: Okay, I'll see if I can get some scoop for you.

Not being in the States when he was there continued to weigh heavily on me. How could I ever repay the family who had taken him under their wing during this time of crisis? I wasn't sure how much longer he would be with them in Virginia Beach, but Gene and I were extremely grateful for the unofficial adoption. I felt like they were the cardinals and I was the cowbird mother. I was beholden to them for welcoming him into their nest and continuing with the care and feeding of our son when we weren't able to do so.

> **Message from Mom**: FYI we have a new (used) car. It has a backup camera and a push-button start. It has Bluetooth so I can listen to my book in the car. Your dad has driven it down to Sarasota to take care of some business for Aunt Babe. Also, you should be getting a Walmart email because we're getting a delivery today.
>
> **Me**: Okay, I'll forward the emails to you. I'm glad you didn't go with Dad. Even though Florida is opening back up, it's still important for you to stay home! Love you.

> **Message to Barbara**: Happy Happy Birthday and Happy Bubble Sunday!
>
> **Barbara**: Thank you for my beautiful flowers; they made my day!
>
> **Me**: You've been wiping down and delivering everyone else's flowers for a while now. It's your turn.

In addition to my sister's birthday, May 31 marked another significant day on the calendar. It had been one hundred days since I told my kindergartners how proud I was of them for being one hundred days smart. It had been one hundred days since this tsunami of events had swept us up, rolled us in the current, and spit us out on a new shore. One hundred days since this swipe of fate changed our lives. Forever.

One hundred days ago.
Pizza night, hold on tight, 2020 hindsight.
One hundred days, one hundred nights.
A lifetime ago. In Vo'.

EPILOGUE

Tuesday, June 9, 2020

From: Mrs. Tramm
To: VES Kindergarten 2019-2020
Subject: Kindergarten in the Kitchen News, Tuesday, June 9, 2020

Dear Kindergarten Families,

This is hard. Ending the year this way is a challenge for all of us. I'm striving to make it meaningful for the children. I've prepared a short slideshow that I'll share with the kids during our regular meeting time. Then I want to give them all some talking time if they want to say anything about kindergarten, their favorite center, song, or activity, something they learned, or whatever is important to them. If your child just wants to listen, that's okay too. Please help your child organize their thoughts on a piece of paper with words or a drawing. This isn't homework or anything I need to see; it's just to remind them what they want to say. When they're finished, I'll read a story, the same one I read on the first day of school. The meeting may run a little long, depending on how the talking time goes. I don't want to cut them short because this part is important. Bring your own tissues.

Thank you all for the privilege of teaching your child this year. Every year my class amazes me at how much they grow during our short time together. And I learned from them, too, every day. I appreciate your support in and out of the classroom. Mrs. Dee and I feel we were all a committed team working toward a common goal. It has been our pleasure to be a part of that community. This year especially.

Good luck to our friends who will be moving this summer. For those who will be here in Vicenza over the break, I hope you can take advantage of the virtual summer reading program at the post library. Please play outside, swim, read books, eat gelato, and write stories! I'll write a story, too. Have a wonderful summer!

Karin Tramm
VES Kindergarten

I read *Leo the Late Bloomer* to the class, finding it so very hard to read this story to the computer screen in my kitchen as opposed to a carpet full of almost first graders in my classroom. Every year I read it cautiously on the first day of kindergarten, and then again, joyfully, and perhaps a bit tearfully, on the last. We talked about school and how much they had learned: to read, write, draw, and eat neatly. We practiced pinkie waves, a communication tool for next year when we see each other in the hall. When they are big first graders.

There were tears and lots of waving but no big hugs. I assured them all I would see them in the commissary, probably the very next day. I reminded them that when we saw each other we could pinkie wave, maybe we could elbow bump, and one day we could hug again.

~

Everyone's pandemic story is unique to time and place, but the collective struggle against COVID-19 is not over. Loved ones lost, financial turmoil, and social and political upheavals are the scars we'll bear far into the future. As predicted, the second COVID-19 wave came hard and fast in the fall. This time we were well prepared.

School started back at Vicenza Elementary, brick and mortar (BAM is the new acronym), in August 2020. While we set up our classrooms, the post clinic offered COVID-19 tests for all teachers. Gene and I both tested negative then, at the end of the summer, but we'd never know if Gene had been positive back in the spring.

In September, Mrs. Dee had a beautiful baby girl. She passed on the names Diamond, Peppermint, and Little Egg, and instead chose Evelina. A new aide was brought on board, jumping in with hand sanitizer and a smile.

School remained open for us, but not as usual. We wore our Hello Kitty and Spiderman masks. We washed our hands. A lot. We figured out how to social distance in our own special kindergarten way.

"Mrs. Tramm, is COVID real?" a student asked me one day.

"Yes, it is, my friend."

"How do you know? Did you have it?"

"No, not me, but my sister did last summer and so did my son. That's why we have to wear masks and have personal space. We have to stay safe and healthy."

Eyes wide, silence, thinking.

"Mrs. Tramm, does Santa have to wear a mask?"

"Of course, he does. He wants to stay safe and healthy, too, so he doesn't miss Christmas."

I smiled as I glanced up at Stella the elf, back on her shelf above the whiteboard. She wore her Christmas mask, telephone up to her ear. I'm sure she had a lot of good things to tell Santa about this class. They had come together as a beautiful community of learners and had taken all of the challenges in stride.

And there certainly had been challenges. All of our carpets were removed so there were no more story time gatherings on the floor. No more rest time, the best time. We sat at tables spaced six feet apart. We ate lunch in our classroom instead of going to the cafeteria. We didn't share books or blocks or crayons.

But we did share hope.

Hope that we can learn to work together to find solutions.

Hope that we can understand that the choices we make and how the actions we take affect others, even sometimes people we don't know.

Hope that we can learn to look beyond ourselves, that we can respect others no matter their background or beliefs, and that we can rebuild our sense of community.

And hope for a time when we can kiss our family and friends without fear, and for a time when masks are once again for *Carnevale*.

AUTHOR'S NOTES

When school was out in June 2020, Italy eased some restrictions, allowing us a somewhat restored freedom of movement within the country. We were able to enjoy outside activities like hiking, biking, and visiting sites without swarms of tourists. However, the same logistics of flights and quarantines that kept the crowds at bay also made it impossible for us to travel back to the States to see our family, or for our family to come see us.

My parents both celebrated their eightieth birthdays in the summer of 2020, bringing the birthday season to a close. They continued to behave, most days, and began to venture out once they were both fully vaccinated.

Ian's swift departure from Thailand initially looked to last only a few months but ended up morphing into a permanent situation. I'm eternally grateful for the sense of community that growing up in a military environment extends. As he sought refuge in the States, many friends stepped up to help out, opening their hearts and homes to him. He went on to work for a joint venture with Peace Corps and FEMA, doing vaccine outreach in Oregon.

Will graduated from Florida International University in December 2020. We enjoyed the virtual commencement ceremony from our sofa in Bolzano Vicentino. Although I grieved the loss of the graduation ceremony, I was glad this chapter of his life was over and we could all move forward. Perhaps we will watch him walk across the stage in a real ceremony another place, another time. With everyone there.

Our first empty nest Christmas came and went. I would have given a million dollars for those boys to come home but it wasn't meant to be. Italy continued to restrict entry and went into another stringent lockdown during the holiday season. The Veneto had a few weeks of glorious freedom before sinking back into the *zona rossa* again the following spring. The red, white, and green flags dotting the city and country are now faded and tattered but still there. Like us all. *Forza.*

In February 2021, we passed the hundredth day of kindergarten and kept right on going, just like I said we would. Vicenza schools remained open and face-to-face all year, the high school being the only one throughout Italy, both Italian and American, never to transition to remote instruction that school year.

~

In a kindergarten classroom, teamwork is crucial to the mission. Teachers, aides, parents, and students each have an important role to play. Writing this book was no different and I'm grateful for all those who came together to support, encourage, and allow me to tell your stories.

Thanks to my students for your resilience, tenacity, and courage that makes me proud of you every single day. I learn so much from you.

Thanks to my students' amazing parents, our home-teachers, for your support in and out of the classroom. Your patience and understanding of my technological challenges was much appreciated.

Utmost thanks and respect to my colleagues at Vicenza Elementary School who rallied and collaborated in the most unprecedented of times. I'm honored to have worked with you.

To friends near and far who checked in on us, thank you for sharing your personal accounts and for your encouragement.

Thanks to those at Elva Resa who fielded my rookie questions and walked me through this process. I appreciate your confidence in me.

Grazie mille to Gene Tramm for tech support, moral support, pizza night, and so much more. *Ti amo.*

And last, but not least, thanks to my family—there's no place like home.

~~~